TELECOMMUNICATIONS ACT: COMPETITION, INNOVATION, AND REFORM

TELECOMMUNICATIONS ACT: COMPETITION, INNOVATION, AND REFORM

CHARLES B. GOLDFARB
EDITOR

Novinka Books
An imprint of Nova Science Publishers, Inc.
New York

For permission to use material from this book please contact us:
Telephone 631-231-7269; Fax 631-231-8175
Web Site: http://www.novapublishers.com

Library of Congress Cataloging-in-Publication Data:
Available Upon Request

ISBN: 1-60021-133-X

Published by Nova Science Publishers, Inc. ✣ New York

CONTENTS

PREFACE

In 1996, Congress enacted comprehensive reform of the nation's statutory and regulatory framework for telecommunications by passing the Telecommunications Act, which substantially amended the 1934 Communications Act. The general objective of the 1996 Act was to open up markets to competition by removing unnecessary regulatory barriers to entry. At that time, the industry was characterized by service-specific networks that did not compete with one another: circuit-switched networks provided telephone service and coaxial cable networks provided cable service. The act created distinct regulatory regimes for these service-specific telephone networks and cable networks that included provisions intended to foster competition from new entrants that used network architectures and technologies similar to those of the incumbents. This "intramodal" competition has proved very limited. But the deployment of digital technologies in these previously distinct networks has led to market convergence and "intermodal" competition, as telephone, cable, and even wireless networks increasingly are able to offer voice, data, and video services over a single broadband platform. There is consensus that the current statutory framework is not effective in the current market environment, but not on how to modify it. The debate focuses on how to foster investment, innovation, and competition in both the physical broadband network and in the applications that ride over that network while also meeting the many non-economic objectives of U.S. telecommunications policy: universal service, homeland security, public safety, diversity of voices, localism, consumer protection, etc. This book explores these issues and includes the act in its entirety.

In: Telecommunications Act: Competition, Innovation and Reform ISBN 1-60021-133-X
Editor: Charles B. Goldfarb, pp. 1-71

Chapter 1

TELECOMMUNICATIONS ACT: COMPETITION, INNOVATION, AND REFORM*

Charles B. Goldfarb

ABSTRACT

In 1996, Congress enacted comprehensive reform of the nation's statutory and regulatory framework for telecommunications by passing the Telecommunications Act, which substantially amended the 1934 Communications Act. The general objective of the 1996 Act was to open up markets to competition by removing unnecessary regulatory barriers to entry. At that time, the industry was characterized by service-specific networks that did not compete with one another: circuit-switched networks provided telephone service and coaxial cable networks provided cable service. The act created distinct regulatory regimes for these service-specific telephone networks and cable networks that included provisions intended to foster competition from new entrants that used network architectures and technologies similar to those of the incumbents. This "intramodal" competition has proved very limited. But the deployment of digital technologies in these previously distinct networks has led to market convergence and "intermodal" competition, as telephone, cable, and even wireless networks increasingly are able to offer voice, data, and video services over a single broadband platform. However, because of the distinct regulatory regimes in the act, services that are provided by different network technologies, but compete with one another, often receive different regulatory treatment. Also, the act created a classification, "information services," that was not subject to either telephone or cable regulation. Today, voice and video services that are provided using Internet protocol technology may be classified as information services and therefore not subject to traditional voice or video regulation.

There is consensus that the current statutory framework is not effective in the current market environment, but not on how to modify it. The debate focuses on how to foster investment, innovation, and competition in both the physical broadband network and in the applications that ride over that network while also meeting the many non-economic objectives of U.S. telecommunications policy: universal service, homeland security, public safety, diversity of voices, localism, consumer protection, etc. Given the underlying cost structure of broadband networks — huge sunk up-front fixed costs — the marketplace will likely support only a limited number of such networks. Today, the market is largely a duopoly: the telephone company network and the cable company network. The physical network providers argue that they will be discouraged from undertaking costly and risky build-outs if their networks are subject to open access and/or non-discrimination requirements. On the other hand, independent applications providers argue that in

* Excerpted from CRS Report RL33034, dated January 13, 2006.

order for them to best meet the needs of end users and offer innovative services they must have nondiscriminatory access to the physical network. There is much debate over the advantages and disadvantages of structural regulation, such as open access, ex ante non-discrimination rules, ex post adjudication of abuses of market power on a caseby-case basis, and reliance on non-mandatory principles. There is general agreement that there would be great benefits from entry by a wireless broadband network to compete with the telephone and cable networks. There also is debate about how to modify the universal service program and intercarrier compensation rules in light of the major market changes. This report will be updated as warranted.

INTRODUCTION

The Big Picture

A comprehensive statutory framework for U.S. communications policy, covering telecommunications and broadcasting, was first created in the Communications Act of 1934 ("1934 Act").[1] That act created the Federal Communications Commission ("FCC" or "Commission") to implement and administer the economic regulation of the interstate activities of the telephone monopolies and the licensing of spectrum used for broadcast and other purposes. It explicitly left most regulation of intrastate telephone services to the states. In the 1970s and 1980s, a combination of technological change, court decisions, and changes in U.S. policy permitted competitive entry into some telecommunications and broadcast markets. In 1996, Congress passed the Telecommunications Act ("1996 Act"),[2] which opened up markets to competition by removing unnecessary regulatory barriers to entry.

The 1996 Act attempted to foster competition among providers that use similar underlying network technologies (for example, circuit-switched telephone networks) to offer a single type of service (for example, voice). Thus, there is one regulatory regime for carriers providing voice telephone service and another regime for cable television providers. Information services[3] are not subject to either regulatory regime. The subsequent deployment of digital broadband technologies in telephone and cable networks has resulted in these networks providing services that compete with one another, but that sometimes are subject to different regulatory requirements. Voice and video services can now be provided using Internet protocol and thus might be classified as unregulated information services, but these services compete directly with regulated traditional voice and video services. Moreover, these digital technologies do not recognize national borders, much less state boundaries.

There is consensus that the current statutory framework is not effective in the current market environment, but not on how to reform that framework. Key issues of contention have been identified, however, and various proposals have been put forward to resolve these issues.

Both houses of Congress have begun debating how to modify the 1996 Act, most of which resides within the Communications Act of 1934, as amended. That debate focuses on how to foster investment, innovation and competition in both the physical broadband network and in the applications that ride over that network while also meeting the many non-economic objectives of U.S. telecommunications policy: universal service, homeland security, public safety, diversity of voices, localism, consumer protection, etc.

The underlying cost structure of broadband networks, huge sunk up-front fixed costs, can only support a limited number of broadband networks, though there generally is no similar cost constraint on the number of applications providers. In this new environment, there will be three broad categories of competition:

1) intermodal competition among a small number of broadband network providers that offer a suite of voice, data, video, and other services primarily for the mass market;
2) intramodal competition among a small number of wireline broadband providers that serve multi-locational business customers who tend to be located in business districts; and
3) competition between these few broadband network providers and a multitude of independent applications service providers.

These three areas of competition will all be affected by a common factor: will there be entry by a third broadband network to compete with the broadband networks of the local telephone company and the local cable operator?

There are four general approaches to the regulation of broadband network providers vis-a-vis independent applications providers: structural regulation, such as open access; *ex ante* non-discrimination rules; *ex post* adjudication of abuses of market power, as they arise, on a case-by-case basis; and reliance on antitrust law and non-mandatory principles as the basis for self-regulation. At present, the FCC follows the last two approaches. In this report, a number of regulatory proposals, sometimes incorporating elements from more than one of these approaches, are discussed.

There is consensus that the current universal service and intercarrier compensation mechanisms need to be modified to accommodate the new market conditions. For example, the current universal service funding mechanism is assessed only on telecommunications services, and carriers can receive universal service funding only in support of telecommunications services. Thus, if services that had been classified as telecommunications services are re-classified as information services, as recently occurred for high-speed digital subscriber line ("DSL") services, then the universal service assessment base will decline and carriers that depend on universal service funding may see a decline in support. It therefore may be timely to consider whether the scope of universal service should be expanded to include universal access to a broadband network at affordable rates, not just to basic telephone service.

Problems with the Current Statutory and Regulatory Framework for Telecommunications

Technological change is driving the convergence of a number of previously distinct telecommunications and media markets. Digital technologies are being deployed in and carried over wireline, cable, and wireless networks that are increasingly capable of providing voice, data, and video services over a single broadband platform.[5] The U.S. communications infrastructure is evolving from circuit-based networks, in which individual applications (such as voice telephony) are tightly woven into the network architecture, to Internet Protocol ("IP") networks, in which multiple applications ride on top of the physical (transmission) network layer. There is consensus that the current statutory and regulatory framework for telecommunications is ill-suited for the current market environment. There is disagreement, however, about what modifications are necessary and how comprehensive those modifications should be.

At the time of the 1996 Telecommunications Act, the last comprehensive review of U.S. telecommunications policy, the environment we live in today was barely contemplated:

- voice, data, and video transported in packets of digitized bits over routes that pay no attention to state or even national boundaries;
- network "usage" measured in terms of bandwidth rather than time;[6]
- an end-user service provided over competing wireline, cable, and/or wireless broadband networks;
- those networks capable of providing multiple services; and
- no knowledge of the next "killer application" (comparable to the World Wide Web or e-mail) that will drive network and software investment.

Given the distinct, service-specific networks then in use, the 1996 Act created distinct vertical regulatory "silos" that equated specific services with specific network technologies. The statutory framework for regulating telecommunications services is found in one title of the 1996 Act[7] and for cable services in another title.[8] In addition, the 1996 Act defines a category of services, "information services," consisting of

> the offering of a capability for generating, acquiring, storing, transforming, processing, retrieving, utilizing, or making available information via telecommunications.[9]

These information services are not subject to any of the specific regulatory regimes in the 1996 Act; FCC jurisdiction over them is limited to its ancillary authority under Title I of the 1934 Act.[10] The distinction in the 1996 Act between telecommunications services and information services was an outgrowth of a line of FCC decisions dating back to the 1970s that distinguished between "basic" services that were subject to regulation and "enhanced" services that the Commission chose not to regulate in order to foster their development and deployment.[11] Keeping with this regulatory history, the Commission has chosen to forbear from regulating information services, again seeking to foster their development and deployment.[12]

These distinct regulatory regimes did not create significant problems so long as technological and market forces did not erode the distinctions between cable, telecommunications, and information services — and so long as it was possible to unambiguously classify services into these categories. But they became problematic when technological change made it more difficult to determine which service category a particular service fell under and when market convergence resulted in competition between services that were classified, and thus regulated, differently.

Since 1996, the distinctions between these service categories have become increasingly blurred. For example, some providers are offering voice over Internet protocol ("VoIP") services that meet the definition of information services while competing directly with traditional voice telecommunications services. Similarly, some providers have begun to offer IP video services that arguably would meet the definition of information services while competing directly with traditional cable services. Those IP-based service providers assert that their offerings should be subject only to the limited regulatory oversight of information services, not to the more intrusive regulation of telecommunications services and cable services, respectively.

It has proven to be an administrative and legal morass to determine whether an information service, which, by definition, provides certain capabilities via telecommunications, is purely an information service, and therefore subject only to a light regulatory regime, or has a distinct telecommunications service component that would make it subject to the more rigorous common carrier regulation imposed on telecommunications services. For example, in 2002 the FCC concluded that the telecommunications functionality in the cable modem service offered by cable companies to provide high speed access to the Internet is integral to the service, and not transparent to the consumer, and therefore cable modem service should be treated as a pure information service, and not subject to the access requirements imposed on telecommunications services.[13] That decision was upheld by the Supreme Court in June 2005.[14] At the same time, although the FCC had tentatively concluded that DSL service, which is offered by telephone companies to provide high-speed access to the Internet, also is an information service, with an integral telecommunications component, rather than a telecommunications service,[15] it had continued to treat the transmission component of DSL as a telecommunications service, and therefore DSL continued for more than three years to be subject to the access and other telecommunications service requirements. Local telephone companies were required to unbundle and separately tariff the underlying transmission component of their DSL Internet access services. On August 5, 2005, the FCC adopted an order that granted DSL Internet access providers the same regulatory classification and treatment as cable modem Internet access providers.[16]

There is an expectation that providers of information services will attempt to configure their service offerings in a fashion that will maximize the likelihood that the FCC will classify them as pure information services for regulatory purposes. As explained in greater detail below in the section on VoIP, however, the Commission continues to make determinations, based on the underlying network architectures used, about whether any specific service offering should be classified and regulated as an information service or as a telecommunications service.

The current siloed statutory and regulatory framework has not been able to accommodate the rapid pace of market convergence; it sometimes treats differently providers or services that are in direct competition with one another. The disparate rules have sometimes created incentives for providers to tailor their investment decisions and product offerings to avoid/exploit artificial regulatory distinctions rather than to efficiently serve customer needs. Similarly, the mechanisms currently embodied in statutes and rules to support such social policy goals as universal service are based on the pre-1996 market environment and are no longer sustainable or as effective as they could be.

Public Policy Issues to Debate

While there are many dimensions to the debate about reform of the statutory and regulatory framework for telecommunications, there appear to be two fundamental underlying issues that affect all others.

First, in this new environment in which applications are no longer tightly woven into the network architecture, what is the best regulatory framework for fostering investment and innovation in both the physical broadband network and in the applications (services) that ride over that network? The physical network providers (local exchange carriers and cable system operators) argue that they will be discouraged from undertaking costly and risky broadband network build-outs and upgrades if their networks are subject to open access and/or non-discrimination requirements that might limit their ability to exploit vertical integration efficiencies or to maximize the return on (or even fully recoup) their investments. On the other hand, the independent applications providers argue that in order for them to best meet the needs of end users and offer innovative services in competition with the vertically integrated network providers and, in some cases, services not offered at all by network providers. They must have the same unfettered open access to the physical networks that the network providers enjoy or, at the least, be protected by non-discrimination rules. Similarly, many end users argue that their broadband network providers should not be allowed to restrict their usage of the broadband network so long as they do not in any way compromise the integrity of the network.

This big-picture issue raises a number of corollary issues:

- In a complex technical environment in which a broadband platform typically consists of a physical (transmission) network layer, a logical layer (usually the TCP/IP[17] suite of protocols), an applications layer, and a content layer,[18] and in which services pass over both the broadband network provider's last-mile network and the Internet, where and how can denied access harm consumers? What does it mean to have nondiscriminatory access? Should access be viewed from the perspective of an end user or of an independent applications provider or of a competing network? Which access restrictions are justifiable to maintain the integrity and operational efficiency of the network? Should access regulation take the form of structural open access requirements or *ex ante* non-discrimination rules or *ex post* adjudication of abuses of market power as they arise on a case-by-case basis?[19] Or should there be no regulation, with industry voluntarily adhering to non-discrimination principles such as the Internet Consumer "four freedoms" enunciated by former FCC Chairman Michael Powell[20] or the principles in the non-binding policy statement adopted by the FCC on August 5, 2005?[21]
- How many competing physical broadband networks are needed for market forces alone to ensure that the network providers lack the incentive and the ability to restrict access or otherwise discriminate against independent applications providers to the detriment of consumers? To what extent can federal spectrum policy and infrastructure programs foster the deployment of multiple competitive broadband networks, thereby alleviating the need for access rules?

Second, while market demand appears to be suficient to generate competitive broadband network deployment in many urban areas without government intervention, that may not be the case in rural or other high cost (or low income) areas, where high costs and/or limited demand may render it economically infeasible to deploy multiple broadband networks, or even a single network, without government intervention. Does Congress want to expand the scope of universal service to include universal access to a broadband network at afordable rates? If so, how can the needed universal service support mechanisms accomplish this in an efficient and sustainable fashion that does not harm other policy goals, such as competitive neutrality? More basically, how "broad" is the "broadband" that should be provided as part of universal service? Bigger may be better, but only at an associated cost. Is it sufficient, for example, to limit a subsidy program in high cost areas to support for broadband service capable of (relatively low quality) video streaming if the unsubsidized market is driving companies to deploy broadband capable of offering (higher quality) broadcast-quality video service in urban areas? Should the universal service subsidy support access to the physical broadband network or should it support specific services provided over that network?

There are corollary issues relating to how the universal service program would be affected by changes in economic regulation. For example, when the FCC recently re-classified DSL service as an information service rather than a telecommunications service, it had two effects on universal service. First, the current universal service assessment base, interstate and international telecommunications revenues, was immediately reduced. Second, currently federal universal service funding is only available to support telecommunications services. If DSL services are no longer telecommunications services, eligible high-cost carriers would no longer be able to obtain universal service funds in support of those services. Thus, reform of economic regulation must be undertaken in conjunction with review of existing universal service programs.

Another important element of the debate is how to develop a regulatory framework that will not quickly become obsolete as the market continues to experience rapid technological change. For example, many technologists envision the development of highly decentralized peer-to-peer networks to efficiently deliver interactive services in the future; these networks would have no major nodes and therefore no single points of failure, making them more secure and robust than current networks that rely on key servers.[22] Already there is discussion of the need to construct a new, more secure Internet.[23] Thus, although it would not be appropriate to base a new regulatory paradigm on a presumption that peer-to-peer network architecture will predominate, it also would not make sense to construct a regulatory framework that cannot accommodate that architecture.

Further complicating these issues, it will be necessary to chart a transitional course as the shift to a digital, broadband environment will not occur instantaneously and some providers and customers will continue to be dependent on old technology for some period of time.[24]

Finally, although the current statutory and regulatory framework allows the FCC to preempt state laws that restrict competition,[25] it generally limits FCC regulatory authority to interstate and international services,[26] leaving jurisdiction over intrastate telecommunications services to the states. It also gives states or localities the authority to grant cable franchises and to regulate rights-of-way.[27] As voice, data, and video services increasingly are provided over technologies and networks that do not follow state, or even national, borders, however, it is becoming less effective to perform certain types of regulation — and especially economic regulation — at the state or local level. *One task of telecom reform is to identify those regulatory elements that can continue to be performed efectively at the state or local level and those that should be centralized.*

The purpose of this report is to provide an analytical overview of the market and technological developments that have rendered the current statutory and regulatory framework ineffective and, in some cases, contrary to stated U.S. telecommunications policy objectives, and to present options for reforming the framework.[28] After a background discussion, it addresses the following issues:

- What are the advantages and disadvantages of the various different approaches to regulating access to broadband networks? Four options are discussed: open access, *ex ante* non-discrimination rules, *ex post* adjudication of abuses of market power, and self-regulation based on non-mandatory principles.
- How might the current statutory framework be modified to address the head-to-head competition developing between the broadband networks of telephone companies and cable operators?
- How might public policy foster the deployment of additional broadband networks?
- How might the rules for intercarrier compensation — the payments that carriers make to one another for terminating the calls originated by their subscribers — be made competitively neutral without impinging on other goals of U.S. telecommunications policy?
- In a broadband environment, which services should be supported by a universal service subsidy, who should receive the subsidy, who should contribute to a universal service fund, and how should the contributors be assessed?
- How do other programs and policies, such as federal grant and loan programs and policies toward municipal provision of broadband networks, contribute to the universal availability of broadband networks?
- How might current policies concerning voice over Internet protocol, access to 911 and E9 11, CALEA, and localism, competition, and diversity of voice in media change to better accommodate the current and future market and technological environment?

BACKGROUND: THE 1996 ACT

In 1996, Congress passed the Telecommunications Act, the first major rewrite of our nation's telecommunications law since the enactment of the 1934 Communications Act. The general objective of the 1996 Act was to open up markets to competition by removing unnecessary regulatory barriers to entry.[29] Congress attempted to create a regulatory framework for the transition from primarily monopoly provision to competitive provision of telecommunications services.

One key provision allowed the FCC to preempt enforcement of any state or local government statute, regulation, or legal requirement that acted as a barrier to entry in the provision of interstate or intrastate telecommunications service.[30]

Since the value of a network service, such as telecommunications service, increases as the number of other parties connected to the network increases,[31] new entrants would have a very difficult time entering the market if they could not interconnect their networks with those of the incumbent carriers. Competitive provision of service would benefit consumers most if all carriers' networks were interconnected. Thus, another key provision of the 1996 Act set obligations for incumbent carriers and new entrants to interconnect their networks with one another, imposing additional requirements on the incumbents because they might have the incentive and ability to restrict competitive entry by denying such interconnection or by setting terms, conditions, and rates that could undermine the ability of the new entrants to compete.[32]

With competitive provision of service, many calls will originate on the network of the carrier to whom the calling party subscribes but end up on the network of another carrier (to whom the called party subscribes). While it might be possible to have the calling party pay its carrier for originating a call and the called party pay its carrier for terminating that call, for various reasons it has been traditional in the United States for the calling party's carrier to pay the called party's carrier for completing the call — this is called intercarrier compensation[33] — and, in turn, for the calling party's carrier to recover those costs in the rates charged to its subscribers. The 1996 Act requires that intercarrier compensation rates among competing local exchange carriers be based on the "additional costs of terminating such calls."[34] However, as discussed below, the framework created by the 1996 Act set different intercarrier compensation rates for services that were not competing at that time but do compete today.

To foster competition in both the long distance and local markets, the 1996 Act created a process by which the Regional Bell Operating Companies ("RBOCs") would be freed from the restriction on their offering long distance service (which was one of the terms of the 1982 Consent Decree settling the government's antitrust case against the former Bell System monopoly)[35] once they made a showing that their local markets had been opened up to competition.[36]

Because Congress did not believe it would be viable for competitive entrants to fully build out their networks immediately, it included a provision requiring the incumbent local exchange carriers to make available to entrants, at cost-based wholesale rates, those elements of their network to which entrants needed access in order not to be impaired in their ability to offer telecommunications services.[37]

Prior to enactment of the 1996 Act, universal service (primarily for high-cost rural service) had been funded through implicit subsidies in above-cost rates for the "access charges" that long distance carriers paid as intercarrier compensation to local telephone companies for originating and terminating their subscribers' long distance calls, above-cost business rates, and above-cost urban rates. Recognizing that new entrants would target those services that had above-cost rates, and thus erode universal service support, Congress included in the 1996 Act a provision requiring universal service support to be explicit, rather than hidden in above-cost rates.[38] This requirement has only been partially implemented, however, and therefore significant implicit universal services subsidies still remain in above-cost rates for certain services.

The regulatory framework created by the 1996 Act was intended to foster "intramodal" competition within distinct markets, that is, competition among companies that used the same underlying technology to provide service, such as the development of competition between the incumbent local and long distance wireline carriers plus new competitive local exchange carriers, all of which used circuit-switched networks to offer voice services. It did not envision the intermodal competition that has subsequently developed, such as wireless service competing with both local and long distance wireline service, VoIP competing with wireline and wireless telephony, IP video competing with cable television. Given the focus on intramodal competition and the lack of intermodal competition, there was little concern about statutory or regulatory language that set different regulatory burdens for different technology modes.

As a result, the current statutory and regulatory framework may be inconsistent with, or unresponsive to, current market conditions in several ways:

- service providers that are in direct competition with one another sometimes may be subject to different regulatory rules because they use different technologies;[39]
- economic regulations intended to protect against monopoly power may not be fully taking into account intermodal competition; and
- the framework may not effectively address interconnection, access, and social policy issues for an IP architecture in which multiple applications ride on top of the physical (transmission) network layer.

At the same time, it might not be wise to simply replace the statutory provisions fostering intramodal competition with provisions fostering intermodal competition on the expectation that intermodal competition will always be effective. For the foreseeable future, the primary source of competition in the telecommunications service market for large business ("enterprise") customers will be intramodal, rather than intermodal. Cable networks were constructed to serve residential customers and therefore tend not to be ubiquitously deployed in business districts. Even the largest cable companies are only in selected geographic markets in the country, and may not be able to meet the needs of large, multi-locational business customers. Also, it is likely to take many years for wireless carriers to construct networks that can meet the bandwidth and security requirements of large corporations. Competitive provision of broadband services to these enterprise customers therefore is most likely to be intramodal. But even intramodal competition may be decreasing in the enterprise market. Until recently, the long distance carriers, in particular AT&T and MCI, were the largest providers of service to enterprise customers, with various competitive local exchange carriers ("CLECs") also offering enterprise service. In addition, as they began to meet the conditions in the 1996 Act that allowed them to offer service outside their regions, the RBOCs were becoming significant competitors to AT&T and MCI in the enterprise market. The recent acquisitions of AT&T by SBC (with the new company renamed AT&T) and of MCI by Verizon have eliminated those two RBOCs as competitors in the enterprise market and also in the Internet backbone market. Also, although the remaining CLECs have built fiber rings in business areas that connect directly to their major customers' locations, they have not captured sufficient traffic to capture the scale economies needed to justify buildout of a ubiquitous transport network. Rather, they have relied on the RBOCs, AT&T, and MCI for transport facilities on many routes. As a result, in approving those mergers, the Department of Justice and the FCC set a number of conditions intended to retain competitive options for enterprise and Internet customers, including the divestiture of some key transport facilities and ensuring CLECs and ISPs access to certain facilities or services at set rates for at least two years.[40] Nonetheless, some enterprise customers and CLECs remain concerned about their reduced options for retail services and transport facilities.

Competition and Innovation in the Internet Protocol Environment

In a relatively short period of time, the telecommunications sector has evolved from monopoly provision of services over service-specific networks, to a brief period of limited intramodal competition (from wireline competitive access providers and competitive local exchange carriers for the provision of telephone services and from a small number of cable "overbuilders") over service-specific networks, to incipient intermodal (wireline, wireless, and cable) competition over increasingly multiple-service broadband platforms. These new broadband networks are the physical vehicle for bringing into the home the applications (services) of both the network providers, themselves, and the independent applications providers. At this stage of the transition, however, most customers continue to receive services over legacy service-specific narrowband networks.

It is important to understand what this new environment — characterized by convergence of previously distinct markets and government policy focused on fostering facilities-based intermodal competition — is likely to yield. The market convergence currently underway will not result in a multitude of broadband networks because the underlying cost structure for such networks, meaning the huge sunk up-front fixed costs that can only be recovered if the company can exploit significant economies of scale and scope, will only support a limited number of networks. This is the case for wireline or wireless networks. Moreover, market convergence is not simply the ability to bundle voice, data, and video services into a single product offering. Rather, it is a technological spillover (from digital technology) that reduces entry costs so that *firms that already have single-use networks* providing voice, data, or video services can now use those networks with relatively inexpensive upgrades to offer multiple services over a single platform.[41] For example, at far less cost than would be required to build an entirely new network, the incumbent local exchange carriers can deploy DSL equipment on their copper networks to offer data and video services or the cable companies can upgrade their networks to offer VoIP. In this situation, in which underlying costs are likely to limit the number of network providers, public policy can nonetheless foster competition by removing impediments to single-use networks expanding into other markets. At the same time, policy makers should remain vigilant that the few network providers not constrain the ability of independent applications providers that do not have their own broadband networks to compete in those applications markets.

In the new environment, there will be three broad categories of competition and innovation issues, tied together by one common issue. These three categories are:

- intermodal competition and innovation among a small number of broadband network providers that offer a suite of voice, data, video, and other services primarily for the mass market;
- intramodal competition and innovation among a small number of wireline broadband providers that serve multi-locational business customers who tend to be located in business districts;[42] and
- competition between those few broadband network providers and a multitude of independent service providers, often for applications that have a more specialized customer base.

The common issue: how many broadband networks will there be and how will that affect competition among network providers and competition between those network providers and the independent applications providers?

Despite all the technological and market changes that have occurred and continue to take place, competition issues in the telecommunications sector will continue to focus on the physical transport link into both business and residential customers' premises. The new network architectures may allow many applications to ride on a single physical transmission layer, but access to that layer and competition among the small number of physical network providers remain the primary competition issues.

Applications Innovation: Competition between Integrated Network Providers and Independent Applications Providers

Integrated network providers and independent applications providers come from very different traditions. The network providers (the local exchange carriers, cable companies, and wireless carriers) come from the tradition of employing a vertically integrated business model, providing, as a single product offering, the network connection and a specific service or suite of services. They are used to developing and deploying their networks in the context of a business plan that jointly maximizes profits from the physical network and the services they provide over that network. Their network rollout and applications product rollout are coordinated. Network architecture is driven, at least in part, by the services they intend to offer. Underlying this approach is the assumption that investment can best be supported and innovation can best be achieved by giving the vertically integrated network provider free rein over network architecture, control of network intelligence, and discretion over the extent to which it gives competing applications providers access to its network.

In sharp contrast, many of the independent applications providers (and their customers) come from the Internet tradition of "network neutrality," that is, an Internet that does not favor one application over others. In practice, even the Internet does not adhere to pure network neutrality; for example, the Internet protocol works well for data applications, which are insensitive to "latency" (delay), and less well for voice and video applications that are sensitive to latency, because it lacks a universal quality of service guarantee.[43] Nonetheless, the assumptions that underlie the Internet tradition are that the innovation process is a survival-of-the-fittest competition among developers of new technologies, that the most promising path of innovation cannot be predicted in advance, and that therefore it is not optimal to allow any private or public entity to direct that path; the network should be "neutral." This reasoning supports the need for "end-to-end" design, by which, whenever possible, communications protocol operations occur at the end-points of a communications system (i.e., a "dumb network" with "smart terminals"). But since until 1995 the Internet was supported by government funding, rather than market funding, this approach has not focused in the past on the task of raising sufficient capital to build out physical networks.

The vertically integrated network providers and the independent applications providers are not inherently at odds with one another, however; they share many goals. The Internet environment is characterized by "indirect network externalities," in which independent actions taken by hardware and software providers benefit one another. The greater the investment in physical network to improve connection speed and quality of service, the greater the opportunities for software providers to develop new, potentially profitable applications. At the same time, the greater the number of software applications available, the greater the end-user demand for broadband connections. A network provider will have an incentive not to restrict applications providers' access to its physical network to the extent that could reduce demand for connections to that network (though that effect could be limited if end users have no alternative broadband networks available to turn to).

At the same time, vertically integrated network providers might face a counter-incentive to restrict or delay network access to applications providers; an example is if the vertically integrated company is developing an application that would compete with the independent provider's application and would like to exploit "first-in" advantages. They also will have the incentive to deploy a network architecture most consistent with their own plans for applications, which may not coincide with the needs of the independent applications providers or with the desire of end users to use their broadband network for applications (telecommuting, home networking, or other purposes) that might undermine the ability of the network provider to price discriminate or in other ways jointly maximize the profits from its network and own suite of applications. For example, some critics have claimed that the RBOCs resisted deploying DSL technology in their networks for more than a decade because of concern that offering a high-speed DSL service would cannibalize the revenues and profits that were being generated by their T-1 (large capacity dedicated pipe) service. According to these critics, despite the fact that the relatively inexpensive DSL technology had been available for a long time, the RBOCs began deploying DSL only once there was significant risk of ceding the mass market high-speed connection market to cable modems. (The RBOCs have responded that they had not deployed DSL because the market had not yet developed for the high-speed service.)

In a market characterized by economic interdependence between a platform and applications made for that platform, sometimes an arm's-length relationship between the platform provider and the applications providers will be less efficient than a closer vertical relationship. Academic economists have employed the concept of internalizing complementary efficiencies ("ICE") to explain vertical competitive effects — why sometimes the platform provider chooses an open architecture and modular design to interact with the full universe of applications providers and sometimes chooses to interact only with its own vertically integrated applications subsidiaries or affiliates.[44] The ICE theorem suggests that a monopolist broadband network provider has incentives to provide independent applications providers access to its broadband platform when it is efficient to do so, and to deny such access only when access is inefficient. But economic theory further explains that platform providers will not always make the optimal choice. There are a number of circumstances when the platform provider's choice might not be efficient or benefit consumers.[45] Economic theory therefore suggests that there may be pitfalls in either a blanket requirement for access to the broadband network or blanket deregulation.

In a market characterized by high sunk up-front fixed costs and very low variable (usage) costs once the up-front costs have been sunk, which is descriptive both of the physical broadband network and the software applications provided over that network, it often is efficient for a firm to employ price discrimination to recover its fixed costs. That is, it may be most efficient to segment customers according to the intensity of their demand for the broadband connection (or application), charging a higher price for the customers with higher intensity of demand. In the case of the broadband connection, that intensity might be measured in terms of the amount of bandwidth demanded. As will be discussed below, such price discrimination based on bandwidth usage need not infringe on network neutrality (need not favor some applications over others) so long as the market segmentation is based on the amount of bandwidth used rather than on the specific application and so long as customers who want to use the network for a bandwidth-intensive application are able to pay more for that additional bandwidth, rather than being prohibited from using the network to access bandwidth-intensive applications.

Broadband Network Restrictions

In 2002, Professor Tim Wu performed a survey of broadband usage restrictions and network designs for the 10 largest cable operators and six major DSL operators.[46] The survey found that, on the whole, broadband providers' networks and usage restrictions favored client-server applications (such as the World Wide Web) and disfavored home networking, peer-to-peer applications, and home telecommuting. Cable operators tended to impose far more restrictions on usage than DSL operators. Specifically,

- Nearly every cable operator and one third of DSL operators restricted end users from operating a server and/or providing content to the public. This restriction is potentially very significant because it affects the broadest class of applications: those where the end user shares content, as opposed to simply downloading content. It favors a "one-to-many" or "vertical model" of applications over a "manyto-many" or "horizontal" model. In application design terms, the restriction favors client-server applications over peer-to-peer designs. The inability to provide content or act as a server could serve to restrict a major class of network applications.
- Every cable operator and most DSL operators had some ban on using a basic residential broadband connection for "commercial" or "enterprise" use. The most controversial of such restrictions barred home users from using virtual public networks, which are used by telecommuters to connect to their work network through a secure connection.
- When home networking became widespread in 2002, four of the ten largest cable operators contractually limited the deployment of home networks by setting restrictions on the number of computers that could be attached to a single connection. In contrast, some DSL operators in their agreements explicitly acknowledged that multiple computers could be connected to the DSL connection, though sometimes only through a single DSL account and a single IP address obtained from the DSL operator.
- Several cable operators sought to control the deployment of home wireless networks by banning the connection of Wi-Fi equipment.
- The practice of designing asymmetric networks, with more downstream bandwidth than upstream bandwidth, favors the development of applications that are one-to-many or client-server in design. Applications that would demand residential accounts to deliver content as quickly as they receive it are limited by asymmetric bandwidth.

It was not clear how actively network providers had attempted to enforce those restrictions in their contracts with subscribers, though there was anecdotal evidence of some enforcement. Nor was it clear whether such restrictions would continue when wireless technology was able to provide greater competition to wireline and cable network providers. In some ways, there appear to be fewer usage restrictions today than there were in 2002. It is noteworthy, however, that the cable networks imposed more usage restrictions than did the DSL network. There are two possible explanations for this: (1) cable is the largest broadband platform provider and can offer greater bandwidth and these "first-in" and technology advantages may allow it to set strategic usage restrictions that other platforms could only set at their peril, and (2) since cable's broadband architecture requires customers to share bandwidth, there is greater need for cable to manage the bandwidth usage of its customers. Yet, cable operators have not barred streaming video, despite its potential for competing with cable television.

It does not appear that these restrictions will go entirely away anytime soon. Vendors are actively marketing equipment designed to facilitate applications-based screening and control for broadcast networks, such as products intended to address peer-to-peer traffic and unauthorized Wi-Fi connections and control over network utilization.[47] Network providers are deploying such equipment, though it is not clear exactly how they are using it.

Access and usage restrictions may be justified if they are needed to protect the integrity of the network or to operate the network efficiently (for example, bandwidth management needed to maintain quality of service). But there may be situations where the network provider has chosen an overly restrictive solution that will discourage applications innovation and competition. For example, if a network provider must manage bandwidth usage in order to maintain quality of service for video and voice services, it would be more efficient for the provider to do so by setting rates that rise as bandwidth usage increases rather than by prohibiting all bandwidth-intensive applications. The former represents an application of price discrimination that most economists recognize as efficient; the latter may be unnecessarily restrictive.

Professor Wu concluded that, on the whole, the evidence from his survey suggested that the operators were often pursuing legitimate goals, such as price discrimination and bandwidth management. The problem was they often used methods, like bans on certain forms of applications, that are likely to unnecessarily distort the market and the future of application development. The use of restrictions on classes of application to pursue bandwidth management and price discrimination may be inefficient and may unnecessarily harm consumers; the objectives may be attainable through less restrictive means.

In November 2005, several ISPs alleged that Verizon restricted their access to its broadband network immediately after the FCC's August 2005 decision that DSL service is an information service and therefore not subject to Title II access requirements.[48] They claimed that, prior to the FCC decision, Verizon had offered them access to its broadband network at the Layer 2 or data link level, which allowed them to offer their own services at a guaranteed a quality of service. But after the FCC decision, Verizon replaced that access offering with an offering that only allowed access at the Layer 3 or network level, which in essence is a complete package that the ISP can only resell, without offering additional services. A Verizon representative conceded the change in service offering, but claimed that "No customers have been cut off and no Internet sites are being blocked, and the customers of these ISPs will have full Internet access under the new service arrangement."[49]

More recently, the three largest RBOCs have announced their intentions to take advantage of new technology that allows them to distinguish among the digitized packets on their high-speed networks to charge those providers of applications who want to be able to guarantee their customers an assured quality of service — for example, for voice or video service — a premium for such assured high quality delivery.[50] The RBOCs claim that even if an end-user customer pays a high price for a lot of bandwidth, that customer could not receive an assured quality of service for voice or video service received over the public Internet. That customer might blame its broadband network provider or the applications provider for the degraded service quality even if the problem resided in the Internet. But today an RBOC can distinguish the packets destined for that provider's end-user customers and, by connecting the provider directly to its proprietary IP networks, can guarantee the quality of service of the provider's offerings. The RBOCs argue that such guaranteed quality of service is of value to the applications provider as well as to the end user, and therefore they should be able to charge the provider a premium for such assured quality. Applications providers have criticized these proposed quality of service charges, arguing that the RBOCs could impose high quality of services charges on them that they do not impose on their own applications. They also have voiced concern that the RBOCs could use the new packet identification equipment to provide better service to their own end-user customers than to competitors' end-user customers, and could strategically deploy network capacity sufficient to meet the quality of service needs of their own applications offerings but not sufficient to meet the needs of their competitors' offerings.

Approaches to Regulating Access to Broadband Networks

There are four general approaches to the regulation of broadband network providers vis-a-vis independent applications providers:

- structural regulation, such as open access;
- *ex ante* non-discrimination rules;
- *ex post* adjudication of abuses of market power, as they arise, on a case-by-case basis; and
- reliance on antitrust law and non-mandatory principles as the basis for self-regulation.

There have been a plethora of proposals for such regulation, with the proposals sometimes incorporating elements from more than one of these approaches.

Ex ante rules and *ex post* adjudication both typically focus on anti-competitive discrimination that harms consumers, but in distinct ways. *Ex ante* rules have been characterized as "positive" anti-discrimination rules in that they create affirmative legal duties that are intended to remedy either past discrimination or the likelihood of future discrimination,[51] prohibiting certain activities before the fact. By contrast, "negative" *ex post* adjudication typically seeks to punish identified episodes of discrimination on a case-by-case basis, after the fact. Positive schemes impose more up-front costs: by restricting certain behaviors, some of which might have proven beneficial to consumers. But, depending on the cost to consumers (in terms of denied access to potentially highly valued applications) of allowing discrimination to occur and then adjudicating after the fact, the ultimate cost of positive *ex ante* rules might prove lower than *ex post* adjudication.

Open Access

Although there is not a single agreed-upon definition of open access, it generally refers to a structural requirement that would prevent a broadband network provider from bundling broadband service with Internet access from its own in-house Internet service provider and would require the network provider to make its broadband transmission capability available to independent ISPs on a nondiscriminatory basis. Proponents of open access argue that if a broadband network provider, such as a cable operator, is allowed to bundle ISP services with its broadband connection at a single price, and not offer the broadband connection separately, it would be in a position to foreclose competition among Internet applications.[52] They claim that as ISPs expand the services they offer, bundling would foreclose competition in an increasing range of services provided over broadband lines. If the customer has no choice but to accept from the broadband provider a single bundle that includes both the broadband connection and ISP service, then an independent ISP would always be at a price disadvantage and could only compete by offering unique capabilities that are sufficient to overcome that price disadvantage. This is likely to limit an independent ISP's customer base to those customers with unique needs that are not met by the mass market broadband provider.

Proponents of open access claim that allowing network providers to restrict independent ISPs' access will (1) eliminate, or at least reduce, ISP competition; (2) allow legacy monopoly networks to improperly affect the architecture of the Internet in an effort to protect their own business plans; (3) discourage innovators from investing in a market in which a dominant player has the power to behave strategically against them; and (4) make government intervention to control certain forms of speech easier and therefore more likely.

Open access has been criticized on several fronts. First, broadband network providers and a number of academics[53] claim that, due to indirect network externalities and internalizing network efficiencies, network providers do not have the incentive to restrict independent applications providers access to their networks, or would do so only where it was efficient. They further argue that even if one group of network providers — for example, the cable companies — were to restrict access, wireline broadband providers and other competitors are unlikely to follow suit, so independent ISPs would have access to customers.

Some critics claim that open access would retard deployment of broadband networks by reducing the ability of network providers to exploit vertical integration efficiencies and also by reducing the revenues network providers could generate from their applications, thereby making some network investments unprofitable. They also suggest that the close coordination between a network provider and as applications provider needed for optimal joint development of network and applications is sometimes only possible through vertical integration. For example, Professor James Speta argues that "Vertical integration of access providers may be necessary. Especially in initial periods of deployment, broadband access providers must ensure a supply of complementary information services.... [A] broadband provider must either provide those goods itself or arrange for a source of supply."[54]

Also, to the extent open access regulation prevents broadband operators from architectural cooperation with independent ISPs for the purpose of providing quality of service ("QOS") dependent applications, it could harm network neutrality. By threatening the vertical relationship required for certain application types, it could maintain IP's discrimination in favor of data applications.

In response to these criticisms of open access, its proponents have pointed out a fundamental contradiction among the criticisms.[55] On one hand, critics argue that, due to indirect network externalities, broadband network providers' self-interest will lead them to place minimal restrictions on customers' usage of, and independent applications providers' access to, their networks. On the other hand, critics argue that restricted access is needed to ensure that the network providers generate enough revenues to recoup their investment in the network.

Ex Ante Non-Discrimination Rules

The basic principle behind a network non-discrimination regime is to give users the right, by rule, to use non-harmful attachments or applications, and give innovators the corresponding right, also by rule, to supply them. Proponents claim that such a regime avoids some of the costs of structural regulation by allowing for efficient vertical integration so long as the rights granted to the users of the network are not compromised.

Proponents contend that the ability of a network provider to discriminate is greater with a digital broadband network than with an analog narrowband network offering dial-up service. Analog network operators cannot easily distinguish between types of digitized packets of information going across their lines. But digital network operators can distinguish among the packets on their high-speed networks.[56] For example, some universities are performing application-specific screening to identify students illegally copying entertainment materials and, presumably, similar capabilities could be used to identify applications the network provider wishes to restrict or prohibit.

Typically proponents of non-discrimination rules are proponents of network neutrality — not favoring one application over another.[57] They argue that network neutrality, as embodied in *ex ante* non-discrimination rules, fosters the goal of stimulating investment and innovation in broadband technology and services in two ways: (1) by eliminating the risk of future discrimination, thereby providing independent applications providers greater incentives to invest in broadband applications, and (2) by facilitating fair competition among applications, ensuring the survival of the fittest.

Proponents claim that a network that is as neutral as possible, with such neutrality ensured by explicit non-discrimination rules, provides entrepreneurs predictability in that all applications are treated alike. This, they argue, will foster investment in broadband applications by eliminating the unpredictability created by potential future restrictions on network usage. Neutrality provides applications designers and consumers alike with a baseline on which they can rely. Proponents allege the recent restrictions that cable operators placed on virtual private networks is indicative of the tendency of some network providers to restrict new and innovative applications they see as either unimportant or a competitive threat. Such usage restrictions, they claim, particularly harm those small and startup developers that are most likely to push the envelope of what is possible using the Internet's architecture.[58]

Proponents also claim that the most promising path of development will be difficult to predict in advance; neutral network development is likely to yield better results than planned innovation directed by a single prospect holder. Any single entity will suffer from cognitive biases (such as a predisposition to continue with current ways of doing business). These proponents conclude that restrictions on usage, however well-intended, tend to favor certain applications over others. A regulatory framework that requires network providers to justify deviations from neutrality would prevent both unthinking and ill-intentioned distortions of the market for new applications. The proponents of non-discrimination rules argue that the restrictions that some network providers have imposed on home networking, online gaming, and VPNs not only directly harm consumers and applications providers today, but also have a chilling effect on innovators and venture capitalists considering future applications development and deployment. They argue that the possibility of discrimination in the future dampens the incentives to invest today.

Two very different proposals for *ex ante* rules merit discussion; one would enact a "pure" *ex ante* regime, the other would enact a hybrid regime that constructs *ex ante* rules only where antitrust enforcement might not be sufficient.

Ex Ante Neutrality Regime

Professor Wu has proposed what he calls a neutrality regime that would set *ex ante* non-discrimination access rules that would apply to the "inter-network" portion of a broadband network provider's network (that is, the portion that it collectively manages with other network providers), but not to the local portion of the network that is under the provider's sole control. Each broadband network provider is a member of two networks: the local network that provides the last-mile of transport to its end-user customers and which it owns and manages by itself, and the inter-network, which it collectively manages with other service providers. If a broadband network provider imposes local network restrictions, usually those restrictions will only affect its local network. Such restrictions are likely to be necessary for good network management. In contrast, restrictions at the inter-network layer or applications layer will affect the entire network, inter-network as well as local network, and can cause externality problems.

The *ex ante* neutrality regime is based on a non-discrimination rule that distinguishes between discrimination at the local network level (acceptable) and at the inter-network level (unacceptable); the rule would make operational the network neutrality principle at the inter-network level.[59] The rule prohibits discrimination based on such inter-network elements as IP addresses, domain name, and cookie information. Its general principle is: absent evidence of harm to the local network or the interests of other users, broadband network providers should not discriminate in how they treat traffic on their broadband network on the basis of inter-network criteria.

Thus, for example, under the *ex ante* neutrality regime, a broadband network provider concerned about managing bandwidth would be prohibited from blocking traffic from game sites based on either application information or the IP address of the application provider. But it would be allowed to invest in policing bandwidth usage; users interested in a better gaming experience would need to buy more bandwidth, not get permission to use a given application. As another example, recently the FCC entered into a consent decree with Madison River Communications, a rural telephone company, which had been blocking ports used for VoIP applications, thereby affecting their customers' ability to use VoIP through VoIP service providers.[60] Under this regime, such discriminatory behavior would be *ex ante* illegal.

Since Professor Wu would not regulate customer access to the local network portion of the broadband network, he would allow cable operators to tie cable modem service (broadband access) to ISP service (an application) and, similarly, would allow ILECs to tie DSL service (broadband access) to voice service (an application). That is, ILECs would not be required to offer end users what is sometimes referred to as "naked DSL" service: DSL service without voice service. But because he would prohibit discriminatory access to the inter-network, Professor Wu would prohibit a cable operator from refusing to allow a customer to use its cable modem to obtain ISP service from another ISP and would prohibit an ILEC from refusing to allow a customer to use its DSL service to obtain voice service from another voice provider.

Ex ante non-discrimination rules have been subject to criticism from parties that argue that such rules would intrude too much into the business plans of broadband network providers. These critics argue that non-discrimination rules impinge on the ability of broadcast network providers to fully exploit efficiencies from vertical integration or to use price discrimination or other pricing strategies to maximize return on investment. Professor Wu responds that his proposal, which limits the non-discrimination prohibition to the inter-network portion, minimizes that effect by allowing the network provider to take advantage of those economies of scope and vertical integration advantages (such as offering service level guarantees not provided on a shared network) that come with building one's own physical network — so long as no restrictions (such as prohibiting access to certain IP addresses) are placed on use of the shared portion of the Internet network. On the other hand, some parties have been concerned that by allowing the broadband network providers unlimited control over the local portion of their networks, those providers still could distort applications markets to their advantage, though it might be more difficult or more expensive to do so.

Another criticism of *ex ante* non-discrimination rules is that they inherently lead to delays, litigation, and other regulatory costs, as parties fight over interpretation of the rules. The complexity of communications networks, it is argued, renders it difficult, if not impossible, to construct clear *ex ante* rules. These critics point to the industry experience implementing the 1996 Act. Professor Wu has responded that delays, litigation, and other regulatory costs of administering an *ex ante* non-discrimination rule could be minimized by identifying only two network layers — the transport infrastructure layer and the application services level[61] — and by restricting the rules to the inter-network portion of the network.

The other major criticism is that *ex ante* rules of any sort, and especially those relating to network access, will artificially aid an independent applications provider in its contractual negotiations with a broadband network provider by allowing it to threaten to bring a regulatory complaint and attendant costs if the network provider does not accept its terms. According to this argument, the network provider often might be forced to accept unfavorable or inefficient access terms to avoid the threat of litigation.

The European Union Framework

The European Union ("EU") has adopted a legislative framework for the regulation of electronic communications ("EU Framework") that includes creation of *ex ante* rules to supplement an antitrust approach to regulation.[62] The EU Framework creates a single regulatory structure that covers all electronic networks and services within its scope, without regard to underlying technology.[63] It aims to "reduce *ex-ante* sector-specific rules progressively as competition in the market develops."[64] The rules, requirements, or obligations imposed on providers are service-specific and are determined by the level of competition in the market.[65] The EU Framework calls for periodic review of all regulatory obligations,[66] although no time period is specified.

Under the EU Framework, specific *ex ante* regulatory obligations are imposed only on those providers that:

- have significant market power; *and*
- are operating in markets where competition is not effective; *and*
- where national and European Community competition law (i.e., antitrust) remedies are not sufficient to address the problem.[67]

The Framework Directive equates "significant market power" with "dominance." It states that a provider "shall be deemed to have significant market power if, either individually or jointly with others, it enjoys a position equivalent to dominance, that is to say a position of economic strength affording it the power to behave to an appreciable extent independently of its competitors, customers, and ultimately consumers."[68]

As required by the Framework Directive, the Commission of the European Communities (a body of the EU) has prepared Commission Guidelines that describe in detail how to measure effective competition and significant market power,[69] and also a Commission Recommendation that identifies 18 product and service markets in which *ex ante* regulation may be warranted because of a lack of effective competition.[70]

The Commission, itself, does not devise specific rules, requirements, and obligations for electronic communications providers. Rather, the National Regulatory Agencies of each of the EU's member states must perform market analysis within their national boundaries to determine which providers have significant market power and, based on that market analysis, create the appropriate specific regulations, rules, or obligations to impose on those providers.[71] To date, very few of the member states have performed this market analysis or implemented regulations, rules, or obligations, and thus there is no empirical evidence on the impact of this regulatory framework.

The Commission Guidelines state that, although a high market share alone is not considered sufficient to establish possession of significant market power, concerns about single firm dominance arise with market shares of 40% or above.[72] Providers with market share of 25% or less are deemed unlikely to have significant market power. Emerging markets, where *de facto* the market leader is likely to have a substantial market share, should not be subject to inappropriate *ex ante* regulation.[73]

Proponents of the EU Framework argue that telecommunications regulation should be viewed as an applied case of antitrust and therefore should adhere to antitrust principles.

Critics of the EU Framework claim that although the rules are set *ex ante,* they fail to provide either network providers or independent applications providers the type of certainty that fosters innovative activity because they are determined on a case-by-case basis and do not take advantage of characteristics common to most communications markets. As one critic explains:

> ...what distinguishes telecommunications problems is that they share consistent features found in some but not all antitrust cases. Most telecommunications problems feature many if not all of the following economic features: (1) a physical infrastructure of high fixed cost, that is (2) a large source of both positive externalities including network externalities, that (3) can be used to provide

a range of services, and (4) in an environment of rapid technological change that makes the infrastructure useful for different services than those for which it was originally designed.[74]

Given these common market characteristics, it might be possible to construct general rules that provide certainty for network providers and independent applications providers alike.

Another criticism of the EU Framework is that reliance on antitrust principles simply replaces the current contentious battle over the classification of services with a new contentious battle over proper market definition, since any determination of whether a firm has significant market power is likely to depend heavily on the geographic and product market definitions chosen.

Ex Post Adjudication of Abuses of Market Power

The Regulatory Framework Working Group of the Digital Age Communications Act Project of the Progress and Freedom Foundation ("PFF Working Group") has proposed replacing the current statutory and regulatory framework that relies heavily on proscriptive rules that set *ex ante* structural and behavioral requirements (such as access requirements or non-discrimination rules) with a system that would adjudicate alleged abuses of market power *ex post,* as they arise, on a case-by-case basis. It proposes enacting a new statute, the Digital Age Communications Act ("DACA"),[75]

modeled after the Federal Trade Commission Act, [76] that would give the FCC (or a successor agency) the authority to adjudicate allegations of "unfair methods of competition ... and unfair or deceptive acts in or affecting electronic communications networks and electronic communications services." These unfair practices could include interconnection-related practices (such as the refusal to interconnect or unfair terms, conditions, and rates of interconnection):

- *if* such practices were shown to pose a substantial and non-transitory risk to consumer welfare;
- *and if* the Commission determined marketplace competition were not sufficient to protect consumer welfare;
- *and if* the Commission considered whether requiring interconnection would affect adversely investment in facilities and innovation in services.

Under the proposal, the Commission could require the guilty party to pay damages to the harmed party if any violation were found. Also under the proposal, the Commission would have very constrained authority to prescribe rules, which would automatically sunset after five years. The FCC's authority to approve an application to assign or transfer control of a license (that is, to review mergers) would be limited to ensuring that any such change in control did not violate existing FCC rules.

The PFF Working Group claims that the potential harm to consumers from bad regulation far exceeds the potential harm from badly functioning markets and therefore the burden of proof must fall on the regulator for imposing any regulation. It seeks to "codif[y] a presumption that regulation is unnecessary to protect consumers and provide[] tools that can adequately address competition problems that arise in communications markets." It states that even inefficient market outcomes are likely to be less problematic than regulatory solution because (1) markets are effective at responding to and overcoming their own inefficiencies, (2) government may not have the incentive to improve matters, and (3) policy makers are likely to lack the information needed to make efficient decisions. Thus, it proposes *ex post* rather than *ex ante* regulation and the five-year sunset provision. The PFF Working Group further argues that a new statute is needed in order to replace the current model of regulation based on vague standards such as the "public interest" and "just and reasonable" with the well-established "unfair competition" standard of the FTC. It explicitly seeks, in each and every provision of its proposed statute, to minimize the FCC's regulatory authority.

The PFF Working Group proposal for *ex post* regulation has been subject to several criticisms. First, it is based on the assumption that consumer welfare loss from bad regulation is always far greater than consumer welfare loss from badly performing markets, and that it is therefore best to err on the side of under-regulating. This may or may not be true in the case of markets characterized by networks where the platform provider and applications providers must cooperate to maximize consumer welfare. There is a large and growing academic law and economics literature on these unique markets; there is no consensus in the literature, or from empirical evidence, that in these markets there is less risk from erring on the side of under-regulation than on the side of over-regulation. Nor is there theoretical or empirical proof that the potential harm to consumers from distortions created by *ex ante* rules are greater than those created by *ex post* adjudication. It is possible that a narrowly crafted *ex ante* non-discrimination rule could create less distortion than *ex post* adjudications that will inherently result in some, and potentially many, innovative independent applications providers being driven from the market, thereby denying customers the benefit of their services. The PFF Working Group proposal appears implicitly to recognize that possibility by giving the FCC rulemaking authority, which, although constrained, would allow the Commission to consider adoption of *ex ante* rules where appropriate.

More generally, critics claim that *ex post* regulation distorts the business plans, and undermines the negotiating position, of independent applications providers by placing the burden of proof for network access on them if they seek to develop and introduce an application that may not fit into the business plan of the network provider. According to this argument, the independent applications provider might be forced to modify its planned application or accept unfavorable or inefficient access terms to avoid the threat of being denied access to the broadband network.

Some critics also oppose the PFF Working Group proposal to eliminate the public interest standard, claiming reliance on what is basically an antitrust standard fails to take into account non-economic objectives of U.S. telecommunications policy, such as localism and diversity of voices.

Antitrust Law and Non-Mandatory Principles as the Basis for Self-Regulation

The broadband network providers have argued that they should not be subject to access regulation because they face strong market incentives not to restrict the access of independent applications providers to their networks. They cite the existence of indirect network efficiencies, which reward network providers for keeping their network open, and the availability to most Americans of at least two broadband networks. They argue that any access regulation would cause harm, by curtailing their ability to vertically integrate to exploit efficiencies such as ensuring quality of service levels needed for video and voice services.[77] They argue that where they have placed usage restrictions on customers those restrictions were needed to ensure quality of service and other bandwidth management objectives and to make it feasible to undertake their huge infrastructure investments. They also claim that they remain subject to the antitrust laws, which would constrain them from undertaking any anticompetitive activities that are harmful to consumers.

These arguments have been subject to a number of attacks. Critics have pointed to the widespread, documented usage restrictions that network providers have placed on end users, which the critics claim have harmed consumers, for example, by denying access to virtual private networks needed for telecommuting. Critics claim that these usage prohibitions are far more restrictive than needed to manage bandwidth, and often are imposed for strategic purposes, not for network efficiency reasons. They also claim that not regulating access will harm innovation by giving the broadband network providers the ability to strategically constrain independent applications.

Former FCC chairman Michael Powell has suggested that it might not be necessary to impose regulations if the industry were to agree to follow certain "Internet Freedom" principles as the basis for self-regulation. Mr. Powell has constructed guiding principles,[78] noting that:

> Promoting competition among high-speed Internet platforms is only half of our task, however. We must ensure that the various capabilities of these technologies are not used in a way that could stunt the growth of the economy, innovation and consumer empowerment. Thus, we must expand our focus beyond broadband networks — the so-called "physical layer" of the Internet's layered architecture.

Referring explicitly to the research and analyses performed by Professors Weiser, Farrell, and Wu, cited earlier, Mr. Powell explained that there are circumstances in which broadband network providers might choose to restrict usage on their network, and that some troubling restrictions have appeared in broadband service plan agreements. But he stated that he did not believe that there was yet a case for government imposed regulations regarding the use or provision of broadband content, applications, and devices. Instead, he challenged the industry to avoid future regulation by embracing what he called the four Internet Freedoms. These are:

- *Freedom to Access Content:* Consumers should have access to their choice of legal content.
- *Freedom to Use Applications:* Consumers should be able to run applications of their choice.
- *Freedom to Attach Personal Devices:* Consumers should be permitted to attach any devices they choose to the connection in their homes.
- *Freedom to Obtain Service Plan Information:* Consumers should receive meaningful information regarding their service plans.

In presenting these principles, Mr. Powell indicated that broadband network providers have a legitimate need to manage their networks and ensure a quality experience; thus reasonable limits sometimes must be placed on service contracts. Such constraints, however, should be clearly spelled out and should be as minimal as necessary. Since no one can know for sure which "killer" applications will emerge to drive deployment of the next generation high-speed technologies, the industry must let the market work and allow consumers to run applications and attach devices unless they exceed service plan limitations or harm the provider's network. (The broadband network providers have not explicitly opposed Mr. Powell's proposal; nor have they explicitly endorsed it.)

In its August 5, 2005 order and related actions, the FCC, in effect, implemented Mr. Powell's proposal. It ruled that DBS service, like cable modem service, is an information service and therefore not subject to any of the access requirements in Title II of the Communications Act. It also adopted a non-binding policy statement consisting of four principles: consumers are entitled to access the lawful Internet content of their choice; consumers are entitled to run applications and services of their choice, subject to the needs of law enforcement; consumers are entitled to connect their choice of legal devices that do not harm the network; and, consumers are entitled to competition among network providers, application and service providers, and content providers.[79]

Critics have challenged Mr. Powell's proposal — and, by extension, the FCC's August 5, 2005, order and policy statement — on several grounds. They point to the many documented instances of usage restrictions placed on end users as proof that, left unregulated, market forces are not robust enough to ensure unrestricted access. They argue that the search for the killer application that might drive investment in both infrastructure and applications is more likely to be successful in a regulatory regime that fosters network neutrality than in a regime that allows the few broadband network providers to determine the direction of the network. They argue that it is impossible to undo harm after it has occurred and that, in light of the identifiable reasons why network providers might have both the incentive and the ability to restrict access, it is dangerous to move forward based on non-mandatory principles that the network providers have not, in any case, endorsed.

Critics also claim that antitrust laws, which generically address monopoly behavior and anticompetitive practices, are inefficient vehicles for addressing the impediments to competition and innovation that are most common in communications markets. These critics argue that there is abundant empirical evidence that there are greater opportunities for firms to erect barriers to entry in "network" markets than in traditional markets and that as a result relying primarily on *ex post* antitrust enforcement leaves consumers subject to unnecessary risk. They also oppose elimination of the public interest standard.

Platform Innovation: Mass Market Competition among Broadband Network Providers

Currently, in most locations, the incumbent local exchange carrier ("ILEC") and the local cable company are the only broadband network providers serving the mass market. Wireless (including satellite) carriers, cable overbuilders, or power companies may provide a relatively ubiquitous third broadband connection some time down the road, but in the next few years are likely to offer mass market customers a competitive option in scattered locations at most. Nor have the ILECs demonstrated tangible plans to extend their broadband networks beyond their current service areas to compete head-on with other ILEC broadband providers.

It appears that the competition that is developing between telephone and cable providers is taking the form of "triple play" offerings of voice, data, and video services. At present and in the near future, some telephone companies will bundle re-sold satellite video services with their voice and DSL services to compete with cable companies' triple play. But the largest ILECs and even many small rural carriers have begun to upgrade their networks to have the bandwidth capacity to offer video services themselves.[80] Broadband network providers will seek to distinguish themselves by offering premium services such as video on demand, bundles that include wireless service (with that service provided over a separate wireless network, though perhaps using hybrid telephones that can be used on wireless and wireline networks), access to advanced electronic games, etc. A key will be to offer a broadband connection with sufficient bandwidth to accommodate whatever service becomes the killer application, or at least an important application.

As explained earlier, these broadband networks actually consist of two parts: the last-mile local network privately owned and operated by the broadband network provider and the inter-network that is jointly operated by multiple Internet backbone providers. Success for any broadband network provider will depend on the bandwidth, security, and service quality it can ensure over its local network.

Although currently all ubiquitous broadband networks provide hard wires into the customer premise, the various network providers are each deploying unique network architectures. Most of the large cable companies have upgraded their coaxial cable networks and now are offering video, data, and voice services in many areas of the country, especially in urban areas. Their cables into customers' premises often have sufficient bandwidth to "broadcast" to customers' premises hundreds of video channels for the customers to choose among and their set-top boxes allow customers to select video on demand, although the video choices available at any particular point in time may be limited. Currently deployed cable modem technology, however, requires clustered customers to share bandwidth capacity, so that connection speeds fall as more neighbors use the network.

Traditional Cable vs. IP Video

The two largest ILECs, AT&T[81] and Verizon, are pursuing quite distinct architectures, with the Verizon architecture in many ways more like cable architecture than like the AT&T architecture. Verizon reportedly will spend $6 billion over five years to bring optical fiber directly to as many as 16 million homes in its service areas.[82] Verizon has begun deployment of its "FiOS TV" network, which will require the replacement of current copper wires into the household premise with optical fiber. This requires a truck roll to physically replace the copper with fiber. But that fiber has such high capacity that it is likely to allow Verizon to bring as much or more bandwidth to the home as cable systems, thus allowing Verizon to simultaneously "broadcast" a large number of video channels and offer video on demand. At the customer premise, the viewer will use the remote control to the set-top box to choose the channel to be watched at any point in time, just as is done for cable service today. Also like cable, the signals for premium channels will be "broadcast" in coded form, and households that do not subscribe to particular premium channels will not be able to decode the signals. Verizon will use a particular wavelength on their fiber to implement QAM, a cable protocol used as a transport mechanism. This architecture appears to be consistent with the definitions of "cable service" and "cable system" in Section 602 of the Communications Act.[83]

In contrast, AT&T reportedly is spending $4 billion over the next three years to string optical fiber cable to neighborhoods totaling as many as 18 million homes, and plans to deliver television services using Internet technology called IPTV.[84] Rather than "broadcasting" a constant stream of all available programs, as cable does and Verizon plans to do, IPTV stores a potentially unlimited number of programs on a central server, which users then call up on demand. AT&T will not replace the copper lines that currently run into customer premises. Instead, to make sure there is sufficient bandwidth between the neighborhood node where the optical fiber terminates and the household premise, it will upgrade the DSL equipment currently at those nodes and in households with VDSL technology. At the household, the viewer will use the IP technology to send a signal to the AT&T end-office to send a particular channel or video on demand selection. That signal will be sent over the same bandwidth used for data and VoIP service. In AT&T's system, a single customer line will have enough bandwidth to support up to four active television sets per household at a time, or up to two HDTV channels at a time.

The Verizon and AT&T broadband network architectures each have their advantages and disadvantages. For example, AT&T's IP approach has greater two-way capability and therefore probably can better accommodate two-way applications than the Verizon architecture. On the other hand, AT&T's architecture provides far less bandwidth into the household, and thus may not be able to accommodate some bandwidth-intensive applications that the Verizon architecture could accommodate. AT&T may face customer resistance to an IP system that may experience some delay when changing channels. AT&T's reliance on DSL technology also may create problems with home networking. Telephone wires currently enter the house and then the inside wiring goes to the various telephones. But television sets may not be located near the telephones. AT&T's plan requires 20-2 5 megabits of bandwidth into the home, but with its architecture — deploying optical fiber to the neighborhood node, and then continuing to use copper into the home with VDSL — bandwidth falls as the distance to a customer's house increases. It may be that only those homes within a couple of thousand feet of the neighborhood node will be able to be fully served. On the other hand, Verizon's choice of deploying optical fiber all the way to the home, which requires a very large investment in optical cable, labor-intensive truck rolls, and in some cases digging up of land to replace the copper with optical cable, will be far more expensive per household served and thus may be constrained both by limits on Verizon's capital budget and by customer resistance to digging up their yards to lay fiber. Some observers have questioned whether Verizon's fiber to the home approach can prove out financially, even as they concede that the huge bandwidth provided could give it a leg up in the long run.

Unlike current copper networks, both the AT&T architecture and the Verizon architecture could leave customers without telephone service if their electricity goes out, though for different reasons. Fiber to the home technology does not incorporate line powering, so Verizon might have to provision the optical interface at its customers' premises with back-up batteries. But even then, the batteries would probably last at most 8 to 16 hours, less time than might be needed in case of natural disruptions such as hurricanes. At the same time, DSL modem systems of the sort used by AT&T require active electric power at the customer premise, which may not be available during emergencies. In both cases, customers might have to rely on wireless telephone service during time of electric power loss.

The marketplace will determine which of these network strengths and weaknesses are most important to end users. These architectural differences, in addition to creating competing platforms for triple play service, offer platform diversity to independent applications providers. Where the competing networks have distinct characteristics that better meet the needs of some sets of applications and are less effective for other sets of applications, applications providers are not constrained in their product development to the characteristics of a single platform. Thus, competing distinct broadband networks fosters applications innovation.

AT&T claims that since it will be using IP technology to offer video service, it is not subject to cable television regulation, most notably, franchising requirements. Under federal law, franchise authorities:[85] may require a cable operator to pay a franchise fee of up to 5% of cable service revenues;[86] may establish requirements for designation of channel capacity for public, educational, or governmental ("PEG") use and for the construction of "institutional networks" that serve educational and governmental functions of the franchiser;[87] may require the franchisee to provide facilities or financial support for PEG access;[88] may require a cable system to designate channel capacity, up to maximum levels based on system capacity, for commercial use by persons unaffiliated with the cable system;[89] must allow the cable system a reasonable period of time to build out its system to cover all households in the franchise area;[90] and must prohibit the redlining of low income neighborhoods.[91]

Clearly, if AT&T were not subject to a 5% franchise fee and other cable franchising requirements, but its competitors were, it would enjoy a significant competitive advantage. To the extent such advantage would artificially raise the relative costs or otherwise harm competing broadband network providers, or otherwise weaken them, then their ability to foster innovation by providing a unique alternative broadband platform could be undermined.

Verizon has agreed that it is subject to franchise requirements, but argues that a streamlined state-wide or nationwide franchising process is needed because the extremely time consuming process of negotiating literally thousands of individual franchise agreements could slow down its entry into video by years and could endanger its planned upgrade to a broadband network.

Reviewing the Current Framework for Cable Franchising

These potential inconsistencies suggest that it is timely to review the current statutory and regulatory framework for cable, found primarily in Title VI of the Communications Act, to determine whether it would be in the public interest to streamline the franchising process (for example, by consolidating it at the state or federal level) and/or to lessen or eliminate some current regulations. For example:

- Is the potential for competition from the new telephone company-based video providers sufficient to lighten or eliminate the remaining economic regulations of cable? (Already, the only cable rates subject to regulation are basic cable rates and cable equipment rates.)
- Is there a need for more stringent economic regulation of the incumbent cable companies than of new subscription video providers?
- Which current regulations are intended to "assure that cable systems are responsive to the needs and interests of the local community"? To what extent can competitive provision of subscription video create market forces that would, on their own, force

video providers to be responsive to local community needs and interests? To what extent can centralized (state or federal) regulation, rather than local franchise regulation, address local needs?

- If there already is a ubiquitous provider of broadband video service — the local cable system — in a municipality, does the public benefit from requiring new entrants also to provide ubiquitous service? On one hand, the existing telephone networks do not conform to municipal boundaries, so even a complete broadband buildout of a telephone company's network might not provide ubiquitous coverage of a particular political jurisdiction. On the other hand, less than ubiquitous coverage might leave some households without a competitive alternative and also might allow the new entrant to strategically "cherry-pick" the most valuable neighborhoods.
- If the underlying public interest objectives that are served by the current PEG and institutional network requirements are fully met by the incumbent cable companies, such that there would be little public benefit to imposing the same requirements on new entrants, how could these requirements be maintained on the incumbents without placing them at a competitive disadvantage?
- With respect to the long-standing media policy objective of diversity of voices, the media ownership rules address horizontal ownership relationships, not vertical ones. Congress enacted sections 611 and 612 of the Communications Act[92] to ensure diverse sources of video programming on cable television if cable companies are vertically integrated into program production. Section 612 allows franchising authorities to require a cable system to designate channel capacity, up to maximum levels based on system capacity, for commercial use by persons unaffiliated with the cable system. Section 611 allows franchising authorities to require the designation of channel capacity for public, educational, or governmental use. The public access channels, in particular, are intended to ensure that diverse voices are heard. How should these be applied to telephone company-based video providers?

Some observers have argued that fairness in the marketplace requires that the new telephone-based video providers be subject to the same requirements as the incumbent cable operators. In particular, some have argued that the new entrants should be subject to the same buildout requirements as the cable operators. But economists have explained that the costs of a particular regulatory requirement may be very different for an incumbent and a new entrant, and if imposed in exactly the same fashion may act as a barrier to entry and increase the "first mover" advantage already enjoyed by the incumbent.[93] For example, a buildout requirement is one of the costs of entry into the market. For the incumbent cable operator, the buildout requirement may have been imposed at a time when cable operators received an exclusive franchise and thus it represented a cost of entry into a monopoly market. Moreover, that cost is now sunk and likely has long since been recovered. In contrast, for a new telephone-based entrant, a buildout requirement would represent an entry cost into a competitive market environment and would not be viewed as sunk when it makes the decision to enter or not enter. Thus, the imposition of identical franchise (or other regulatory) requirements on an incumbent and a new entrant might not represent an equal burden in the marketplace.

At the same time, the advent of IP video potentially raises a new regulatory issue. While it is unlikely that an independent applications provider would be able to put together a suite of video programming to compete head-on with AT&T, Verizon, or cable operators for the provision of multiple channels of subscription video service, it is possible that an independent applications provider might be able to offer specialty video programming, perhaps independent films or local sports programming, using IP technology. While a single applications provider of this sort might not be a threat to the business plan of the large cable and telephone companies, a plethora of such independent video providers — or, in the future, the development of a direct link between content providers and end users via peer-to-peer connections — might be a threat. The network providers might then have the incentive to restrict end user access to these services. This raises the non-discrimination issues discussed earlier: should vertically integrated broadband network providers have the right to restrict IP video or other applications that challenge their own video services or should end users' have nondiscriminatory access to all applications that do not threaten the integrity of the network be mandatory?

Fostering Additional Broadband Networks

Intermodal Competition from Advanced Wireless Networks

In the debate among proponents of the various approaches to regulation of broadband networks — structural requirements, *ex ante* non-discrimination rules, *ex post* adjudication of abuses, and reliance on antitrust law and non-binding principles — the only point of agreement is that end users would benefit, and the need for regulation would be reduced, if customers had more than two broadband networks to choose among.[94]

In almost all geographic markets today, however, the mass market broadband market structure is characterized by duopoly provision of broadband network services (cable modem service from the local cable system or DSL service from the local telephone company), plus competition among independent applications service providers and the two vertically integrated broadband network providers for the provision of broadband applications (services). All parties agree that the dynamics in both the network market and the applications market would likely change if there were three or more network providers. For example, as discussed earlier, network providers face countervailing incentives. On one hand, due to indirect network externalities, they have the incentive to minimize restrictions on independent applications providers' access to their networks. On the other hand, they sometimes have the incentive to restrict such access when to do so would yield them first-in advantages or other strategic advantages in the applications market or would aid in their ability to bolster profits through price discrimination. A third network provider, entering the market after the first two have been established, is likely to seek customers by pursuing the strategy of offering access to those independent applications providers that had been denied access by the incumbents and allowing end users to use the network for applications that they were not allowed to use on the incumbents' networks.[95] Thus, a third network is likely to strengthen the market forces for nondiscriminatory network access and to reduce the need for regulatory intervention.

Entry by a third broadband network provider would threaten the profits of incumbent wireline and cable broadband network providers to the extent they lose customers to the entrant and to the extent a third network reduces their negotiating strength vis-a-vis independent applications providers and end users. The incumbent network providers might benefit, however, if such entry justified the easing of regulatory requirements. The incumbents have argued that regulation of their networks inevitably introduces inefficiencies, distortions, and unnecessary costs. If entry of a third broadband network created market forces that decreased both the perceived and the actual need for regulation of the broadband networks, and if such regulation did indeed impose those inefficiencies on network providers, then regulatory relief induced by competitive entry could benefit the incumbents.

While ultimately broadband may be provided over power lines ("BPL") and/or satellite, there is general agreement that a third ubiquitous broadband network option is most likely to be provided using terrestrial wireless technology. In recognition of that fact, the FCC created a Wireless Broadband Access Task Force that issued a report in February 2005.[96] The report identified two policy reasons for fostering deployment of wireless broadband networks:[97]

- Terrestrial wireless technology provides both mobility and portability, efficiently connects devices within short distances, and bridges longer distances more efficiently than wireline and cable technologies. Wireless technologies frequently are a more cost-effective solution for serving areas of the country with less dense population, and provide rural and remote regions new ways to connect to critical health, safety, and educational services.
- Terrestrial wireless networks can provide competition to existing broadband services delivered through the currently more prevalent wireline and cable technologies. Wireless broadband can create a competitive broadband marketplace and bring the benefits of lower prices, better quality, and greater innovation to consumers.

There appears to be consensus that one objective of U.S. telecommunications policy should be to foster the deployment of wireless broadcast networks. But any actions to foster deployment should not take the form of industrial policy favoring any specific wireless technology, since there are a variety of technologies that can offer broadband capability. Nor should it provide wireless technology an artificial advantage over other broadband technologies.

Wireless broadband can be provided using fixed or portable technologies (such as Bluetooth or ultra-wide band for short-range communications, Wi-Fi for medium-range, and WiMAX for longer-range) or by using mobile technologies (such as those used for third-generation ("3G") or forthcoming fourth-generation ("4G") mobile cellular service). Currently, Wi-Fi primarily provides wireless Internet access for laptop computers and personal digital assistants; WiMAX expands networks with wireless links to fixed locations; and 3G brings Internet capabilities to wireless mobile phones.[98] Over time, the capabilities of all these technologies are likely to expand. The short and medium range technologies share unlicensed spectrum with other technologies. WiMAX and 3G operate on designated, licensed frequencies (though it may soon be possible for WiMAX to operate on unlicensed spectrum). Proponents of each of these technologies share the concern that there may be insufficient spectrum available for their technologies to be developed to full market potential, though recent FCC actions have at least started the process for making such spectrum available. It is not yet clear whether these various wireless technologies ultimately will be competing for customers or complementing one another by providing a broader base and greater choice of devices for wireless communications and networking.

Wi-Fi, or wireless fidelity, is the most widely employed of the family of Institute of Electrical and Electronics Engineers ("IEEE") standards for frequency use in the unlicensed 2.4 GHz and 5.4/5.7 GHz spectrum bands. Those are the bands on which wireless local area networks operate. The FCC's Wireless Broadband Access Task Force and others have identified a variety of actions to foster Wi-Fi usage, including managing spectrum in a fashion that eliminates artificial restrictions on the availability of unlicensed spectrum, promoting voluntary frequency coordination efforts by private industry, considering increasing the power limits in certain bands available for use by unlicensed devices in order to improve their utility for license-exempt wireless Internet service providers.

WiMAX is an industry coalition of network and equipment suppliers that have agreed to develop interoperable broadband wireless based on IEEE standard 802.16. It can transmit data up to 30 miles and may ultimately be used to provide the broadband "last mile" to end users, that is, a means to provide fixed wireless services to locations that are not connected to networks by cable or high-speed wires. WiMAX uses multiple frequencies around the world, an impediment to interoperability. In the United States, the 700 MHz band is being used in some WiMAX deployments and there is industry interest in expanding to additional 700 MHz frequencies to create national access. But the 700 MHz band is currently held by television broadcasters and will not be available until the transition from analog to digital television has been completed. That transition is one of the most contentious communications policy issues before Congress today.[99] But the potential benefits to business customers, and perhaps individual consumers as well, of making a portion of that spectrum available sooner rather than later for fixed or portable broadband wireless access are huge.

Today's mobile wireless networks can only provide voice and limited data service. The next major advance in mobile technology, referred to as 3G, has been deployed overseas and is beginning to be introduced in the United States. It dramatically increases communications speed. Fourth generation networks, which may be available in the near future, are expected to deliver wireless connectivity at speeds up to 20 times faster than 3G. Some U.S. providers may choose to leapfrog directly from second to fourth generation technology. Third generation and future developments in wireless technology will be able to support many services for business and consumer markets, such as: enhanced Internet links, digital television and radio broadcast reception, high-quality streaming video, and mobile commerce, including the ability to make payments.

The National Telecommunications and Information Administration ("NTIA"), within the Department of Commerce, has responsibility for the management of spectrum used by the federal government, and the FCC has responsibility for management of spectrum used commercially and by state and local governments. Aided by an Intra-Government 3G Planning Group, in 2001 the FCC and NTIA announced plans to reallocate the 1710-1755 MHz and 2110-2155 MHz spectrum bands to use for commercial advanced wireless services ("AWS"), including 3G. Since the 1710-1755 MHz band was being used by federal agencies, particularly the Department of Defense, the plan included a process for making new spectrum available for the government users who would have to give up spectrum and for funding those users' transfer costs. In addition, use of the 2110-2155 MHz band required moving certain commercial multipoint distribution service licensees from the 2150-2150 MHz band to new spectrum (as part of a larger reorganization plan creating the broadband radio service and educational broadband service in the 2.5 GHz band)[100] and certain fixed microwave licensees (using a long-established process for moving these licensees).

Frequencies in the 1710-1755 MHz and 2110-2155 MHz bands will be made available to the private sector through spectrum auctions conducted by the FCC, and the auction proceeds will be placed in a Spectrum Reallocation Fund to be used to cover the costs of transferring the government users to new spectrum. This required modification of the Communications Act of 1934 to permit the affected agencies direct access to the auction funds, which was accomplished with the passage of the Commercial Spectrum Enhancement Act, Title II of P.L. 108-494. Key provisions of that act include the requirements that the auctions recoup at least 110% of the projected transfer costs and that unused funds revert to the Treasury after eight years.[101] The Spectrum Relocation Fund was created within the Treasury to hold auction proceeds as designated. The fund is to be administered by the Office of Management and Budget. The Commercial Spectrum Enhancement Act requires that the FCC start the process by notifying the NTIA at least 18 months in advance of a planned auction. The FCC notified the NTIA of plans to auction frequencies in the 17 10-1755 MHz band as early as June 2006.

In addition, in September 2004, the FCC provided an additional 20 megahertz of spectrum for advanced wireless services, including 3G. It redesignated the 1915-1920 MHz band for advanced wireless services from unlicensed personal communications services and paired this block of spectrum with the 1995-2000 MHz band, which was previously allocated for the mobile satellite service. Also, it concluded that an additional ten megahertz of spectrum at 2020-2025 MHz and 2175-2180 MHz, previously allocated for mobile satellite service, should be made available for AWS.[102] The Commission adopted a reimbursement plan to compensate UTAM, Inc. for relocation expenses it will incur to relocate incumbents from the 1915-1920 MHz band. The FCC is still developing service rules needed to implement this spectrum reallocation.

The FCC has taken steps to make other licensed and unlicensed spectrum available for advanced wireless services. As mentioned earlier, much of the spectrum in the 700 MHz band that will be affected by the broadcast television digital transition is expected to be used for AWS, including WiMAX. Some spectrum will be available in the 70, 80, and 90 GHz bands on a quasi-licensed basis capable of providing pencil beams between commercial office buildings of as much as a mile in length. In addition, ultra wide band technology, using small amounts of available spectrum across multiple bands, will allow users to employ Bluetooth and other technologies for wireless personal area networks.

The reallocation of spectrum to make more available for advanced wireless services is a specific example of a broader public policy objective: the management of spectrum in a fashion that promotes its efficient use to provide innovative services to Americans. There is a very lively debate about how best to manage the spectrum to maximize consumer welfare. There has been much criticism that legacy command-and-control regulation of spectrum — under which spectrum is assigned to specific uses and access to that spectrum for other uses is prohibited — does not take into account advances in technology that have created the potential for systems to use spectrum more intensively and to be much more tolerant of interference than in the past.[103] Two proposed alternative approaches have been the subject of much discussion: the granting of exclusive, tradeable spectrum usage rights through market-based mechanisms and creating open access to unlicensed spectrum "commons." The three approaches are not necessarily mutually exclusive; some portions of the spectrum could remain subject to command-and-control, while other portions are allocated by the market and the remainder is held as commons. The debate about how best to allocate spectrum, however, is beyond the scope of this report.

Some observers have suggested that a third network provider might have less incentive to provide strong price and service competition — to challenge the network access status quo — if it shared ownership or a strategic alliance with one of the incumbent networks. For example, if the new network were an advanced wireless network that shared ownership with one of the RBOCs (Verizon Wireless/Verizon or Cingular/AT&T/BellSouth) or if the wireless network had a strategic relationship with the major cable companies (an alliance has been formed between four of the major cable companies and Sprint/Nextel to offer bundled "quadruple play" voice/data/video/wireless in competition with the RBOCs),[104] then there might be some reluctance on the part of the new entrant to employ an entry strategy that disrupts the market. This might suggest that, in any auction of spectrum for 3G or 4G services, some preference be given to bidders that are independent of the RBOCs, Sprint/Nextel, and major cable companies, or that some portion of the auctioned spectrum be set aside for independent providers.

On the other hand, there appear to be strong incentives for any broadband wireless network provider, even if it were owned by a telephone company or in a marketing relationship with a cable company, to be an aggressive competitor. First, wireless service is growing faster than wireline service, so it would not seem to be in a company's long term strategic interest to constrain its wireless activities to protect its wireline business. Second, the broadband wireless networks are likely to extend geographically beyond the geographic reach of any telephone company or cable company network and therefore wireless providers will in many instances not be competing against an affiliated network. It would be difficult for a national wireless carrier to strategically provide two levels of competition: aggressive competition outside an affiliated network's region and passive within. Third, there will probably be multiple broadband mobile wireless networks — at the national level, Cingular, Verizon, Sprint/Nextel, and perhaps T Mobile, and at the regional level Alltel/Western Wireless — so any single network will face intramodal competitive pressure on price and service access.

Intramodal Competition from CLECs for Large Business Customers

Much of the criticism of the 1996 Act has focused on those provisions that attempted to facilitate the transition from monopoly to competitive provision of telecommunications services, most notably the provisions requiring the incumbent local exchange carriers to make elements of their networks available to new entrants under certain conditions. Those provisions were intended to foster intramodal competition with the understanding that new entrants could not instantaneously build out ubiquitous networks like those of the incumbent monopolies.

Nine years after enactment of the 1996 Act, no intramodal entrant has been able to construct a ubiquitous network. It has not proven viable to replicate the local loop ("last mile" connection) between a network's switch and a customer's premise, except in the case of large business customers whose traffic volume is sufficient to justify deploying a large pipe to the premise. As a result, the competitive local exchange carriers' ("CLECs") networks typically consist largely of fiber rings in business areas that connect directly to their major customers' locations. Nor has it proven viable for the CLECs to fully replicate the RBOCs' transport networks, the connections between the nodes in their networks, through which aggregated traffic is routed. Even the CLECs that had been serving the most multi-locational business customers, AT&T and MCI, and which have now been acquired by SBC and Verizon, respectively, had not been able to capture sufficient traffic to create the scale economies needed to support a ubiquitous transport network. Rather, they continued to rely on the RBOCs for transport facilities on many routes.

Cable networks were constructed to serve residential customers and therefore tend not to be ubiquitously deployed in business districts. Even the largest cable companies are only in selected geographic markets in the country, and may not be able to meet the needs of large, multi-locational business customers. Also, it is likely to take many years for wireless carriers to construct networks that can meet the bandwidth and security requirements of large corporations. Competitive provision of broadband services to large business market customers therefore is most likely to be intramodal. But the recent acquisitions of AT&T by SBC and of MCI by Verizon have eliminated two significant competitors in the enterprise market and also in the Internet backbone market. In approving those mergers, the Department of Justice and the FCC set a number of conditions intended to retain competitive options for enterprise and Internet customers, including the divestiture of some key facilities and ensuring CLECs and ISPs access to certain facilities or services at set rates for at least two years.[105] Nonetheless, some enterprise customers and CLECs remain concerned about their reduced options for retail services and transport facilities.

It therefore might not be wise to simply replace the statutory provisions fostering intramodal competition with provisions fostering intermodal competition on the expectation that intermodal competition will always be effective. Intramodal competition will remain important, especially for large business markets. But given the inability of facilities-based CLECs to attain the economies of scale needed to support ubiquitous transport networks, there might be reason to maintain some of the current statutory provisions intended to foster that competition.

Antitrust Savings Clause: The *Trinko* Decision

The 1996 Act includes an "antitrust savings clause" stating that neither the act nor any amendments made by it "shall be construed to modify, impair, or supersede the applicability of any of the antitrust laws."[106] In a recent decision,[107] involving an antitrust suit brought against Verizon, an incumbent telephone company that had been disciplined by both the FCC and the New York Public Service Commission ("P SC") for breaching its duty under the 1996 Act to adequately share its network with competitive providers, in which the plaintiff alleged that such breaches represented exclusionary and anticompetitive behavior, the Supreme Court ruled that the breached FCC and PSC rules affirmatively required Verizon to aid its competitors and that failing to meet those requirements was not a sufficient basis for finding a violation of antitrust law. The Court found that "the act does not create new claims that go beyond the existing antitrust standards." The Court also found that the plaintiff, a customer of one of the CLECs, did not have standing to bring the case.

Congressional reaction to the *Trinko* decision was mixed. House Judiciary Committee Chairman Sensenbrenner stated concern that the decision not be "perceived as giving a green light to all manner of anticompetitive behavior by the Bells.... The Committee on the Judiciary ... will not hesitate to develop legislative responses to competitive problems that may arise as a result of this decision."[108] House Judiciary Committee ranking minority member Conyers called for legislation to address the "Supreme Court's horrible blunder."[109] On the other hand, Representative Tauzin, then-chairman of the House Energy and Commerce Committee, expressed his approval that the Supreme Court had "decisively reiterated ... that the regulation of the telecommunications industry should be the purview of the FCC and the state [public utility commissions], rather than judges all across the country.[110]

It may be that, when Congress inserted the "antitrust savings" clause in the 1996 Act, many Members believed that the clause was preserving an unlimited private right of action on the part of other-than-directly affected parties to sue under the antitrust laws. But, as this case indicates, the clause may be of little effect in instances such as this in which it is found that traditional antitrust principles/standards are not implicated. Given the Verizon decision, there are at least three congressional options that might have the effect of providing the breadth of private action some members of Congress apparently thought they had assured. First, Congress could amend the savings clause to clarify that the phrase, "the antitrust laws," means the literal words of the statutory provisions, but excludes any judicial interpretation of them. Second, Congress could amend the "enforcement" provisions of the 1996 Act so that even if there had already been regulatory action, certain provisions of the act would remain enforceable by private individuals who are not competitors of local exchange carriers, but, rather, their customers or customers of would-be or actual competitors. Third, Congress could characterize a violation of any (or some) mandatory, competitive obligation(s) of the act as *prima facie* evidence of violation of the antimonopoly provision of the antitrust laws (15 U.S.C. § 2). Congress could also choose to allow the current law to remain unchanged.

Intercarrier Compensation

Since the value of access to a network or of a network service, such as a telecommunications service, increases as the number of other parties connected to the network increases, new entrants would have a very difficult time entering the market if they could not interconnect their networks with those of the incumbent carriers under nondiscriminatory terms and conditions. Thus a key provision of the 1996 Act set obligations for incumbent carriers and new entrants to interconnect their networks with one another, imposing additional requirements on the incumbents because they might have the incentive and ability to restrict competitive entry by denying such interconnection or by setting terms, conditions, and rates that could determine the ability of the new entrants to compete.[111]

With multiple networks interconnecting to provide service, a necessary component of a competitively neutral regulatory regime is nondiscriminatory intercarrier compensation — the payments that interconnected carriers make to one another when more than one carrier's network must be used to complete a call or other electronic communication.[112] When Congress passed the 1996 Act, there was very limited competition across the boundaries of local exchange service, long distance service, and wireless service, and thus the act did not focus on intercarrier compensation rates, though it did prescribe that intercarrier compensation rates between competing local exchange carriers be based on the "additional costs of terminating such calls."[113] Primarily, though, the 1996 Act left in place existing intercarrier compensation rates.

But that system of intercarrier compensation was implemented on a piecemeal basis, as specific existing telecommunications services were opened to competitive provision or providers offering entirely new services (such as wireless service) were allowed to interconnect with the public switched telephone network. Today, these intercarrier compensation payments vary widely, depending on the following:

- whether the interconnecting party is a local exchange carrier ("LEC"),[114] an interexchange (long distance) carrier, a commercial mobile radio service ("CMRS" or wireless) carrier, or an information service provider, and
- whether the service is classified as telecommunications or information, local or long distance, or interstate or intrastate,

even though in each case basically the same transport and switching functions are provided.

As shown in Figure 1, a chart prepared by the Intercarrier Compensation Forum ("ICF"),[115] today the *average* intercarrier compensation rate ranges from 0.1 cents per minute for traffic bound to an ISP to 5.1 cents per minute for intrastate traffic bound to a subscriber of a small (rural) incumbent local exchange carrier; individual rates can be as low as zero and as high as 35.9 cents per minute.[116] These intercarrier compensation charges can represent a substantial portion of the costs of providing certain services and, in the case of long distance calls that interexchange carriers are required by statute and FCC rule to offer at a single rate nationally,[117] can exceed the retail price for the service.[118]

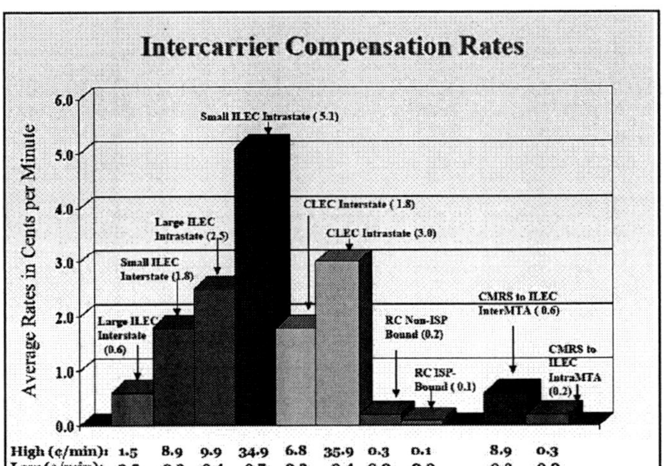

Figure 1. Current Intercarrier Compensation Rates; Source: Intercarrier Compensation Forum

Given the wide variation in intercarrier compensation rules applied to carriers and technologies that are now competing with one another, the FCC adopted a Further Notice of Proposed Rulemaking in February 2005 to review and reform its rules with the goal of constructing a unified intercarrier compensation regime.[119] The FCC seeks public comment on nine comprehensive intercarrier compensation reform proposals or sets of principles that have been submitted to the FCC as well as a staff proposal.[120] The issues raised in the ICC FNPRM are not new to the Federal Communications Commission. In 2001, the FCC opened a rulemaking proceeding and adopted a Notice of Proposed Rulemaking seeking information on how to develop a unified intercarrier compensation regime.[121]

There is general agreement that intercarrier compensation reform is needed because:

- The current regime distorts investment decisions and undermines efficient competition by providing artificial advantages/disadvantages to those service providers that happen to be subject to favorable/unfavorable intercarrier compensation rules. For example, for non-local calls made within any of the 51 Metropolitan Trading Areas ("MTAs") in the United States,[122] if the caller uses a wireless telephone, the caller's wireless carrier is subject to a cost-based "reciprocal compensation" charge for the termination of that call; but if the caller made an identical call, from the same location to the same called party, using a wireline telephone (and hence a wireline long distance carrier), that carrier would be subject to an above cost "access charge" for the termination of the call. As another example, when a long distance call is made to a called party's wireline telephone, that party's wireline local exchange carrier can charge the calling party's long distance carrier an above-cost access charge for terminating the call; but if an identical long distance call were made to the same called party, from and to the same physical location, but to the called party's wireless telephone, the called party's wireless carrier is not allowed to charge the calling party's long distance carrier any access charge for terminating the call.
- The current regime fails to provide innovators certainty about the intercarrier compensation regime to which their services will be subject. For example, since VoIP service is, on one hand, an application of an information service and, on the other hand, functionally equivalent to a traditional voice telephone call, it arguably fits into two different classifications for the purposes of intercarrier compensation. Information services are not subject to access charges; long distance telephone calls are. As discussed in the section on VoIP below, the FCC has begun to make decisions, on a case-by-case basis, about the classification of specific voice product offerings that use IP technology to varying degrees. The business plans of VoIP providers will be strongly affected by the ultimate decision about how they are classified for intercarrier compensation purposes.
- The current regime encourages uneconomic arbitrage; that is, providers making business decisions based on the artificial rates set for intercarrier compensation, rather than on true underlying costs. For example, because of the traffic patterns of ISPs and some anomalies in the rules,[123] some CLECs have pursued the market strategy of targeting ISPs as customers. They have offered ISPs service at what may have been below-cost rates because they could more than recoup any losses by charging above-cost rates to the carriers of the ISPs' subscribers for terminating the large volume of subscriber calls to those ISPs.[124] Regulators also may seek to exploit uneconomic arbitrage. For example, state regulators as well as rural LECs may have the incentive to limit the scope of rural local calling areas since calls that are classified as long distance will generate more revenues (through toll charges or access charges) than they would if classified as local and also will tend to move the burden of cost recovery from local rural customers to urban long distance customers (since long distance rates are

averaged and thus urban customers who can be served at low cost face higher averaged rates that contribute to the recovery of higher rural costs).

- The current regime creates an artificial cost structure, based on minutes of use, which appears to be inconsistent with actual cost causation in networks and which renders it difficult for carriers to meet the preferences of many consumers for offerings consisting of large baskets of minutes or unlimited calling at a fixed price. For example, under the current access charge regime, interexchange carriers are charged on a per-minute-of-use basis for the switching used to originate and terminate their customers' calls, making the interexchange carriers' underlying cost structure usage-sensitive even though the preponderance of those switching costs appear not to be usage-sensitive.[125] But by facing these artificially imposed usage-based costs, long distance carriers are discouraged from offering large baskets of minutes or unlimited calling at a fixed price since they would lose money when serving high usage customers, who are the customers most likely to select such packages.[126]
- The current regime requires carriers to expend millions of dollars and scarce information technology resources developing systems to identify, measure, monitor, bill, reconcile, audit and dispute the classification of trafic as local or toll, intrastate or interstate, intraMTA or interMTA,[127] information service or telecommunications service, etc., in order to determine which intercarrier compensation rules apply. It also encourages wasteful litigation as carriers fight among themselves about that classification of traffic. These costly nonproductive activities will continue to grow as providers respond to consumer demand for bundled offerings of services that fit into different classifications.
- The current regime undermines the stability of universal service subsidy funds. Where ILECs rely at least in part on the profits from above cost access charges to defray the cost of providing universal service, this funding source is in jeopardy because the number of minutes subject to access charges is declining as carriers with more favorable intercarrier compensation treatment (for example, wireless and VoIP carriers) are gaining market share and traditional long distance carriers have an incentive to manipulate the complex packages of services that they offer to minimize their exposure to access charges.

At the same time, in some quarters there is resistance to comprehensive intercarrier compensation reform because of concerns that some carriers and some consumers may be harmed by the changes. In this view:

- If the access charges currently imposed by local exchange carriers on interexchange carriers to originate and terminate long distance calls were reformed to more accurately reflect the low proportion of switching costs that appear to be usage-sensitive (and the high proportion that appear to be fixed), per-minute access charges imposed on the long distance carriers would fall, but the fixed costs of switching would likely be recovered by raising the subscriber line charge imposed on end users for connecting to the network. Consumer groups have consistently opposed line charges of any sort, arguing that such charges unfairly burden low usage and low income customers.[128]

- The access charges that long distance carriers must pay to small rural local exchange carriers for originating or terminating the long distance calls of the rural carriers' customers tend to be higher than the access charges paid to urban carriers. This is in part because the small rural carriers' underlying costs are higher than those of urban carriers due to the lack of population density and lack of scale economies and in part due to efforts by regulators to keep rural end users' local rates low. Also, the rural carriers' local calling areas tend to be narrowly defined and to serve only a small number of households. Many of their customers' incoming and outgoing calls therefore are classified as toll (long distance) calls, for which the rural LECs receive above-cost minute-of-use access charges from long distance carriers, rather than the fixed end-user charge typical of local service. As a result, the small rural LECs historically have generated a much larger portion of their total revenues from access charges than have urban LECs.[129] Since the access charges of rural LECs exceed costs by more than those of urban LECs, and since rural LECs have depended on access charges more than urban LECs, reforming access charges to bring them down to cost would place a greater revenue burden on rural LECs than on urban LECs. Absent another revenue source, end-user line charges would have to be raised more in rural areas than in urban areas. To keep line charges from growing to the point where local service becomes unaffordable or non-comparable with urban rates, a new universal service funding mechanism would be needed to replace the implicit universal service funding currently in the rural carriers' access charges. Although all the proposals for intercarrier compensation reform have included new universal service funding mechanisms, the rural LECs prefer not to have to rely so heavily on an explicit universal service funding mechanism. They generally prefer to have three revenue sources — line charges, universal service funds, and above-cost access charges — rather than just the first two. In part, this is because they prefer to recover a larger portion of their costs from long distance carriers (whose averaged rates subsidize rural customers) than from their own end-user customers in subscriber line charges. And in part it is because they are concerned about relying too heavily on universal service funds, which they consider a potentially unstable source of revenue, especially now that rural wireless carriers are seeking these same universal service funds.
- Although section 254(e) of the 1996 Act requires universal service support to be explicit and sufficient,[130] many state regulators continue to set intrastate access charges, and especially the intrastate access charges of rural carriers, at above-cost rates that exceed interstate access charges, in order to create a revenue source (ultimately borne primarily by customers of long distance carriers that do not live in rural areas) that will help keep local rates low. Some parties question whether the FCC has the authority to modify intrastate access charges (as part of comprehensive intercarrier compensation reform) without the formal involvement of the states.

The rural telephone companies have an additional problem relating to intercarrier compensation. They claim that they are unable to receive compensation for the termination of a very substantial portion of the traffic they receive from outside their service areas because they are unable to identify the originating carrier. This problem, referred to as "phantom traffic," has grown in recent years. Typically, it occurs when traffic is passed from an originating local or long distance carrier to an intermediate or "transiting" carrier (most typically the Regional Bell

Operating Company located closest to the rural telephone company), which then passes the traffic on to the terminating rural carrier. The transiting carriers sometimes, however, will not pay the rural carrier for terminating the call, but rather will insist that the terminating carrier seek payment directly from the originating carrier. Unfortunately, at times the information identifying the originating carrier has been stripped away before the call reaches the terminating carrier.[131] This allegedly happens most frequently when the originating carrier is a long distance or wireless carrier, which must pay above-cost access charges for the termination of the call but would prefer to transit the call through an intermediate local exchange carrier, since the latter would only have to pay cost-based reciprocal compensation rates for the termination of the call.[132] It is likely that intercarrier compensation reform that equalizes the termination rates for long distance and local calls would reduce this phantom traffic problem, but it still is essential that the identification problem be corrected as it places an unfair burden on rural carriers.

Given the many affected interests with conflicting views and the impact of intercarrier compensation on such fundamental public policy objectives as competition and universal service, Congress might choose to use its deliberations on reform of the Communications Act as an opportunity to provide the FCC statutory guidance on how to proceed with its intercarrier compensation reform efforts.

Universal Service in a Broadband Environment

The universal availability of basic telecommunications service at affordable rates has been a fundamental element of telecommunications policy in the United States since the enactment of the Communications Act in 1934. To achieve this, a universal service subsidy system has been employed to keep end user rates affordable for low income households and for households and small businesses in high cost areas (and, since 1996, to provide discounts to schools and libraries for telephone service, Internet access, and internal network wiring, and to public and non-profit rural health care providers for telecommunications services and installations and for long distance Internet connections).

This policy goal can be fully compatible with the development of a competitive market for telecommunications services, including the last mile into customers' premises, so long as the universal service funding mechanism is constructed in a competitively neutral and efficient fashion. That cannot be accomplished if any of the universal service subsidy is hidden in above-cost rates for certain services that are intended to subsidize the below cost rates for other services. In that situation, a competitor could successfully enter the market by undercutting the above-cost prices for those services whose rates are raised to include implicit subsidies, but could not compete in the provision of those services whose rates are set below cost.

The policy goal also cannot be achieved if the universal service subsidy is not available on the same basis to all competitors in the market. This is especially important today, with competing wireline, cable, mobile wireless, and fixed wireless technologies all potentially able to offer service to rural customers. In addition, if the universal service funding mechanism is not efficient — and therefore requires more resources than is necessary to provide universal availability — it will place an unnecessary burden on telecommunications markets (or on the general public, if supported by general tax revenues).

The 1996 Act took a major step in the direction of reconciling universal service with competitive markets by requiring that "[a]ny such support should be explicit and sufficient to achieve the purposes...."[133] This requirement has not yet been achieved, however. Although competitive market forces have driven some above-cost rates down toward cost, especially for business services, and an explicit Federal Universal Service Fund ("FUSF") funding mechanism has been created that provides a significant portion of total universal service subsidies,[134] many rates continue to be set above cost in order to include hidden universal service subsidies; for example, the intrastate access charges of many rural telephone carriers discussed earlier in the section on intercarrier compensation.

Which Services Should Be Supported By A Universal Service Subsidy And Who Should Receive The Subsidy?

The 1996 Act instructs the FCC and a Federal-State Joint Board on Universal Service to base policies for the preservation and advancement of universal service on seven principles. One of those principles is: "Access to advanced telecommunications and information services should be provided in all regions of the Nation."[135] The act is not specific about how this should be accomplished and does not explicitly include advanced services among those that should be subsidized to achieve universal service. To date, the Joint Board and the FCC have not included advanced services in the definition of universal service. But there has been considerable national discussion of the role of broadband networks in stimulating economic development and some Members of Congress believe the time is ripe to debate the inclusion of access to a broadband network in universal service.

While market demand appears to be sufficient to generate competitive broadband network deployment in many urban areas without government intervention, that may not be the case in rural or other high cost (or low income) areas, where high costs and/or limited demand may render it economically infeasible to deploy multiple broadband networks, or even a single network, without government intervention.

If Congress wants to expand the scope of universal service to include universal access to a broadband network at affordable rates, it must address a number of issues. Most basically, how "broad" is the "broadband" that should be provided as part of universal service? Bigger may be better, but only at an associated cost. As explained earlier, one of the primary drivers of broadband deployment has been network providers' desire to bring sufficient bandwidth to customer premises to support the triple play of voice, data, and subscription video services. Of these three applications, video is the one that requires the most bandwidth, but it also is the one that has the least nexus to public safety or economic development. Thus, it may be difficult to establish a public interest justification for subsidizing the additional bandwidth needed for video. On the other hand, one of the principles in the universal service section of the 1996 Act states that "Consumers in all regions of the Nation ...should have access to telecommunications and information services, including interexchange services and advanced information services, that are reasonably *comparable* to those services provided in urban areas and that are available at rates that are reasonably comparable to rates charged for similar services in urban areas."[136] Is it sufficient, for example, to limit a subsidy program in high cost areas to support for broadband service capable of (relatively low quality) video streaming if the unsubsidized market is driving companies to deploy broadband capable of offering (higher quality) broadcast-quality video service in urban areas — even though subscription video is needed neither for public safety nor for economic development?

Also, the sparse population and longer distances in rural areas translate into low density of demand, limited economies of scale, and hence higher costs, such that there is uncertainty whether even a single broadband network can be sustained. Is it possible, then, to construct a universal service subsidy program that is open to all competing technologies (and thus competitively neutral) without creating incentives for the deployment of multiple networks, none of which can exploit economies of scale to constrain costs?

Historically, universal service has been limited to basic telephone service, but the subsidy has been given to the provider, rather than to the end user. (The latter might be accomplished in the form of a voucher that could be used to reduce a cost-based rate to an affordable rate.). Since wireline, wireless, and cable companies all may offer local telephone service in a particular high cost area, all three can potentially qualify as "eligible telecommunications carriers" ("ETCs") in that locality and receive universal service funds. The competing carriers only receive funds for those customers they capture, but since a customer can elect to obtain service from more than one carrier at the same time, more than one carrier can receive universal service funding for serving that customer. Typically, customers do not receive basic voice service from both the local telephone company and the local cable operator, so it is unlikely that those two carriers would each receive universal service funds for serving the same customer. But many customers do receive both fixed telephone service (from a telephone company or a cable operator) and mobile telephone service (from a wireless carrier), and in that case both the fixed and the mobile telephone service provider would receive the universal service subsidy. Thus, competitive entry in that situation will increase the total size of the universal service fund. Data from the 2004 annual report of the Universal Service Administrative Corporation ("USAC"), which administers the federal universal service fund, corroborates this.[137] High cost funds in 2004 were distributed as follows: $3,154 million to local exchange carriers, $323 million to wireless carriers, and $10 million to competitive access providers.[138]

The potential growth in the size of the federal universal service fund from customers being able to subscribe for services from multiple carriers, with more than one of those carriers becoming eligible for FUSF payments, might be exacerbated if the scope of universal service were expanded to include advanced services or the connection (access) to a broadband network. One possible way to limit the increase in subsidy requirements would be to expand the definition of universal service to include the connection to a broadband network, but, at the same time, to require each customer in a high cost area eligible for universal service support to choose a single broadband provider as its "principal" provider and only that chosen provider would be eligible for the subsidy.[139] This approach would have the advantage of constraining the size of the universal service fund. But it also likely would reduce the total flow of subsidy dollars to rural areas and might distort the market by encouraging consumers to choose broadband service even if they do not seek it.

Having invested in a broadband network, each network provider will seek to maximize its return from that investment, most likely by enticing its customers to choose bundled packages of "value added" services for which it can charge prices that reflect that value. Network providers are likely to avoid the alternative pricing strategy of setting separate charges for the network connection (access) and for individual services for several reasons: (1) most consumers prefer a single bill; (2) there is risk that network access could become a low-markup commodity if competing networks eventually are deployed and the revenues generated by value-added applications then might flow to independent services providers; and, (3) it might not be easy to set up a discriminatory pricing scheme for access that would allow them to maximize their profits. This raises an interesting issue. Today, universal service is defined in terms of providing basic local telephone service and typically only providers that offer, as one option, basic voice service (a connection plus limited local service) are eligible for FUSF funds. If the universal service definition were changed to cover access to broadband, would it be appropriate to make universal service funds available only to those carriers that offer their customers, as one option, a basic service package consisting only of the broadband connection (or of the connection plus basic local voice service)? If that were a requirement for receiving FUSF support, however, network providers would not be able to tie broadband access to the purchase of value-added services and thus might not be able to compel customers to select those service packages that maximize the providers' profits.

Currently, the Federal Universal Service Fund subsidy is made directly to those carriers that qualify as ETCs. The specific payments made to individual carriers are subject to a number of very arcane accounting rules, some of which limit funding to wireline providers because only those providers are eligible for certain pools of money.[140] The various mechanisms use different costing methodologies, but where the subsidy is available to the incumbent wireline telephone company and new entrants, the payments to all are based on the costs of the wireline company. The latter have complained that some of the new entrants, in particular the wireless carriers, have lower costs and therefore should receive lower subsidies; otherwise, they claim, the wireless carriers will enjoy a windfall. The lower cost carriers have countered that, for competitive neutrality, each provider should be given the same level subsidy and then allowed to compete on an equal footing in the market. A low cost provider might be able to set lower rates since it needs less subsidy to meet the higher cost provider's rates, and over time the subsidy could be reduced or eliminated if lower cost rural providers could offer affordable service with little or no need for a subsidy. Economists argue that to base universal service payments on providers' costs — so that high cost providers receive higher subsidy payments — is to subsidize the inefficient at the expense of whoever is paying the subsidy.

The incumbent local exchange carriers have made another argument for why they should enjoy superior, or even exclusive, access to the universal service subsidy: they have made a commitment to be the carrier of last resort and serve every customer in their serving area. But those states that have awarded ETC status to other carriers have tended to require such a commitment from those carriers as well (though there may remain issues of the geographic reach of each ETC's services).

Who Should Contribute to a Universal Service Subsidy Fund and How Should Contributors be Assessed?

There are several sources of universal service funding. At the federal level, there is currently a 10.2% assessment on interstate and international telecommunications service revenues.[141] This assessment provides the bulk of universal service funds. In addition, at the federal level, some interstate access charges and other service charges, particularly those of some rural carriers, may still be set above cost in a fashion to contribute to universal service.

At the state level, some states have created state universal service funds financed by assessments on certain intrastate and interstate telecommunications revenues. Also, most states maintain some intrastate rates, in particular the intrastate access charges imposed by rural carriers, above cost to contribute to universal service.

There is consensus in the industry that continued reliance on interstate and international telecommunications revenues as the funding base would threaten the predictability, sufficiency, competitive neutrality — and very stability — of the Federal Universal Service Fund, for a variety of reasons.

- Total end-user interstate and international telecommunications service revenues reached a peak of $81.7 billion in 2000 and fell to an estimated $76.7 billion in 2004.[142] They appear to be falling at a rate of about 1% per year. The precipitous fall in the interstate and international telecommunications revenues of the traditional long distance carriers has been partially, but not completely, countered by an increase in interstate and international telecommunications revenues among wireless carriers and incumbent local exchange carriers. The downward trend in total end-user interstate and international telecommunications revenues is expected to continue as a result of a number of factors: the continued fall in rates for interstate and international calls as VoIP service grows, continued substitution of e-mail and other Internet applications for long distance service, and the classification of DSL service and certain VoIP services as information services, rather than telecommunications services.
- It has become increasingly difficult to identify (and audit) individual companies' interstate and international telecommunications service revenues because these services are being offered to both business and residential customers as part of bundled packages that include other services. Both customers and service providers have the incentive to understate the proportion of total revenues generated by these bundled services that are attributable to interstate and international telecommunications services.
- The convergence of formerly distinct markets and the introduction of new technologies have resulted in some interstate and international telecommunications services, which are subject to the 10.2% assessment, having to compete directly with VoIP and other services that are not subject to the assessment. Thus, the current assessment mechanism is not competitively neutral. Moreover, indirect substitutes, such as e-mail, are not subject to the assessment.
- As a result of the significant market changes and substantial revenue shifts, the assessment percentage has not been predictable, further complicating business decisions by adding a regulatory uncertainty to the mix.

There are a number of alternatives to an assessment on interstate telecommunications revenues to provide the funding needed for universal service that might better meet the policy objectives articulated by Congress. Some of these could not be implemented without congressional action. These include:

- an assessment on all telecommunications service revenues: interstate, international, and intrastate. Since telecommunications services increasingly are being offered as bundled packages of interstate and intrastate minutes, at a fixed price, expanding the assessment base in this fashion would have the advantages of both increasing the total subsidy base and eliminating the problem of determining the proportion of a fixed monthly charge that should be attributed to interstate service. Assessing all telecommunications service revenues would not eliminate the problem of competitive non-neutrality, however, as those VoIP services that are classified as information services, but compete directly with traditional voice services that are classified as telecommunications services, would be given an artificial competitive advantage. Because of a court decision prohibiting the FCC from assessing intrastate revenues,[143] Congress would have to modify the Communications Act before the FCC could include intrastate revenues in the assessment base.

- as assessment on all telecommunications service and information service revenues. This would increase the assessment base and eliminate the disparate treatment of telecommunications services and information services that compete directly with one another. But it would impose an assessment on information services, which would be inconsistent with congressional and FCC policy to foster the development of these services by minimizing regulatory burdens on them. It also might prove very difficult to determine which information services should be subject to the assessment since information services cover such a wide range of applications. This option also would require modification of the Communications Act before the FCC could include all these revenues in the assessment base.
- an assessment on the revenues of all services and equipment that benefit from the subsidies provided by the Federal Universal Service Fund, such as revenues from the services and products that receive discounts under the schools and libraries fund, as well as on services. This option would assess not only telecommunications and information service providers, but also companies that manufacture goods or provide other services that are subsidized by the Fund. This would increase the assessment base, but it would be inconsistent with congressional and FCC policy to foster the development of information services and it likely would be extremely difficult to identify the portion of revenues of non-telecommunications service companies that would be subject to the assessment. This option, too would require modification of the act before the FCC could include all these equipment and service revenues in the assessment base.
- an assessment on all connections to the public switched network, weighted by the bandwidth of those connections. Ultimately, all telecommunications users must connect to the public switched network to complete communications. Thus, a per connection assessment, based on bandwidth, would significantly widen the assessment base and could be structured in a way that is competitively neutral.[144] There would be issues about how to assign different assessment weights to connections of various capacity (bandwidth). Consumer groups have opposed this approach, arguing that it harms end users who have very low network usage, including low income households. Proponents have responded that since universal service is intended to subsidize connection to the public switched network, a per connection charge is appropriate. They also argue that many low income households are actually large telecommunications users; many of them make calls to family members in the military or (for immigrants) living overseas or calls from retirees living in the Sun Belt to family members living in more northern climes. There are differences of opinion about

whether the Communications Act would have to be modified before the FCC could use connections as the assessment base.

- an assessment on all telephone numbers in use. Just as every end user needs a connection to the public switched network, every end user needs a telephone number identifier. A per telephone number connection would significantly widen the assessment base and could be structured in a way that is competitively neutral.[145] Consumer groups have had the same criticisms of a per number assessment as they had for a per connection assessment, and proponents have made the same responses. There is also some possibility that future technological changes will lead to use of a customer identifier other than the telephone number. There are differences of opinion about whether the Communications Act would have to be modified before the FCC could use telephone numbers as the assessment base.
- dedicating the existing 3% federal excise tax on all telephony revenues to funding the FUSF. Depending on the potential growth of the FUSF, the federal excise tax might raise sufficient revenue to meet all or most universal service subsidy needs. It is easy to collect, imposing virtually no administrative costs. But the federal excise tax, which was originally enacted during the Spanish-American War on what was then a luxury item, currently funnels revenue into the general tax fund and many parties argue either that these revenues are needed to address the federal deficit or that this tax is ripe for elimination. It also might prove difficult to increase the tax rate if revenues did not prove great enough to meet FUSF needs. This option would require Congress to pass tax legislation before it could be implemented.
- using funds from general tax revenues. Since universal service is a subsidy program that is intended to benefit all sectors of the U.S. economy and all segments of the population, some have argued that it should be funded from general tax revenues. This would eliminate the market distortions inevitable when an assessment is imposed only on a subset of competitors or consumers and thus economists have argued this is the most efficient option. But this would make universal service funding subject to annual appropriations, which particularly in times of budget deficits might place such funding at risk. This option requires annual or multi-year appropriations action by Congress to be implemented.
- continue to fund universal service in part by allowing rural carriers to set above-cost intercarrier compensation rates as a way to maintain lower local rates. Some rural carriers are very concerned about relying entirely on external sources of universal service funding, especially at a time when competitors, such as wireless carriers, are seeking certification as ETCs to compete for those funds. These rural LECs would prefer to be able to ensure an internal funding source by maintaining above-cost rates for originating or terminating certain traffic where the other carrier involved with the call is a captive customer. This, however, would maintain the market distortions that exist today that hamper competition. This option would not require prior congressional action, but it might be challenged in court by parties that seek to remove all implicit universal subsidies from the rates of telecommunications services.

Transition Issues

As explained earlier, in order not to disrupt markets, when the FCC adopted an order on August 5, 2005, changing the classification of DSL from a telecommunications service to an information service, it created a 270 day transition period (which could be extended) during which the DSL revenues would continue to be treated as interstate telecommunications service revenues for the purposes of funding universal service. In addition, because a blanket re-classification of DSL to information service would, under current rules relating to National Exchange Carrier Association ("NECA") tariffs and pools that help fund universal service, reduce the universal service support available to certain rural telephone companies for the provision of DSL services, those carriers were given the option of continuing to treat DSL as a common carrier (telecommunications) service. Whichever universal service reforms are adopted, given the heavy reliance of rural telephone companies and their customers on universal service funding, there will have to be a transition period to minimize disruptions.

Other Programs and Policies that Contribute to the Universal Availability of Broadband Networks

According to the latest FCC data[146] on the deployment of high-speed Internet connections,[147] as of December 31, 2004, high-speed Internet subscribers were reported to be present in 99% of the most densely populated zip codes and in 74% of zip codes with the lowest population densities.[148] The FCC found that 99% of the U.S. population lives in the 95% of zip codes where a provider reports having at least one high-speed service subscriber.

Section 706 of the 1996 Act requires the FCC to determine whether "advanced telecommunications capability [i.e., broadband or high-speed access] is being deployed to all Americans in a reasonable and timely fashion." If this is not the case, the act directs the FCC to "take immediate action to accelerate deployment of such capability by removing barriers to infrastructure investment and by promoting competition in the telecommunications market."[149] In its most recent report pursuant to Section 706, the Commission concludes that "the overall goal of section 706 is being met, and the advanced telecommunications capability is indeed being deployed on a reasonable and timely basis to all Americans."[150] Two commissioners, however, dissented from that conclusion, claiming that the FCC's continuing definition of broadband as 200 kilobits per second is outdated and is not comparable to the much higher speeds available to consumers in other countries, and that the use of zip code data does not sufficiently characterize the availability of broadband across geographic areas.[151]

Many rural telephone companies already are deploying broadband networks, and some of those are deploying networks capable of offering IP video. According to an article in *Rural Telecommunications*,[152] by the end of 2003, 100 independent telephone companies were offering digital video content services, another 60 were expected to do so by the end of 2004, and it was projected that between 500 and 800 additional independent telephone companies would be doing so in the next four to five years. According to a report in *Broadcasting & Cable,*[153] two small, rural telephone companies — Farmers Telephone Cooperative in Kingstree, SC, and Progressive Rural Telephone in central Georgia — are upgrading their copper networks with IPTV technology to offer video service as well as voice and data services, and will be offering service before SBC and Verizon do. Farmers will send three video streams to member households so each can have up to three television sets receiving IPTV signals. It will send standard-definition video signals over DSL lines and high-definition television content over ADSL lines.[154] Progressive will deliver IPTV and music content across its access lines. Its service will include 141 television networks, six local channels, and 35 music channels. Similarly, *Rural Telecommunications* reports that Dakota Central Telecommunications ("DCT") of Carrington, ND, is using IPTV to offer voice, data, and video services both to the 5,000 customers in its own service area and to 16,000 customers in the neighboring city of Jamestown.[155] A Yankee Group analyst reportedly has stated that, while smaller, rural telephone companies have a disadvantage in terms of available capital and the ability to get the best rates for cable networks, they are likely to be competing with a local cable system that, even if it is owned by a large cable operator, is not technologically cutting-edge.[156] This suggests that the scope of the current universal service subsidy program, in conjunction with various grant and loan programs targeted on rural development, may be sufficient to support deployment of broadband network platforms capable of offering triple play voice, data, and video bundles in many rural areas.

At the same time, some industry observers have claimed that broadband deployment is occurring more rapidly in those rural areas served by small telephone companies and cooperatives than in those rural areas served by the RBOCs and other large incumbent telephone companies. For example, in their announcements concerning deployment of broadband networks capable of offering video as well as voice and data services and in their testimonies before Congress, neither Verizon nor SBC was willing to commit to deployment in their more rural service areas.[157]

Grant and Loan Programs

In addition to the Federal Universal Service Fund, there are a number of federal programs intended to foster deployment of broadband networks and services.[158]

- The Farm Security and Rural Investment Act of 2002 (P.L. 107-171) authorized the Rural Broadband Access Loan and Loan Guarantee Program for eligible entities for facilities and equipment providing broadband service in rural communities. Section 6103 makes available, from the funds of the Commodity Credit Corporation, a total of $ 100 million through FY2007 ($20 million for each of fiscal years 2002 through 2005, and $10 million for each of fiscal years 2006 and 2007). P.L. 107-171 also authorizes any other funds appropriated for the broadband loan program. The FY2005 Consolidated Appropriations Act (P.L. 108-447) provided $11.71 5 million for the cost of broadband loans, representing $550 million in lending authority. On March 4, 2005, the Rural Utilities Service ("RUS") announced the availability of $2.1 57 billion, consisting of $2.032 billion in direct cost-of-money loans, $46 million for direct 4 percent loans, and $79 million for loan guarantees. The FY2006 Department of Agriculture Appropriations Act (P.L. 109-97) provides $10.75 million for the cost of broadband loans.
- Complementing the broadband loan program, the RUS has established a broadband pilot grant program that issues grants to applicants proposing to provide broadband

service on a "community-oriented connectivity" basis to rural communities of under 20,000 inhabitants. The program targets rural, economically-challenged communities by providing support for broadband service to schools, libraries, education centers, health care providers, law enforcement agencies, public safety organizations, residents, and businesses. The FY2005 Consolidated Appropriations Act (P.L. 108-447) provided $9 million for broadband grants.

- The Telecommunications Development Fund, created in Section 714 of the 1996 Act, is a private, non-governmental venture capital corporation whose purpose is threefold: to promote access to capital for small businesses in order to enhance competition in the telecommunications industry; to stimulate new technology development and promote employment and training; and to support universal service and enhance the delivery of telecommunications services to rural and underserved areas. It is authorized to provide financing to eligible small businesses in the telecommunications industry through loans and investment capital. At this time the TDF is focusing on providing financing in the form of equity investments ranging from $375,000 to $1 million per investment. Initial funding for this program is derived from interest earned from the up-front payments bidders submit to participate in FCC auctions. As of December 1, 2004, the TDF had $50 million under management.[159]

In addition to these programs, RUS, NTIA, the Economic Development Administration in the Department of Commerce, several offices in the Department of Education, several organizations in the Department of Health and Human Services, several offices in the Department of Homeland Security, the National Foundation on the Arts and Humanities, the Appalachian Regional Commission, and the Denali Commission all have programs that could help fund the deployment of broadband network infrastructure or of broadband customer premises equipment.

These programs are being used by rural telephone companies to construct broadband networks. For example, Dakota Central Communications ("DCT"), a telephone cooperative serving 5,000 customers has used the RUS broadband program to fund its deployment of IPTV architecture to offer triple play service both to its own customers and to 16,000 households in a nearby town. As reported in *Rural Telecommunications,*[160]

> When money became available through the Rural Utilities Service (RUS) broadband program, moving into triple-play services with residential customers seemed like a natural next step. "We applied for and received a loan from RUS totaling $15.5 million, then supplied an additional $3.5 million of our own, [DCT general manager Keith] Larson said.

Municipal Provision of Broadband Networks

A growing number of municipalities, in both rural and urban areas, have announced plans to undertake deployment, or already have begun deployment, of broadband networks in their jurisdictions. Some have taken this step to provide broadband access in locations that the private sector has not shown an inclination to serve, typically small towns or low income neighborhoods in larger cities. Others have chosen to follow the model of Starbucks and other retailers by providing Wi-Fi hot spots as a "loss-leader" to attract upscale customers to retail districts. These municipal networks have used a variety of technologies, ranging from optical fiber to Wi-Fi. But at least 15 states have adopted laws banning or limiting these municipal networks.[161]

Proponents of municipal broadband networks argue that the marketplace, on its own, will steer broadband network to those locations that will be most profitable to serve, leaving less financially attractive locations unserved and placing those locations at a disadvantage in terms of attracting and supporting businesses and providing first quality education and health care. They claim government intervention is justified in support of economic development.[162]

Critics of municipal broadband networks argue that it is too soon to conclude that the marketplace will not serve all locations, that municipal networks enjoy an artificial advantage over private networks because of cost of capital and rights-of-way advantages, that many of the proposed broadband networks are based on unrealistic financial assumptions that will leave local taxpayers paying for mistakes, and that municipal networks are less likely than private networks to be upgraded as technological advances make improvements possible.[163] Some critics are concerned that with the development of WiMax technology, municipalities with small Wi-Fi networks will upgrade and expand to WiMax, which is potentially capable of providing the "last mile" connection to residents in competition with private networks. The RBOCs and cable companies have been supporting efforts at the state and federal level to prohibit municipal broadband networks.

In an interview with the *Wall Street Journal*,[164] FCC chairman Kevin Martin stated:

> I grew up in what was then a rural area in North Carolina and my parents lived on a gravel road. I think it's critical that we make sure that people who live in rural areas are able to be connected to all the advances in technology that are available. If you're asking about the role that local and city governments can play trying to deploy their own equipment, I think there is, at times, a role for them in that. There's always a balance. You prefer private sector deployment whenever possible and you want to make sure we don't get in a situation where the private sector players are trying to compete with government-sponsored players who have easier access to rights-of-way and government-backing. On the other hand, there are instances and communities where there aren't any private companies that want to deploy. No one is coming to deploy and I think in those instances people need to be able to make sure they can provide a service to their citizens. You have to have the right balance.

Corollary Issues

Voice over Internet Protocol (VoIP)

Today, the vast majority of Americans still obtain voice services over traditional circuit-switched networks that are subject to the common carrier regulations in Title II of the Communications Act. These regulations include specific network interconnection, access, intercarrier compensation, public safety, and law enforcement requirements, as well as assessments on all interstate and international telecommunications services to fund universal service. At the same time, a small, but growing number of customers obtain voice services from VoIP service providers. The FCC has ruled that a particular type of VoIP service — provided only to customers that already separately receive broadband Internet access service, so that their VoIP provider does not, itself, offer transmission service or transmission capacity, and requiring the customer to have enhanced premise equipment or downloaded software — (1) is neither a "telecommunications service" nor "telecommunications," but rather is an "information service" that should be unregulated; and (2) cannot be characterized as purely intrastate and therefore is subject only to federal jurisdiction.[165] As a result, that service is not subject to the interconnection, access, intercarrier compensation, public safety, law enforcement, and universal service requirements in Title II. But the FCC has ruled that voice services that are provided partly through IP technology, but that use ordinary customer premises equipment without enhanced functionality, originate and terminate on the public switched telephone network, undergo no net protocol conversion, and provide no enhanced functionality to end users due to the provider's use of IP technology, are telecommunications services and subject to Title II regulation.[166]

As a result, today competing voice services are subject to different regulatory regimes depending on whether they are classified by the FCC as telecommunications services or information services. The Commission is attempting to address one aspect of this issue — how to determine the classification of IP-enabled services — through a rule making proceeding.[167] But it is constrained by current statute in its ability to provide regulatory parity to competing voice services when one subset of those services clearly meets the current statutory definition of telecommunications service, a second subset clearly meets the current statutory definition of information service, and a third subset is ambiguous as to its classification. While the FCC can choose to forbear from regulating those competitive interstate services that are classified as telecommunications services, it may not have the authority to require state jurisdictions to forbear on regulation of intrastate telecommunications services.

This suggests that it may be timely to review the Title II telecommunications requirements. That review might address which requirements may be applicable to all voice services, regardless of the technology and network architecture used to provide those services, which may only be relevant for dominant firms, and which may not be relevant at all with the advent of competition.

Access to 911 and E911

Competition in the provision of applications (services) is developing today between integrated network providers that have ubiquitous networks and independent applications providers that have more limited networks and capabilities. In some situations, it would be inefficient, if not impossible, for a new entrant to replicate the facilities of a network provider. For example, for public safety reasons, the FCC has determined that all interconnected VoIP providers must be able to provide their customers access to 911 and E9 11 service, and that for this to happen there is need for cooperation between VoIP providers and ILECs. The FCC thus has required all interconnected VoIP providers to:

- deliver all 911 calls to the customer's local emergency operator (as a standard, not optional, feature);
- provide emergency operators with the call back number and location information of their customers (i.e., E91 1) where the emergency operator is capable of receiving it. Although the customer must provide the location information, the VoIP provider must provide the customer a means of updating this information, whether he or she is at home or away from home; and

- inform their customers, both new and existing, of the E91 1 capabilities and limitations of their service.[168]

At the same time, the FCC has required ILECs to provide access to their E91 1 networks to any requesting telecommunications carrier. They must continue to provide access to trunks, selective routes, and E9 11 databases to competing carriers.

Although some proponents of minimal government intervention have argued that customers should be allowed to choose low-cost options that do not include public safety features such as access to 911 and E9 11 service, the FCC had determined that in this case government intervention was justified by the public safety concern. At the same time, without rules in place to ensure all voice providers access to the E91 1 network, new entrants could be denied entry into the market. Some observers have argued that the VoIP providers currently are enjoying a "free ride" and an artificial marketplace advantage because their services are not subject to state taxes imposed on telecommunications services to support the E91 1 call centers (sometimes referred to as public safety answering points or "P SAPs") run by municipalities or states. These PSAPs are the physical locations where emergency calls are received and then routed to the proper emergency services.

Law Enforcement (CALEA)

In 1994, Congress enacted the Communications Assistance for Law Enforcement Act ("CALEA"),[169] to preserve the ability of law enforcement officials to conduct electronic surveillance effectively and efficiently despite the deployment of new digital and wireless technologies that have altered the character of such surveillance.[170] CALEA requires telecommunications carriers to modify their equipment, facilities, and services, wherever achievable, to ensure that they are able to comply with authorized electronic surveillance actions. In implementing CALEA, the FCC adopted an order on August 5, 2005 concluding that CALEA applies to facilities-based providers of any type of broadband Internet access service — including wireline, cable modem, satellite, wireless, and power line — and to VoIP providers that offer services permitting users to receive calls from, and place calls to, the public switched public network (these providers are sometimes referred to as "interconnected VoIP providers") because these providers offer services that are a replacement for a substantial portion of the local telephone exchange service."[171] The FCC also adopted a Further Notice of Proposed Rulemaking that will seek more information about whether certain classes or categories of facilities-based broadband Internet access providers, notably small and rural providers and providers of broadband networks for educational and research institutions, should be exempt from CALEA.

The important law enforcement objectives of CALEA potentially can conflict with the goals of competition and innovation. Some technologies and network architectures may be able to accommodate the CALEA requirements more readily — more quickly, less expensively, or with less impact on efficiency — than others. Also, CALEA requirements might impose substantial up-front costs on new technologies, architectures, or services that could be an impediment to their successful entry into the market, thus slowing innovation. There may be some tension in the future if network technologies and architectures migrate away from centralized networks to peer-to-peer networks, which have potential benefits to consumers both in terms of security and of allowing service providers and end users to interact more directly, but which may not be very accommodating to law enforcement concerns.

Media Policy: Localism, Competition, and Diversity of Voices

Localism,[172] competition, and diversity of voices have long been the fundamental goals of U. S. media policy. With the convergence of media, telecommunications, and information service markets, these goals may now have to be considered when developing telecommunications policy as well.

Subscription Multi-Channel Video Services

As discussed earlier, Section 601 of Title VI of the Communication Act explicitly identifies a local purpose for regulation of cable television: "[to] establish franchise procedures and standards which ... assure that cable systems are responsive to the needs and interests of the local community." Key sections in Title VI related to localism and diversity of voices allow franchise authorities to (1) require cable systems to set aside channels for public, educational, or governmental ("PEG") use and to provide facilities and/or financial support for PEG access;[173] (2) set aside channels for commercial use by persons unaffiliated with the cable system;[174] and (3) place safety and convenience restrictions on the construction of cable systems over public rights-of-way and easements.[175] If new entrants begin to offer subscription multi-channel video services in a fashion that does not meet the definition of cable service — for example, as an IP application that might meet the definition of an information service that is not subject to Title VI regulation — policy makers might want to consider whether the new service offering should be subject to the requirements in these provisions in order to foster the policy goal of localism, or whether the localism concerns are being fully met by the incumbent.

In addition, as discussed earlier, policy makers might want to consider the implications, from the perspective of diversity of voices, of a broadband network provider that offers its own subscription multi-channel video service refusing to allow its customers access to the IP video services provided by an independent applications provider.

Multicasting and "Must Carry" Requirements

As part of the transition to digital television, television broadcast licensees have been given 6 MHz of spectrum on which to operate digitally and at some point in time will have to return the spectrum on which they currently operate in analog mode. With digital technology, one option available to licensees is to use their 6 MHz of spectrum for multicasting — that is, to broadcast multiple programming streams. In support of the goal of localism, cable operators have been required to carry the "primary" signals of the local broadcast stations in their service areas. The FCC recently ruled that a television broadcaster that is multicasting video signals must identify one signal as its primary signal that cable systems must carry, but that cable systems have no obligation to carry additional multicast signals.[176] This decision was based in part on the concern that multicast "must carry" might infringe on the first amendment rights of cable operators and in part on the concern that the multicast signals might tend to be duplicative and might not meet the desires of viewers as well as cable channels.

Some observers have suggested that limiting must carriage to a single, primary signal might result in missing an opportunity to foster localism. For example, in considering what public interest obligations might be consistent with allowing broadcasters to air multiple signals, the FCC might consider modifying the current rule that requires cable operators to carry only the primary programming stream of each local television broadcaster by requiring cable operators to carry each programming stream that offers distinct programming aimed at a different, previously unserved geographic portion of the broadcaster's serving area. This could explicitly address those situations in which a broadcaster's serving area crosses state borders, awarding the broadcaster must carry rights for a second signal if the programming on that signal specifically addresses the needs and interests of the viewing households in the second state. If the FCC were to consider this approach, it would want to take into account the impact on cable systems of requiring them to carry additional broadcast channels.[177] It also would want to determine how best to construct a rule that did not artificially encourage or discourage broadcasters from choosing multicasting over other potential applications of digital technology to their 6 MHz of spectrum, such as high definition television. Congress might choose to direct the FCC to study and construct recommendations for rules (and, if necessary, statutory changes) to address the potentially related issues of mandatory carriage of multiple broadcast signals and better serving the needs and interests of viewers in different governmental jurisdictions.

ENDNOTES

[1] 47 U.S.C. 151 *et. seq.*

[2] P.L. 104-104, 110 Stat. 56.

[3] The act defines "information service" as the offering of a capability for generating, acquiring, storing, transforming, processing, retrieving, utilizing, or making available information via telecommunications." (Title I, Section 3(20) of the 1934 Act)

[4] In addition, there will continue to be niche providers that offer consumers users competitive options for specific services.

[5] There is no single, agreed-upon definition of "broadband." In its data collection, the Federal Communications Commission defines "high-speed lines" as connections that deliver services at speeds exceeding 200 kilobits per second ("kbps") in at least one direction and "advanced service lines" as connections that deliver services at speeds exceeding 200 kbps in both directions. (See "Federal Communications Commission Releases Data on High-Speed Services for Internet Access," FCC News release, July 7, 2005.) These speeds would not be sufficient to offer broadcast-quality video service. Thus, for example, telephone companies that currently offer digital subscriber line ("DSL") broadband connections would have to upgrade those connections in order to offer video service.

[6] In circuit-based networks, for the duration of any communication, a circuit is tied up from the calling party's premise all the way to the called party's premise. In IP-based networks, a communication is converted into digital bits and small packets of bits are

transmitted over whatever route is available. With broadband in place, even the "last-mile" into the calling and called parties' premises may accommodate multiple simultaneous applications, depending on each application's bandwidth requirements.

[7] Title I of the 1996 Act, which is incorporated into Title II of the Communications Act as amended, 47 U.S.C. 151 ("1934 Act").

[8] Title II of the 1996 Act, which is incorporated into Title VI of the 1934 Act.

[9] Title I, Section 3(20) of the 1934 Act.

[10] 47 U.S.C. § 154(i) states: "The Commission may perform any and all acts, make such rules and regulations, and issue such orders, not inconsistent with this Act, as may be necessary in the execution of its functions."

[11] See *Regulatory and Policy Problems Presented by the Interdependence of Computer and Communication Services and Facilities,* Docket No. 16979, Notice of Inquiry, 7 FCC 2d 11, 1966, (known as the "Computer I Notice of Inquiry"); *Regulatory and Policy Problems Presented by the Interdependence of Computer and Communications Services and Facilities,* Docket No. 16979, Final Decision and Order, 28 FCC 2d 358, 1971, (known as the "Computer I Final Decision"); *Amendment of Section 64.702 of the Commission 's Rules and Regulations (Second Computer Inquiry),* Docket No. 20828, Tentative Decision and Further Notice of Inquiry and Rulemaking, 72 FCC 2d 358, 1979, (known as the "Computer II Tentative Decision"); *Amendment of Section 64.702 of the Commission 's Rules and Regulations (Second Computer Inquiry),* Docket No. 20828, Final Decision, 77 FCC 2d 384, 1980, (known as the "Computer II Final Decision"); *Amendment of Section 64.702 of the Commission 's Rules and Regulations (Third Computer Inquiry),* CC Docket No. 85-229, Report and Order, 104 FCC 2d 958, 1986, (known as "Computer III"). In its Computer II Final Decision at pp. 432-435, paras. 126-132, the Commission found that the enhanced services market was highly competitive with low barriers to entry and therefore declined to treat providers of enhanced services as common carriers subject to regulation under Title II of the act.

[12] See, for example, *In the Matter of Inquiry Concerning High-Speed Access to the Internet Over Cable and Other Facilities; Internet Over Cable Declaratory Ruling; Appropriate Regulatory Treatment for Broadband Access to the Internet Over Cable Facilities,* 17 FCC Rcd. 4798, 4799 (March 15, 2002).

[13] *In the Matter of Inquiry Concerning High-Speed Access to the Internet Over Cable and Other Facilities; Internet Over Cable Declaratory Ruling; Appropriate Regulatory Treatment for Broadband Access to the Internet Over Cable Facilities,* 17 FCC Rcd. 4798, 4799 (March 15, 2002).

[14] *National Cable & Telecommunications Association v. Brand X Internet Services,* 125 S. Ct. 2688 (2005). This decision does not preclude the FCC from regulating information services, such as cable modem service or DSL services, based on its ancillary authority under Title I of the act.

[15] *Appropriate Framework for Broadband Access to the Internet over Wireline Facilities, Universal Service Obligations of Broadband Providers,* CC Docket Nos. 02-33 and 01-337, Notice of Proposed Rulemaking, adopted February 14, 2002.

[16] *Appropriate Framework for Broadband Access to the Internet over Wireline Facilities; Universal Service Obligations of Broadband Providers,* CC Dockets Nos. 02-33 and 01-337, Report and Order, adopted August 5, 2005 and released September 23, 2005. In order not to disrupt markets, however, the FCC created a one-year transition period

during which independent ISPs would continue to be able to obtain DSL transmission service from incumbent local exchange carriers and also a 270-day transition period (which could be extended) during which the DSL revenues would continue to be treated as interstate telecommunications service revenues for the purposes of funding universal service. The FCC also stated that it retained ancillary authority to regulate DSL service and adopted a Further Notice of Proposed Rulemaking to determine whether it should construct consumer protection rules for broadband services. In addition, the Commission adopted a non-binding policy statement consisting of four principles: consumers are entitled to access the lawful Internet content of their choice; consumers are entitled to run applications and services of their choice, subject to the needs of law enforcement; consumers are entitled to connect their choice of legal devices that do not harm the network; and, consumers are entitled to competition among network providers, application and service providers, and content providers.

[17] TCP/IP stands for Transmission Control Protocol/Internet Protocol. IP is responsible for moving packets of data from node to node. IP forwards each packet based on a four byte destination address (the IP number). The Internet authorities assign ranges of numbers to different organizations. The organizations assign groups of their numbers to departments. IP operates on gateway machines that move data from department to organization to region and then around the world. TCP is responsible for verifying the correct delivery of data from client to server. Data can be lost in the intermediate network. TCP adds support to detect errors or lost data and to trigger retransmission until the data are correctly and completely received.

[18] Since the 1970s, engineers have developed various network design models incorporating protocols in a layered manner. While the network configurations have varied somewhat (there may be different numbers of layers if, for example, network functions are combined in some network designs and separated in others), there is general agreement that the broadband networks currently being deployed consist of layers or tiers, starting with the lowest layer of physical infrastructure and ending with the highest layer of content, with a logical TSP/IP layer that both can accommodate every type of physical network (DSL, cable modem, ethernet, fiber optics, satellite, Wi-Fi, Bluetooth, etc.) as well as a multitude of applications and content. See, for example, Richard S. Whitt, "A Horizontal Leap Forward: Formulating a New Public Policy Framework Based on the Network Layers Model," December 2003, available at [*http://global.mci.com/about/publicpolicy/presentations/ horizontallayerswhite paper.pdf*], viewed on January 13, 2006. Professor Tim Wu has suggested, however, that in order to construct simple regulatory rules that would be subject to minimal administrative and litigative encumbrances, it might be preferable to construct a regulatory framework that defines just two layers: a physical transport infrastructure layer and an application services layer. See Tim Wu, "A Flat Model of Telecommunications Regulation," forthcoming, *Journal on Telecommunications and High Technology Law,* available from Professor Wu, who can be contacted at the website [http://faculty.virginia. edu/timwu/].

[19] *Ex ante* rules impose explicit requirements, restrictions, or prohibitions to which parties know in advance they are required to adhere. The regulatory agency typically need not analyze the impact of a party's failure to comply with the rule before taking remedial action. By contrast, *ex post* adjudication of abuses of market power typically requires the

regulatory agency to make a finding of abuse of market power before taking any remedial action.

[20] These four Internet Consumer Freedoms are: freedom to access content, freedom to use applications, freedom to attach personal devices, and freedom to obtain service plan information.

[21] *Appropriate Framework for Broadband Access to the Internet over Wireline Facilities,* CC Docket No. 02-33, Policy Statement, FCC 05-151, released September 23, 2005.

[22] See, for example, the research projects listed on the website of the Parallel and Distributed Operating Systems Group at MIT, available at [http://pdos.csail.mit.edu] (viewed on January 13, 2006).

[23] See, for example, Ariana Eunjung Cha, "Viruses, Security Issues Undermine Internet," *Washington Post,* June 26, 2005, at pp. A1, A15.

[24] For example, in order not to disrupt markets, when the FCC adopted an order on August 5, 2005, changing the classification of DSL from a telecommunications service to an information service, it created a one-year transition period during which independent ISPs would continue to be able to obtain DSL transmission service from incumbent local exchange carriers and also a 270-day transition period (which could be extended) during which the DSL revenues would continue to be treated as interstate telecommunications service revenues for the purposes of funding universal service. In addition, because a blanket re-classification of DSL to information service would, under current rules relating to National Exchange Carrier Association ("NECA") tariffs and pools that help fund universal service, reduce the universal service support available to certain rural telephone companies for the provision of DSL services, those carriers were given the option of continuing to treat DSL as a common carrier (telecommunications) service.

[25] 47 U.S.C. § 253.

[26] 47 U.S.C. §§ 151-152.

[27] 47 U.S.C. § 522.

[28] This report does not address specific proposed legislation. For a brief discussion of a number of issues potentially under consideration by Congress, please see CRS Report RL32949, *Communications Act Revisions: Selected Issues for Consideration,* by Angele A. Gilroy which provides, by topic, a listing of relevant available CRS reports.

[29] The conference report refers to the bill "to provide for a pro-competitive, de-regulatory national policy framework designed to accelerate rapidly private sector deployment of advanced services and information technologies and services to all Americans by opening all telecommunications markets to competition....", Conference Report, Telecommunications Act of 1996, House of Representatives, 104th Congress, 2d Session, H.Rept. 104-458, at p. 1.

[30] 47 U.S.C. § 253.

[31] Economists call this phenomenon "direct network externalities." A positive/negative externality is a benefit/cost that is not accounted for in the price of a good or service. Direct network externalities are positive externalities because a network connection is more valuable if it can be used to reach more people, but the subscriber is not charged more as the number of other subscribers increases. In most situations, pollution is an example of a negative externality, because it imposes costs on others but the perpetrator generally is not forced to compensate the harmed parties.

[32] 47 U.S.C. § 252.

[33] For a detailed discussion of intercarrier compensation, see CRS Report RL32889, *Intercarrier Compensation: One Component of Telecom Reform,* by Charles B. Goldfarb.

[34] 47 U.S.C. § 252(d)(2)(A)).

[35] Modification of Final Judgment, *United States v. American Telephone and Telegraph Company,* 552 F. Supp 131 (D.D.C. 1982).

[36] 47 U.S.C. § 271.

[37] 47 U.S.C. §§ 251(c)(3) and 252(d)(1).

[38] 47 U.S.C. § 254(e).

[39] For example, for certain long distance calls, if the caller uses a wireless telephone number, the caller's wireless carrier is subject to a cost-based "reciprocal compensation" intercarrier compensation charge for the termination of that call. But if the caller made an identical call, from the same location to the same called party, using a wireline telephone (and hence a wireline long distance carrier), that carrier would be subject to above cost "access charges" for the completion of the call. As another example, when a long distance call is made to a called party's wireline telephone, that party's wireline local exchange carrier can charge the calling party's long distance carrier an above-cost access charge for terminating the call; but if an identical long distance call were made to ths same called party, from and to the same physical location, but to the called party's wireless telephone, the called party's wireless carrier is not allowed to charge the calling party's long distance carrier any access charge for terminating the call. Indeed, the average intercarrier compensation rate ranges from 0.1 cents per minute for traffic bound to an information service provider ("ISP") to 5.1 cents per minute for intrastate traffic bound to a subscriber of a small (rural) incumbent local exchange carrier; individual rates can be as low as zero and as high as 35.9 cents per minute — even though in each case basically the same transport and switching functions are provided. (See CRS Report RL32889, *Intercarrier Compensation: One Component of Telecom Reform.)* As another example of distortions in intermodal competition caused by current rules, the Federal Universal Service Fund is funded through an assessment on interstate telecommunications service revenues that exceeds 10% (the exact assessment rate varies from quarter to quarter); information services, even if they compete directly with the interstate telecommunications services, are not assessed.

[40] These conditions include divesting connections to more than 350 buildings in their respective territories, using long-term leases known as indefeasible rights of use; freezing special access rates for 30 months; offering stand-alone DSL service; continuing settlement-free peering arrangements with at least as many Internet backbone providers as they had prior to the merger; posting their peering policies on publicly accessible websites for two years; abiding by the FCC's network neutrality goals; not seeking increases in unbundled network element rates for two years; and not increasing the rates paid by existing in-region customers of AT&T and MCI for wholesale DS 1 and DS3 local private line services.

[41] For a full discussion of this, see George Ford, Thomas Koutsky, and Lawrence Spiwack, "Competition After Unbundling: Entry, Industry Structure and Convergence," Phoenix Center Policy Paper Number 21, July 2005, available at [http://www.phoenix-center.org], viewed on January 13, 2006.

[42] The large business customers are likely to have such great bandwidth demands that they will have dedicated pipes to their maj or locations with broadband capability and will be reliant on the broadband network providers' general buildout only to connect to their smaller locations or to their customers' locations. Some parties have expressed concern, however, that with the completion of the SBC-AT&T and Verizon-MCI mergers, these large business customers may not have many alternative sources, especially to the extent that cable networks tend to be built out to residential neighborhoods rather than business districts.

[43] For a more detailed discussion of the issues of network neutrality, open access, and broadband discrimination, see Tim Wu, "Network Neutrality, Broadband Discrimination," *Journal on Telecommunications & High Technology Law,* Vol 2, 2003, pp. 141-178 Professor Wu's article is one of many in a very lively debate in the academic economic and legal literature. See footnote 1 and other citations in the Wu article for a list of other academic articles.

[44] See Joseph Farrell and Philip Weiser, "Modularity, Vertical Integration, and Open Access Policies: Towards a Convergence of Antitrust and Regulation in the Internet Age," *Harvard Journal of Law and Technology,* Fall 2003, pp. 85-133.

[45] Farrell and Weiser identify 8 such circumstances: (1) if its rates for platform access are regulated; (2) if the platform monopolist can use otherwise efficient price discrimination to make even inefficient vertical leveraging profitable; (3) if an applications provider is a potential competitor at the platform level that the monopoly platform provider wants to weaken; (4) if the monopoly platform provider can use its market bargaining power to impose a licensing or other arrangement on an applications provider that discourages future applications innovations; (5) if the platform monopolist is incompetent and therefore cannot recognize optimal choices; (6) if the platform monopolist perceives that allowing open access today would undermine its ability to close access in the future even if it would be efficient to do so; (7) if, for regulatory strategy considerations, the platform monopolist is afraid that agreeing to open access for, say ISPs, would raise the risk of having open access imposed in another market, such as cable video programming; and (8) if the platform is not essential for all uses of the application and there are economies of scale or network effects in the application.

[46] See Tim Wu, "Network Neutrality, Broadband Discrimination," *Journal on Telecommunications & High Technology Law,* Vol. 2, 2003, at pp. 158-168.

[47] Tim Wu, "Network Neutrality, Broadband Discrimination," *Journal on Telecommunications & High Technology Law,* Vol. 2, 2003, at pp. 165-166. One manufacturer claims its product is used on hundreds of university campuses to control peerto-peer traffic, but those universities may be motivated by concern about intellectual property rights infractions as well as by bandwidth management issues.

[48] Louis Trager, "ISPs Accuse Verizon of Double-Cross on FiOS Wholesaling," *Communications Daily,* November 3, 2005, at pp. 5-7.

[49] *Communications Daily,* November 8, 2005, at p. 8.

[50] See, for example, Dionne Searcey and Amy Schatz, "Phone Companies Set Off a Battle Over Internet Fees," *Wall Street Journal,* January 6, 2006, at p. A1.

[51] See Tim Wu, "A Flat Model of Telecommunications Regulation," forthcoming, *Journal on Telecommunications and High Technology Law,* available from Professor Wu, who can be contacted at the website [http://faculty.virginia.edu/timwu/].

[52] See, for example, Mark Lemley and Lawrence Lessig, *The End of End-to-End: Preserving the Architecture of the Internet in the Broadband Era,* 48 UCLA Law Review 925 (2001).

[53] See, for example, James B. Speta, "Handicapping the Race for the Last Mile? A Critique of Open Access Rules for Broadcast Platforms, *17 Yale Journal on Regulation* (2000), at p. 76; Joseph Farrell and Philip Weiser, "Modularity, Vertical Integration, and Open Access Policies: Towards a Convergence of Antitrust and Regulation in the Internet Age," *17 Harvard Journal of Law and Technology* (2003), at pp. 4-6; Glen Robinson, "On Refusing to Deal with Rivals," *87 Cornell Law Review* (2002), at pp. 1216-1217.

[54] James B. Speta, "Handicapping the Race for the Last Mile: A Critique of Open Access Rules for Broadband Platforms," Yale Journal on Regulation, Volume 17, 2000, at p. 83.

[55] See, for example, Mark Lemley and Lawrence Lessig, "The End of End-to-End: Preserving the Architecture of the Internet in the Broadband Era," UCLA Law Review, Volume 48, April 2001, at p. 968.

[56] See, for example, Amy Schatz and Anne Marie Squeo, "As Web Providers' Clout Grows, Fears Over Access Take Focus," *Wall Street Journal,* August 8, 2005, at p. A1.

[57] The most detailed discussion of network neutrality and non-discrimination rules can be found in Tim Wu, "Network Neutrality, Broadband Discrimination," *Journal on Telecommunications & High Technology Law,* Vol. 2, 2003, at pp. 141-178 and in an *ex parte* letter from Tim Wu and Lawrence Lessig, dated August 22, 2003, submitted to the FCC in CS Docket No. 02-52, which is available online at [http://faculty.virginia.edu/ timwu/wu_lessig_fcc.pdf], viewed on January 13, 2006. The discussion in this report draws heavily from those analyses.

[58] The independent applications providers and other supporters of enforceable network neutrality rules are not all small players, however. When the FCC was considering re-classifying DSL services as information services rather than telecommunications services, in early August, 2005, representatives from Microsoft, Dell, Yahoo, and the Consumer Electronics Association ("CEA"), as well as consumer organizations, met with FCC commissioners and "explained the need for 'net neutrality' provisions because network operators have the opportunity, incentive and ability to violate these net neutrality principles." See, for example, the *ex parte* letter, dated August 2, 2005, from Veronica O'Connell, Senior Director, Government Affairs, Consumer Electronics Association, to Marlene H. Dortch, Secretary, Federal Communications Commission, on behalf of Microsoft Corporation, Media Access Project, Vonage, Dell, and CEA. Similarly, as entertainment companies seek ways to distribute movies and television shows over the Internet, they have expressed concern about having to rely on broadband networks owned by competitors, such as Time Warner, for access to end users. See Amy Schatz and Anne Marie Squeo, "As Web Providers' Clout Grows, Fears Over Access Take Focus," *Wall Street Journal,* August 8, 2005, at p. A1.

[59] The specific rule would be as follows: Forbidding Broadcast Discrimination (a) Broadband Users have the right reasonably to use their Internet connection in ways which are privately beneficial without being publicly detrimental. Accordingly, Broadband Operators shall impose no restrictions on the use of an Internet connection except as necessary to: 1. Comply with any legal duty created by federal, state or local laws, or as necessary to comply with any executive order, warrant, legal injunction,

subpoena, or other duly authorized governmental directive; 2. Prevent physical harm to the local Broadband Network caused by any network attachment or network usage; 3. Prevent Broadband users from interfering with other Broadband or Internet User's use of their Internet connections, including but not limited to neutral limits on bandwidth usage, limits on mass transmission of unsolicited email, and limits on the distribution of computer viruses, worms, and limits on denial-of-service or other attacks on others; 4. Ensure the quality of the Broadband service, by eliminating delay, jitter or other technical aberrations; 5. Prevent violations of the security of the Broadband network, including all efforts to gain unauthorized access to computers on the Broadband network or Internet; 6. Serve any other purpose specifically authorized by the Federal Communications Commission, based on weighing of the specific costs and benefit of the restriction. (b) As used in this section, 1. "Broadband Operators" means a service provider that provides high-speed connections to the Internet using whatever technology, including but not limited to cable networks, telephone networks, fiber optic connections, and wireless transmission; 2. "Broadband Users" means residential and business customers of a Broadband Operator; 3. "Broadband Network" means the physical network owned and operated by the Broadband Operator; 4. "Restrictions on the Use of an Internet Connection" means any contractual, technical, or other limits placed with or without notice on the Broadband user's Internet Connection.

[60] *In the Matter of Madison River Communications, LLC and afiliated companies,* DA 05-543, File No, EB-05-IH-01 10, Acct. No. FRN: 0004334082, Consent Decree, undated. Under this decree, Madison River agreed not to block ports used for VoIP applications or to otherwise prevent customers from using VoIP applications, and paid a fine of $15,000. It is possible that Madison River's primary incentive for blocking Vonage service was to protect against the loss of access charge revenues. As explained below in the section on *Intercarrier Compensation,* rural telephone companies currently get a large portion of their revenues from above-cost access charges imposed on long distance carriers for originating or terminating long distance calls. If intercarrier compensation reform were enacted that removed the implicit subsidies from access charges and placed those subsidies in an expanded Federal Universal Service Fund, the incentive to block VoIP calls would be significantly reduced.

[61] Tim Wu, "A Flat Model of Telecommunications Regulation," forthcoming, *Journal on Telecommunications and High Technology Law,* available from Professor Wu, who can be contacted at the website [http://faculty.virginia.edu/timwu/].

[62] The single document most concretely laying out the Framework is Directive 2002/21/EC of the European Parliament and of the Council of 7 March 2002 on a common regulatory framework for electronic communication networks and services, OJ L 108, 24.4.2002, pp. 33-50. The complete Framework consists of four additional EU directives plus two documents prepared by the Commission of the European Communities, as required by Article 15, paragraphs 1 and 2, of the Framework Directive (at p. 44).

[63] All transmission infrastructures used to offer electronic communications services to the public (including those used to carry broadcasting content, such as cable television networks, terrestrial broadcasting networks, and satellite broadcasting networks) are within the scope of the new regulatory Framework. (Framework Directive at p. 33, paragraph 5.) Content services (such as broadcast content and e-commerce services),

electronic communications equipment, and private networks that are not used to offer services to the public, are outside the scope of the Framework (Framework Directive at pp. 33-34, paragraphs 5-6 and 8-10, and p. 39, Article 2, Definition d.)

[64] Commission of the European Communities, "Commission Recommendation of 11 February 2003 on relevant product and service markets within the electronic communications sector susceptible to ex ante regulation in accordance with Directive 2002/21/EC of the European Parliament and of the Council on a common regulatory framework for electronic communication networks and services" (Commission Recommendation), OJ L 114, at p. 45, paragraph 1.

[65] Framework Directive at p. 45, Article 16, paragraphs 3-4.

[66] Framework Directive at p. 36, paragraph 27, and at p. 38, paragraph 39.

[67] Framework Directive at p. 36, paragraph 27.

[68] Framework Directive at p. 44, Article 14, paragraph 2.

[69] "Commission guidelines on market analysis and the assessment of significant market power under the Community regulatory framework for electronic communications networks and services," (Commission Guidelines), OJ C 165, 11.7.2002, pp. 6-30. These detailed guidelines describe the relationship between the Framework and EU competition law. They include discussions of the criteria for defining the relevant product market (including demand-side substitution and supply-side substitution) and relevant geographic market, and criteria for assessing significant market power (including dominance, collective dominance, and the leverage of market power).

[70] Commission of the European Communities, "On Relevant Product and Service Markets within the electronic communications sector susceptible to ex ante regulation in accordance with Directive 2002/21/EC of the European Parliament and of the Council on a common regulatory framework for electronic communication networks and services" (Commission Recommendations), OJ L 114, pp. 45-49.

[71] Commission Guidelines at p. 7, paragraph 9, and p. 8, paragraph 19.

[72] Commission Guidelines at p. 15, paragraph 75.

[73] Commission Guidelines at p. 10, paragraph 32.

[74] Tim Wu, "A Flat Model of Telecommunications Regulation," forthcoming, *Journal on Telecommunications and High Technology Law,* available from Professor Wu, who can be contacted at the website [http://faculty.virginia.edu/timwu/].

[75] Digital Age Communications Act: Proposal of the Regulatory Framework Working Group of the Digital Age Communications Act Project of the Progress and Freedom Foundation, June 2005, available at [http://www.pff.org/issues-pubs/other/0506 1 7regframework.pdf], viewed on January 13, 2006.

[76] 15 U.S.C. §§ 41-51.

[77] See, for example, *ex parte* letter dated February 21, 2003, from Daniel L. Brenner and Michael Schooler, counsel for the National Cable & Telecommunications Association, to Marlene Dortch, Secretary of the Federal Communications Commission, submitted in CS Docket No. 02-52, available at [http://www.ncta.com/pdf_files/0221 03_02-52_exparte.pdf], viewed on January 13, 2006.

[78] Remarks of Michael K. Powell, Chairman, Federal Communications Commission, at the Silicon Flatirons Symposium on "The Digital Broadband Migration: Toward a Regulatory Regime for the Internet Age," University of Colorado School of Law, February 8, 2004.

[79] "FCC Eliminates Mandated Sharing Requirement on Incumbents' Wireline Broadband Internet Access Services," FCC News, August 5, 2005.

[80] Deployment by small rural telephone companies of broadband networks capable of providing voice, data, and video is discussed below in the section entitled "Other Programs and Policies that Contribute to the Universal Availability of Broadband Networks."

[81] When SBC acquired AT&T in 2005, it changed its corporate name to AT&T.

[82] Michael Totty, "Who's Going to Win the Living-Room Wars?", *Wall Street Journal,* April 25, 2005, at p. R4, citing a UBS analyst report.

[83] 47 U.S.C. § 522.

[84] Michael Totty, "Who's Going to Win the Living-Room Wars?", *Wall Street Journal,* April 25, 2005, at p. R4, citing a UBS analyst report.

[85] Although franchising is most commonly performed by local jurisdictions, and it is common to talk of "local franchising authorities," there is no statutory language explicitly requiring that franchising be performed at the local level, as opposed to the state level. According to Sec. 601 of the Communications Act, "the term 'franchising authority' means any governmental entity empowered by the Federal, State, or local law to grant a franchise." (47 U.S.C. § 521) At the same time, Sec. 601 also explicitly identifies a local purpose for regulation of cable television: "[to] establish franchise procedures and standards which encourage the growth and development of cable systems and which assure that cable systems are responsive to the needs and interests of the local community" (47 U.S.C. § 521)

[86] 47 U.S.C. §§ 542(a) and 542(b).

[87] 47 U.S.C. § 531.

[88] 47 U.S.C. § 541(a)(4)(B).

[89] 47 U.S.C. § 532.

[90] 47 U.S.C. § 541(a)(4)(A).

[91] 47 U.S.C. § 541(a)(3).

[92] 47 U.S.C. § 531 and 532.

[93] See, for example, George Ford, Thomas Koutsky, and Lawrence Spiwack, "Competition After Unbundling: Entry, Industry Structure and Convergence," Phoenix Center Policy Paper Number 21, July 2005, at pp. 36-39, available at [http://www.phoenix-center.org], viewed on January 13, 2006.

[94] Some parties that have voiced concern about a duopoly market structure have pointed to the history of the wireless telephone industry. According to those commentators, for a decade, when there were only two cellular telephone providers in any geographic area (the incumbent local exchange carrier and a second carrier), there was little investment, innovation, or market success and no attempt to position wireless service as a direct competitor with wireline telephone service. Only when the FCC made additional spectrum available for wireless service (allocating spectrum in the 1900 MHz band for personal communications service), allowing several additional carriers to offer service in most geographic areas, did wireless begin to experience rapid technological and market advances that redounded to the benefit of consumers. Other commentators, however, claim that the rapid changes of the 1 990s were due to technological change lowering costs to the point that wireless service could become a substitute for traditional fixed telephone service, not due to change in the market structure.

[95] See, for example, Christine Vestal, "Wireless Is Key to Post-*Brand X* Broadband Competition, FCC Staffers Say," *Communications Daily,* June 30, 2005, at pp. 2-4, and Dinesh Kumar, "Utilities Set to Benefit from Brand X Ruling, BPL Officials Say," *Communications Daily,* June 30, 2005, at pp. 5-6.

[96] "Connected on the Go: Broadband Goes Wireless," Report by the Wireless Broadband Access Task Force ("FCC Wireless Broadband Task Force Report"), Federal Communications Commission, GN Docket No. 04-163, February 2005.

[97] FCC Wireless Broadband Task Force Report, at pp. 13-14.

[98] For a more detailed discussion of terrestrial wireless technologies, see CRS Report RS20993, *Wireless Technology and Spectrum Demand: Advanced Wireless Services;* and CRS Report RS2 1508, *Spectrum Management and Special Funds,* both by Linda K. Moore.

[99] For a full discussion of the Digital Television Transition, see CRS Report RL3 1260, *Digital Television: An Overview,* by Lennard G. Kruger.

[100] One gigahertz is 1,000 times one megahertz. Thus 2.5 GHz is the same as 2500 MHz.

[101] Specific frequencies mentioned in the act include not only the 1710-1755 MHz band but also other federally-used frequencies scheduled for reallocation and possible auction.

[102] *In the Matter of Amendment of Part 2 of the Commission 's Rules to Allocate Spectrum Below 3 GHz for Mobile and Fixed Services to Support the Introduction of New Advanced Wireless Services, including Third Generation Wireless Systems,* ET Docket No. 00-25 8, Sixth Report and Order, adopted September 9, 2004, released September 22, 2004.

[103] For a detailed discussion of spectrum management issues, see Spectrum Policy Task Force Report, Federal Communications, ET Docket No. 02-135, November 2002.

[104] See, for example, "Cable's Cell Deal," *Broadcasting & Cable,* November 7, 2005, at p. 8.

[105] See footnote 40.

[106] P.L. 104-104, § 601(b)(1).

[107] *Verizon Communications v. Law Ofices of Curtis V. Trinko,* 540 U.S. 398 (2004). For a full discussion of this case, see CRS Report RS2 1723, *Verizon Communications, Inc. v. Trinko: Telecommunications Consumers Cannot Use Antitrust Law to Remedy Access Violations of Telecommunications Act,* by Janice E. Rubin.

[108] "Sensenberenner Statement on Supreme Court's Trinko Decision," U.S. House of Representatives Committee on the Judiciary, January 14, 2004, available at [http://judiciary.house.gov/legacy/news011404.htm], viewed on January 13, 2006.

[109] "Conyers Disheartened by Supreme Court Decision Obliterating Antitrust Law in Telecom Industry," U.S. House Committee on the Judiciary, January 13, 2004, available at [http://www.house.gov/judiciary_democrats/supremecttrinkopr11 304 .pdf], viewed on January 13, 2006.

[110] "Sensenbrenner: Verizon Ruling May Require Legislation," *Congress Daily,* January 14, 2004.

[111] 47 U.S.C. § 252.

[112] For a detailed discussion of intercarrier compensation issues, see CRS Report RL32889, *Intercarrier Compensation: One Component of Telecom Reform,* by Charles B. Goldfarb.

[113] 47 U.S.C. § 252(d)(2)(A).

[114] These payments vary even among LECs, depending on whether the carrier is an incumbent local exchange carrier, that is one of the legacy LECs that was a government sanctioned local monopoly provider prior to the implementation of the 1996 Act; a small LEC (sometimes referred to as a rural LEC), that is an ILEC serving a small rural area; or a competitive local exchange carrier, that is a new competitive provider of local exchange service that was allowed to enter the market as a result of enactment of the 1996 Act.

[115] The ICF is a group of carriers from different segments of the telecommunications industry that has submitted a proposal for comprehensive intercarrier compensation reform in a proceeding currently open at the FCC: *In the Matter of Developing a Unified Intercarrier Compensation Regime,* CC Docket No. 01-92, Ex-Parte Brief of the Intercarrier Compensation Forum in Support of the Intercarrier Compensation and Universal Reform Plan ("ICF Plan"), October 5, 2004.

[116] ICF Plan at Appendix C, p. 2. In Figure 1, "RC" refers to "reciprocal compensation," the cost-based system for intercarrier compensation between providers of local service mandated by the 1996 Act (47 U.S.C. §§ 251(b)(5), 252(d)(1)(A), and 252(d)(2)(A)). "IntraMTA" and "InterMTA" refer to the distinction between those calls originating on wireless networks that are treated as local vs. long distance for intercarrier compensation purposes, as discussed in greater detail below. All classifications with the words "intrastate" or "interstate" refer to intercarrier compensation rates for long distance calls.

[117] In section 254(g) of the 1996 Act, 47 U.S.C. § 254(g), Congress instructed the FCC to "adopt rules to require that the rates charged by providers of interexchange telecommunications services to subscribers in rural and high cost areas shall be no higher than the rates charged by each such provider to its subscribers in urban areas. Such rules shall also require that a provider of interstate interexchange telecommunications services shall provide such services to its subscribers in each State at rates no higher than the rates charged to its subscribers in any other State." To implement this statutory instruction, the FCC adopted a geographic rate averaging rule and a rate integration rule. (47 C.F.R. § 64.180.)

[118] The "access charges" that some rural local exchange carriers charge long distance carriers for originating the long distance calls made by customers located in those rural areas, or for terminating the long distance calls made to customers located in those rural areas, exceed the nationally averaged price that the long distance carriers charge their subscribers for those calls, and thus the long distance carriers lose money on each long distance call into or out of those rural exchanges. As a result, long distance carriers are reluctant to make available to customers in those areas service packages that are likely to be attractive to heavy long distance users.

[119] *In the Matter of Developing a Unified Intercarrier Compensation Regime,* Further Notice of Proposed Rulemaking ("ICC FNPRM"), adopted February 10, 2005, released March 3, 2005.

[120] See the following documents filed with the FCC in the Intercarrier Compensation proceeding: The National Association of Regulatory Utility Commissioners ("NARUC") Study Committee on Intercarrier Compensation Goals for a New Intercarrier Compensation System, May 5, 2004; Cost Based Intercarrier Compensation Coalition ("CBICC") Proposal, September 2, 2004; Ex Parte Brief of the Intercarrier

Compensation Forum in Support of the Intercarrier Compensation and Universal Service Reform Plan, October 5, 2004; The Intercarrier Compensation and Reform Plan of the Alliance for Rational Intercarrier Compensation, October 25, 2004; A Comprehensive Plan for Intercarrier Compensation Reform Developed by the Expanded Portland Group, November 2, 2004; Western Wireless Intercarrier Compensation Reform Plan, December 1, 2004; Updated Ex Parte of Home Telephone Company, Inc. and PBT Telecom, November 2, 2004; Ex Parte of CTIA — The Wireless Association, November 29, 2004; the National Association of State Utility Consumer Advocates ("NASUCA") Intercarrier Compensation Plan, December 17, 2004; "A Bill-and-Keep Approach to Intercarrier Compensation Reform," ICC FNPRM, Appendix C.

[121] *In the Matter of Developing a Unified Intercarrier Compensation Regime,* Docket No. 01-92, Notice of Proposed Rulemaking ("ICC NPRM"), 16 FCC Rcd at 965.

[122] Rand McNally & Co. has formulated 493 non-overlapping Basic Trading Areas ("BTAs") that cover the entire United States and its territories. Each BTA represents a geographic region, defined by a group of counties that surround a city, which is the area's basic trading center. The FCC has used these BTAs to determine service areas for PCS wireless licenses. In turn, these 493 BTAs are aggregated into 51 Major Trading Areas ("MTAs"), usually composed of several contiguous basic trading areas. Individual MTAs are quite large, and can encompass several states. For a map showing the MTA boundaries, see [http://wireless.fcc.gov/auctions/data/maps/mta.pdf] (viewed on 4/14/05). The intercarrier compensation rules are different for intraMTA wireless calls that originate and terminate within an MTA and interMTA wireless calls that originate and terminate in different MTAs.

[123] Specifically, (1) ISPs are treated like end users; (2) ISPs receive far more calls than they make, so an ISP's LEC will terminate far more calls from the ISP's subscribers than it originates from the ISP; (3) for many of those terminated calls, the ISP's LEC can charge the carriers serving the ISP's end user customers above-cost access charges; and (4) the ISP's LEC can choose a single point of interconnection with the carriers serving the ISP's end user customers in a way that requires those carriers to bear most of the costs of transporting the traffic to the ISP. The specifics of this are discussed in the section below on "Where should networks be allowed, or required, to interconnect with one another?"

[124] In its 2001 ISP Report and Order, the FCC found that "under the current carrier-to-carrier recovery mechanism, it is conceivable that a carrier could serve an ISP free of charge and recover all of its costs from originating carriers." The ILECs were somewhat constrained in their ability to compete with the CLECs for these ISP customers because in certain situations they are not allowed to negotiate individual contracts with customers, but rather are limited to offering services through tariffs that are generally available to all customers.

[125] A more detailed discussion of switching costs in presented below in the section entitled, "What is the underlying cost structure of the transport and switching functions?"

[126] The long distance carriers assert that the Bell operating companies, which are now allowed to offer long distance service and typically do so as part of a package of local and long distance service, do not face the same problem. The long distance carriers claim that, even if the Bell companies' long distance arms must pay the same usage-based access charges to their local operating companies as the long distance carriers pay, the

underlying costs to the Bells are not usage-sensitive. That is, any losses that the Bells' long distance arms might suffer, when serving a high usage customer, by having to pay minute-of-use access charges while offering large baskets of minutes or unlimited calling at a fixed price, are matched by the additional profits that the Bells' local operating companies generate from those minute-of-use access charges (since their underlying costs are not increasing with usage).

[127] The intercarrier compensation rules are different for intraMTA wireless calls that originate and terminate within an MTA and interMTA wireless calls that originate and terminate in different MTAs.

[128] See, for example, "Jessica Zufolo: Emerging VoIP Policy is Driving Investment," *Telecom Policy Report,* September 29, 2004.

[129] The ICC FNPRM, at paragraph 107, states: "According to NTCA [the National Telecommunications Cooperative Association], rural LECs receive on average 10 percent of their revenue from interstate access charges and 16 percent from intrastate access charges. In comparison, it asserts that the BOCs [Bell Operating Companies] receive only four percent of their revenue from interstate access charges and six percent from intrastate access charges."

[130] The 1996 Act states at § 254(e): "Any such support should be explicit and sufficient to achieve the purposes of this section."

[131] See, for example, Josh Long, "Rural Telcos Grapple to Identify Phantom Traffic," posted April 1, 2004, available at [http://www.xchangemag.com/articles/441coverstory3.html]. viewed on January 13, 2006.

[132] The long distance and wireless carriers claim that the rural telephone companies are responsible for the phantom traffic problem because they have not deployed facilities with the signaling system (SS-7) capable of identifying the originating carrier and have chosen to route traffic in a fashion that does not transfer billing information. See *Communications Daily,* August 5, 2005, at pp. 6-7.

[133] 47 U.S.C. § 254(e).

[134] The FCC has reported that, for the third quarter of 2005, total projected FUSF program support will be $1 .770 billion, and the total FUSF program collection will be $1 .679 billion. See "Proposed Third Quarter 2005 Universal Service Contribution Factor," CC Docket No. 96-45, Federal Communications Commission Public Notice DA 05-1664, released June 14, 2005, at p. 2.

[135] 47 U.S.C. § 254(b)(2).

[136] 47 U.S.C. § 254(b)(3). Emphasis added.

[137] Universal Service Administrative Corporation 2004 Annual Report at p. 27.

[138] According to a chart in the USAC 2004 Annual Report (at p. 2), total high cost funding increased from approximately $1.6 billion in 1998 to just under $3.5 billion in 2004. Total funding to wireless carriers and other new competitors in 2005 was only $333 million. The bulk of the increase in the fund is attributable to two proceedings at the FCC that removed implicit universal service funds from two categories of rural local exchange carriers — very small carriers subject to rate-of-return regulation and somewhat larger carriers subject to price cap regulation — and replaced those implicit subsidies with new or expanded explicit universal service funding mechanisms.

[139] This approach, requiring the end user to identify a single "principal" carrier eligible to receive FUSF, could be followed even if the definition of universal service were not expanded to include broadband services or broadband access.

[140] There currently are a number of components of the high cost fund, each with specific eligibility requirements. A competitive ETC is only eligible to receive a particular component if the ILEC in its service area is eligible to receive support for that component. The components are: high cost loop support, safety net additive support, safety valve support, local switching support, interstate access support, high cost model support, and interstate common line support.

[141] See "Proposed Third Quarter 2005 Universal Service Contribution Factor," CC Docket No. 96-45, Federal Communications Commission Public Notice DA 05-1664, released June 14, 2005, at p. 2. The assessment rate is modified quarterly, to take into account changes both in the size of the revenue base and in the quantity of subsidy dollars needed. Some international revenues are excepted from the assessment and some interstate telecommunications revenues that are recovered as part of a bundled offering of interstate telecommunications services and other services, for example those from wireless carriers, are assumed to be a specific percentage of the total revenues, and only that percentage is assessed the 10.2%.

[142] See *December 2005 Monitoring Report,* Federal/State Joint Board on Universal Service, Table 1.1, total Telecommunications Industry Revenues, at p. 1-13, released December 5, 2005, available at [http://hraunfoss.fcc.gov/edocs_public/attachmatch/DOC-262986A3 .pdf], viewed on January 13, 2006. In order to avoid duplicative assessments, only end-user interstate and international telecommunications revenues are assessed; the "carrier's carrier" interstate and international telecommunications revenues generated when a wholesale carrier sells services to retail carriers as inputs into the provision of end-user services are not assessed.

[143] In *Texas Ofice of Public Utility Counsel v. FCC,* 183 F.3d 393 (5th Cir. 1999), the U.S. Court of Appeals for the Fifth Circuit overturned the FCC order assessing intrastate as well as interstate revenues to fund the schools and libraries portion of the FUSF.

[144] For example, a medium or large business customer may receive service either by installing its own switch (called a PBX), which requires a smaller number of lines into the premise because traffic is aggregated into a smaller number of large pipes at the PBX, or by using a portion of the local telephone company's end office switch (known as Centrex service), which requires a larger number of lines because the traffic is not aggregated at the customer premise. An appropriate weighting ratio would have to be set for Centrex vs. PBX service, but such weighting has been performed many times in FCC rules.

[145] Just as in the case for connections, the number of telephone numbers required by a medium or large business customer will depend on the internal telecommunications architecture chosen by that customer, with certain configurations requiring more, and certain fewer, telephone numbers. This might require construction of weights for business customer telephone numbers.

[146] *High-Speed Services for Internet Access: Status as of December 31, 2004,* Industry Analysis and Technology Division, Wireless Competition Bureau, Federal Communications Commission, released July 7, 2005, available at

[http://www.fcc.gov/Bureaus/ Common_Carrier/Reports/FCC-State_Link/IAD/hspd0705.pdf], viewed on January 13, 2006.

[147] The FCC defines a high-speed line as a connection to an end-user customer that is faster than 200 kilobits per second ("kbps") in at least one direction.

[148] The FCC identified the most densely populated zip codes as the top decile, with more than 3,147 persons per square mile, and the least densely populated zip codes as the bottom decile, with fewer than 6 persons per square mile.

[149] P.L. 104-104, § 706. See 47 U.S.C. § 157 note.

[150] *Availability of Advanced Telecommunications Capability in the United States,* Fourth Report to Congress, Federal Communications Commission, GN Docket No. 04-54, FCC 04-208, September 9, 2004, at p. 8. Available at [http://hraunfoss.fcc.gov/edocs_public/attachmatch/FCC-04-208A1 .pdf], viewed on January 13, 2006.

[151] Id., pp. 5, 7.

[152] Rachel Brown, "Now Playing: Television Over the Telephone Lines," *Rural Telecommunications,* July-August 2004, at pp. 14-20.

[153] Ken Kerschbaumer, "Telco TV: Smaller is Quicker," *Broadcasting & Cable,* Volume 135, Issue 24, June 13, 2005, at p. 28.

[154] Asymmetric digital subscriber line is a DSL technology that is expected to be especially effective for the provision of video on demand and similar services.

[155] See John Griffin, "Bundling for Success: A Pitch for the Triple Play," *Rural Telecommunications,* March-April 2005, at pp. 14-19.

[156] Ken Kerschbaumer, "Telco TV: Smaller is Quicker," *Broadcasting & Cable,* Volume 135, Issue 24, June 13, 2005, at p. 28.

[157] See, for example, the testimonies and responses to questions of Lea Ann Champion, Senior Executive Vice President, IP Operations and Services, SBC Services, Inc., and of Robert E. In galls Jr., President, Retail Markets Group, Verizon Communications, on "How Internet Protocol-Enabled Services are Changing the Face of Communications: A Look at Video and Data Services," before the House Committee on Energy and Commerce, Subcommittee on Telecommunications and the Internet, April 20, 2005.

[158] For a detailed discussion of these programs, see CRS Report RL307 19, *Broadband Internet Access and the Digital Divide: Federal Assistance Programs,* by Lennard G. Kroger and Angele A. Gilroy.

[159] For additional information on this program, see the TDF website at [http://www.td fund.com].

[160] John Griffin, "Bundling for Success: A Pitch for the Triple Play," *Rural Telecommunications,* March-April 2005, at p. 16.

[161] "Principles for an Open Broadband Future: A Public Knowledge White Paper," Public Knowledge, July 6, 2005, at p. 5, available at [http://www.publicknowledge.org/pdf/openbroadband-future.pdf], viewed on January 13, 2006.

[162] For example, on October 24, 2003, the High Tech Broadband Coalition and Fiber-to-the-Home Council filed an *amicus* brief with the Supreme Court in the case of *Jeremiah W. Nixon, Attorney General of Missouri, et.al., v. Missouri Municipal League, et. al.,* supporting the continued deployment of municipal broadband communications networks. In their brief, the two organizations argued that municipalities are an

important link in enhancing broadband penetration, especially in rural and less densely populated areas that are not an investment priority for private sector service providers.

[163] See, for example, Thomas M. Lenard, "Wireless Philadelphia: A Leap Into the Unknown," The Progress & Freedom Foundation, Release 12.3, April 2005, available at [http://www.pff.org/issues-pubs/pops/pop 1 2.3lenardwifi.pdf], viewed on January 13, 2006.

[164] Amy Schwarz, "Questions for Kevin J. Martin," *Wall Street Journal Online,* July 18, 2005.

[165] *In the Matter of Pet ition for Declaratory Ruling that pulver. com's Free World Dialup is Neither Telecommunications Nor a Telecommunications Service,* WC Docket No. 03-45, Memorandum Opinion and Order, adopted on February 12, 2004 and released February 19, 2004, at paragraph 5.

[166] *In the Matter of Petition for Declaratory Ruling that AT&T's Phone-to-Phone IP Telephony Services are Exempt from Access Charges,* WC Docket No. 02-361, Order, 19 FCC Rcd 7457 (2004), at paragraph 1.

[167] *In the Matter of IP-Enabled Services,* WC Docket No. 04-3 6, Notice of Proposed Rulemaking, FCC 04 28 (March 10, 2004).

[168] *In the Matter of E911 Requirements for IP-Enabled Service Providers,* WC Docket No. 05-196, First Report and Order and Notice of Proposed Rulemaking, FCC 05-116, released June 3, 2005.

[169] P.L. 103-414, 47 U.S.C. 1001-1010.

[170] For a detailed discussion of CALEA, see CRS Report RL3 0677, *Digital Surveillance: The Communications Assistance for Law Enforcement Act,* by Patricia Moloney Figliola.

[171] "FCC Requires Certain Broadband and VoIP Providers to Accommodate Wiretaps," FCC News, August 5, 2005, *In the Matter of Communications Assistance for Law Enforcement Act and Broadband Access and Services.*

[172] For a detailed discussion of statutes and rules affecting localism, see CRS Report RL3 2641, *"Localism ": Statutes and Rules Afecting Local Programming on Broadcast, Cable, and Satellite Television,* by Charles B. Goldfarb.

[173] Section 611, 47 U.S.C. § 531 and Section 621(a)(4)(B), 47 U.S.C. § 541(a)(4)(B).

[174] Section 612, 47 U.S.C. § 532.

[175] Section 621(a)(2), 47 U.S.C. § 541(a)(2).

[176] *In the Matter of Carriage of Digital Television Broadcast Signals: Amendments to Part 76 of the Commission's Rules,* CS Docket No. 98-120, Second Report and Order and First Order on Reconsideration, released February 23, 2005.

[177] For example, in his July 12, 2005 testimony (at pp. 3-4) on "The Digital TV Transition" before the Senate Commerce, Science, and Transportation Committee, Kyle McSlarrow, president and chief executive officer of the National Cable and Telecommunications Association, claimed that cable systems only have finite capacity and mandatory carriage of multicast broadcast signals would command channel capacity that could be better used providing innovative new applications sought by consumers.

In: Telecommunications Act: Competition, Innovation and Reform ISBN 1-60021-133-X
Editor: Charles B. Goldfarb, pp. 73-167

Chapter 2

TELECOMMUNICATIONS ACT OF 1996

ONE HUNDRED FOURTH CONGRESS OF THE UNITED STATES OF AMERICA

At the Second Session

Begun and held at the City of Washington on Wednesday, the third day of January, one thousand nine hundred and ninety-six.

AN ACT

To promote competition and reduce regulation in order to secure lower prices and higher quality services for American telecommunications consumers and encourage the rapid deployment of new telecommunications technologies.

Be it enacted by the Senate and House of Representatives of the United States of America in Congress assembled,

Section 1. Short Title; References

a) SHORT TITLE- This Act may be cited as the `Telecommunications Act of 1996'.

b) REFERENCES- Except as otherwise expressly provided, whenever in this Act an amendment or repeal is expressed in terms of an amendment to, or repeal of, a section or other provision, the reference shall be considered to be made to a section or other provision of the Communications Act of 1934 (47 U.S.C. 151 et seq.).

Sec. 2. Table of Contents

The table of contents for this Act is as follows:

PART II--DEVELOPMENT OF COMPETITIVE MARKETS

Sec. 102. Eligible telecommunications carriers.

Sec. 103. Exempt telecommunications companies.

Sec. 104. Nondiscrimination principle.

SUBTITLE B--SPECIAL PROVISIONS CONCERNING BELL OPERATING COMPANIES

Sec. 151. Bell operating company provisions.

PART III--SPECIAL PROVISIONS CONCERNING BELL OPERATING COMPANIES TITLE II--BROADCAST SERVICES

Sec. 201. Broadcast spectrum flexibility.

Sec. 202. Broadcast ownership.

Sec. 203. Term of licenses.

Sec. 204. Broadcast license renewal procedures.

Sec. 205. Direct broadcast satellite service.

Sec. 206. Automated ship distress and safety systems.

Sec. 207. Restrictions on over-the-air reception devices.

TITLE III--CABLE SERVICES

Sec. 301. Cable Act reform.

Sec. 302. Cable service provided by telephone companies.

PART V--VIDEO PROGRAMMING SERVICES PROVIDED BY TELEPHONE COMPANIES

Sec. 303. Preemption of franchising authority regulation of telecommunications services.

Sec. 304. Competitive availability of navigation devices.

Sec. 305. Video programming accessibility.

TITLE IV--REGULATORY REFORM

Sec. 401. Regulatory forbearance.

Sec. 402. Biennial review of regulations; regulatory relief.

Sec. 403. Elimination of unnecessary Commission regulations and functions.

TITLE V--OBSCENITY AND VIOLENCE SUBTITLE A--OBSCENE, HARASSING, AND WRONGFUL UTILIZATION OF TELECOMMUNICATIONS FACILITIES

Sec. 501. Short title.

Sec. 502. Obscene or harassing use of telecommunications facilities under the Communications Act of 1934.

Sec. 503. Obscene programming on cable television.

Sec. 504. Scrambling of cable channels for nonsubscribers.

Sec. 505. Scrambling of sexually explicit adult video service programming.

Sec. 506. Cable operator refusal to carry certain programs.

Sec. 507. Clarification of current laws regarding communication of obscene materials through the use of computers.

Sec. 508. Coercion and enticement of minors.

SEC. 3. DEFINITIONS.

(a) ADDITIONAL DEFINITIONS- Section 3 (47 U.S.C. 153) is amended—

(1) in subsection (r)—

(A) by inserting (A) after means; and

(B) by inserting before the period at the end the following: , or (B) comparable service provided through a system of switches, transmission equipment, or other facilities (or combination thereof) by which a subscriber can originate and terminate a telecommunications service; and

(2) by adding at the end thereof the following:

(33) AFFILIATE- The term affiliate means a person that (directly or indirectly) owns or controls, is owned or controlled by, or is under common ownership or control with, another person. For purposes of this paragraph, the term own means to own an equity interest (or the equivalent thereof) of more than 10 percent.

(34) AT&T CONSENT DECREE- The term AT&T Consent Decree means the order entered August 24, 1982, in the antitrust action styled United States v. Western Electric, Civil Action No. 82-0192, in the United States District Court for the District of Columbia, and includes any judgment or order with respect to such action entered on or after August 24, 1982.

(35) BELL OPERATING COMPANY- The term Bell operating company—

(A) means any of the following companies: Bell Telephone Company of Nevada, Illinois Bell Telephone Company, Indiana Bell Telephone Company, Incorporated, Michigan Bell Telephone Company, New England Telephone and Telegraph Company, New Jersey Bell Telephone Company, New York Telephone Company, U S West Communications Company, South Central Bell Telephone Company, Southern Bell Telephone and Telegraph Company, Southwestern Bell Telephone Company, The Bell Telephone Company of Pennsylvania, The Chesapeake and Potomac Telephone Company, The Chesapeake and Potomac Telephone Company of Maryland, The Chesapeake and Potomac Telephone Company of Virginia, The Chesapeake and Potomac Telephone Company of West Virginia, The Diamond State Telephone Company, The Ohio Bell Telephone Company, The Pacific Telephone and Telegraph Company, or Wisconsin Telephone Company; and

(B) includes any successor or assign of any such company that provides wireline telephone exchange service; but

(C) does not include an affiliate of any such company, other than an affiliate described in subparagraph (A) or (B).

(36) CABLE SERVICE- The term cable service has the meaning given such term in section 602.

(37) CABLE SYSTEM- The term cable system has the meaning given such term in section 602.

(38) CUSTOMER PREMISES EQUIPMENT- The term customer premises equipment means equipment employed on the premises of a person (other than a carrier) to originate, route, or terminate telecommunications.

(39) DIALING PARITY- The term dialing parity means that a person that is not an affiliate of a local exchange carrier is able to provide telecommunications services in such a manner that customers have the ability to route automatically, without the use of any access code, their telecommunications to the telecommunications services provider of the customers designation from among 2 or more telecommunications services providers (including such local exchange carrier).

(40) EXCHANGE ACCESS- The term exchange access means the offering of access to telephone exchange services or facilities for the purpose of the origination or termination of telephone toll services.

(41) INFORMATION SERVICE- The term information service means the offering of a capability for generating, acquiring, storing, transforming, processing, retrieving, utilizing, or making available information via telecommunications, and includes electronic publishing, but does not include any use of any such capability for the management, control, or operation of a telecommunications system or the management of a telecommunications service.

(42) INTERLATA SERVICE- The term interLATA service means telecommunications between a point located in a local access and transport area and a point located outside such area.

(43) LOCAL ACCESS AND TRANSPORT AREA- The term local access and transport area or LATA means a contiguous geographic area-- (A) established before the date of enactment of the Telecommunications Act of 1996 by a Bell operating company such that no exchange area includes points within more than 1 metropolitan statistical area, consolidated metropolitan statistical area, or State, except as expressly permitted

under the AT&T Consent Decree; or (B) established or modified by a Bell operating company after such date of enactment and approved by the Commission.

(44) LOCAL EXCHANGE CARRIER- The term local exchange carrier means any person that is engaged in the provision of telephone exchange service or exchange access. Such term does not include a person insofar as such person is engaged in the provision of a commercial mobile service under section 332(c), except to the extent that the Commission finds that such service should be included in the definition of such term.

(45) NETWORK ELEMENT- The term network element means a facility or equipment used in the provision of a telecommunications service. Such term also includes features, functions, and capabilities that are provided by means of such facility or equipment, including subscriber numbers, databases, signaling systems, and information sufficient for billing and collection or used in the transmission, routing, or other provision of a telecommunications service.

(46) NUMBER PORTABILITY- The term number portability means the ability of users of telecommunications services to retain, at the same location, existing telecommunications numbers without impairment of quality, reliability, or convenience when switching from one telecommunications carrier to another.

(47) RURAL TELEPHONE COMPANY- The term rural telephone company means a local exchange carrier operating entity to the extent that such entity—

(A) provides common carrier service to any local exchange carrier study area that does not include either—

(i) any incorporated place of 10,000 inhabitants or more, or any part thereof, based on the most recently available population statistics of the Bureau of the Census; or

(ii) any territory, incorporated or unincorporated, included in an urbanized area, as defined by the Bureau of the Census as of August 10, 1993;

(B) provides telephone exchange service, including exchange access, to fewer than 50,000 access lines;

(C) provides telephone exchange service to any local exchange carrier study area with fewer than 100,000 access lines; or

(D) has less than 15 percent of its access lines in communities of more than 50,000 on the date of enactment of the Telecommunications Act of 1996.

(48) TELECOMMUNICATIONS- The term telecommunications means the transmission, between or among points specified by the user, of information of the users choosing, without change in the form or content of the information as sent and received.

(49) TELECOMMUNICATIONS CARRIER- The term telecommunications carrier means any provider of telecommunications services, except that such term does not include aggregators of telecommunications services (as defined in section 226). A telecommunications carrier shall be treated as a common carrier under this Act only to the extent that it is engaged in providing telecommunications services, except that the Commission shall determine whether the provision of fixed and mobile satellite service shall be treated as common carriage.

(50) TELECOMMUNICATIONS EQUIPMENT- The term telecommunications equipment means equipment, other than customer premises equipment, used by a carrier to provide telecommunications services, and includes software integral to such equipment (including upgrades).

(51) TELECOMMUNICATIONS SERVICE- The term telecommunications service means the offering of telecommunications for a fee directly to the public, or to such classes of users as to be effectively available directly to the public, regardless of the facilities used..

(b) COMMON TERMINOLOGY- Except as otherwise provided in this Act, the terms used in this Act have the meanings provided in section 3 of the Communications Act of 1934 (47 U.S.C. 153), as amended by this section.

(c) STYLISTIC CONSISTENCY- Section 3 (47 U.S.C. 153) is amended—

(1) in subsections (e) and (n), by redesignating clauses (1), (2), and (3), as clauses (A), (B), and (C), respectively;

(2) in subsection (w), by redesignating paragraphs (1) through (5) as subparagraphs (A) through (E), respectively;

(3) in subsections (y) and (z), by redesignating paragraphs (1) and (2) as subparagraphs (A) and (B), respectively;

(4) by redesignating subsections (a) through (ff) as paragraphs (1) through (32);

(5) by indenting such paragraphs 2 em spaces;

(6) by inserting after the designation of each such paragraph-- (A) a heading, in a form consistent with the form of the heading of this subsection, consisting of the term defined by such paragraph, or the first term so defined if such paragraph defines more than one term; and (B) the words The term;

(7) by changing the first letter of each defined term in such paragraphs from a capital to a lower case letter (except for United States, State, State commission, and Great Lakes Agreement); and

(8) by reordering such paragraphs and the additional paragraphs added by subsection (a) in alphabetical order based on the headings of such paragraphs and renumbering such paragraphs as so reordered.

(d) CONFORMING AMENDMENTS- The Act is amended—

(1) in section 225(a)(1), by striking section 3(h) and inserting section 3;

(2) in section 332(d), by striking section 3(n) each place it appears and inserting section 3; and

(3) in sections 621(d)(3), 636(d), and 637(a)(2), by striking section 3(v) and inserting section 3.

TITLE I--TELECOMMUNICATION SERVICES

SUBTITLE A--TELECOMMUNICATIONS SERVICES

SEC. 101. ESTABLISHMENT OF PART II OF TITLE II.

(a) AMENDMENT- Title II is amended by inserting after section 229 (47 U.S.C. 229) the following new part:

PART II--DEVELOPMENT OF COMPETITIVE MARKETS SEC. 251. INTERCONNECTION

(a) GENERAL DUTY OF TELECOMMUNICATIONS CARRIERS- Each telecommunications carrier has the duty—

(1) to interconnect directly or indirectly with the facilities and equipment of other telecommunications carriers; and

(2) not to install network features, functions, or capabilities that do not comply with the guidelines and standards established pursuant to section 255 or 256.

(b) OBLIGATIONS OF ALL LOCAL EXCHANGE CARRIERS- Each local exchange carrier has the following duties:

(1) RESALE- The duty not to prohibit, and not to impose unreasonable or discriminatory conditions or limitations on, the resale of its telecommunications services.

(2) NUMBER PORTABILITY- The duty to provide, to the extent technically feasible, number portability in accordance with requirements prescribed by the Commission.

(3) DIALING PARITY- The duty to provide dialing parity to competing providers of telephone exchange service and telephone toll service, and the duty to permit all such providers to have nondiscriminatory access to telephone numbers, operator services, directory assistance, and directory listing, with no unreasonable dialing delays.

(4) ACCESS TO RIGHTS-OF-WAY- The duty to afford access to the poles, ducts, conduits, and rights-of-way of such carrier to competing providers of telecommunications services on rates, terms, and conditions that are consistent with section 224.

(5) RECIPROCAL COMPENSATION- The duty to establish reciprocal compensation arrangements for the transport and termination of telecommunications.

(c) ADDITIONAL OBLIGATIONS OF INCUMBENT LOCAL EXCHANGE CARRIERS- In addition to the duties contained in subsection (b), each incumbent local exchange carrier has the following duties:

(1) DUTY TO NEGOTIATE- The duty to negotiate in good faith in accordance with section 252 the particular terms and conditions of agreements to fulfill the duties described in paragraphs (1) through (5) of subsection (b) and this subsection. The requesting telecommunications carrier also has the duty to negotiate in good faith the terms and conditions of such agreements.

(2) INTERCONNECTION- The duty to provide, for the facilities and equipment of any requesting telecommunications carrier, interconnection with the local exchange carriers network—

(A) for the transmission and routing of telephone exchange service and exchange access;

(B) at any technically feasible point within the carriers network;

(C) that is at least equal in quality to that provided by the local exchange carrier to itself or to any subsidiary, affiliate, or any other party to which the carrier provides interconnection; and

(D) on rates, terms, and conditions that are just, reasonable, and nondiscriminatory, in accordance with the terms and conditions of the agreement and the requirements of this section and section 252.

(3) UNBUNDLED ACCESS- The duty to provide, to any requesting telecommunications carrier for the provision of a telecommunications service, nondiscriminatory access to network elements on an unbundled basis at any technically feasible point on rates, terms, and

conditions that are just, reasonable, and nondiscriminatory in accordance with the terms and conditions of the agreement and the requirements of this section and section 252. An incumbent local exchange carrier shall provide such unbundled network elements in a manner that allows requesting carriers to combine such elements in order to provide such telecommunications service.

(4) RESALE- The duty—

(A) to offer for resale at wholesale rates any telecommunications service that the carrier provides at retail to subscribers who are not telecommunications carriers; and

(B) not to prohibit, and not to impose unreasonable or discriminatory conditions or limitations on, the resale of such telecommunications service, except that a State commission may, consistent with regulations prescribed by the Commission under this section, prohibit a reseller that obtains at wholesale rates a telecommunications service that is available at retail only to a category of subscribers from offering such service to a different category of subscribers.

(5) NOTICE OF CHANGES- The duty to provide reasonable public notice of changes in the information necessary for the transmission and routing of services using that local exchange carriers facilities or networks, as well as of any other changes that would affect the interoperability of those facilities and networks.

(6) COLLOCATION- The duty to provide, on rates, terms, and conditions that are just, reasonable, and nondiscriminatory, for physical collocation of equipment necessary for interconnection or access to unbundled network elements at the premises of the local exchange carrier, except that the carrier may provide for virtual collocation if the local exchange carrier demonstrates to the State commission that physical collocation is not practical for technical reasons or because of space limitations.

(d) IMPLEMENTATION-

(1) IN GENERAL- Within 6 months after the date of enactment of the Telecommunications Act of 1996, the Commission shall complete all actions necessary to establish regulations to implement the requirements of this section.

(2) ACCESS STANDARDS- In determining what network elements should be made available for purposes of subsection (c)(3), the Commission shall consider, at a minimum, whether—

(A) access to such network elements as are proprietary in nature is necessary; and

(B) the failure to provide access to such network elements would impair the ability of the telecommunications carrier seeking access to provide the services that it seeks to offer.

(3) PRESERVATION OF STATE ACCESS REGULATIONS- In prescribing and enforcing regulations to implement the requirements of this section, the Commission shall not preclude the enforcement of any regulation, order, or policy of a State commission that—

(A) establishes access and interconnection obligations of local exchange carriers;

(B) is consistent with the requirements of this section; and

(C) does not substantially prevent implementation of the requirements of this section and the purposes of this part.

(e) NUMBERING ADMINISTRATION-

(1) COMMISSION AUTHORITY AND JURISDICTION- The Commission shall create or designate one or more impartial entities to administer telecommunications numbering and to make such numbers available on an equitable basis. The Commission shall have exclusive jurisdiction over those portions of the North American Numbering Plan that pertain to the

United States. Nothing in this paragraph shall preclude the Commission from delegating to State commissions or other entities all or any portion of such jurisdiction.

(2) COSTS- The cost of establishing telecommunications numbering administration arrangements and number portability shall be borne by all telecommunications carriers on a competitively neutral basis as determined by the Commission.

(f) EXEMPTIONS, SUSPENSIONS, AND MODIFICATIONS-

(1) EXEMPTION FOR CERTAIN RURAL TELEPHONE COMPANIES-

(A) EXEMPTION- Subsection (c) of this section shall not apply to a rural telephone company until (i) such company has received a bona fide request for interconnection, services, or network elements, and (ii) the State commission determines (under subparagraph (B)) that such request is not unduly economically burdensome, is technically feasible, and is consistent with section 254 (other than subsections (b)(7) and (c)(1)(D) thereof).

(B) STATE TERMINATION OF EXEMPTION AND IMPLEMENTATION SCHEDULE- The party making a bona fide request of a rural telephone company for interconnection, services, or network elements shall submit a notice of its request to the State commission. The State commission shall conduct an inquiry for the purpose of determining whether to terminate the exemption under subparagraph (A). Within 120 days after the State commission receives notice of the request, the State commission shall terminate the exemption if the request is not unduly economically burdensome, is technically feasible, and is consistent with section 254 (other than subsections (b)(7) and (c)(1)(D) thereof). Upon termination of the exemption, a State commission shall establish an implementation schedule for compliance with the request that is consistent in time and manner with Commission regulations.

(C) LIMITATION ON EXEMPTION- The exemption provided by this paragraph shall not apply with respect to a request under subsection (c) from a cable operator providing video programming, and seeking to provide any telecommunications service, in the area in which the rural telephone company provides video programming. The limitation contained in this subparagraph shall not apply to a rural telephone company that is providing video programming on the date of enactment of the Telecommunications Act of 1996. (2) SUSPENSIONS AND MODIFICATIONS FOR RURAL CARRIERS- A local exchange carrier with fewer than 2 percent of the Nations subscriber lines installed in the aggregate nationwide may petition a State commission for a suspension or modification of the application of a requirement or requirements of subsection (b) or (c) to telephone exchange service facilities specified in such petition. The State commission shall grant such petition to the extent that, and for such duration as, the State commission determines that such suspension or modification—

(A) is necessary—

(i) to avoid a significant adverse economic impact on users of telecommunications services generally;

(ii) to avoid imposing a requirement that is unduly economically burdensome; or

(iii) to avoid imposing a requirement that is technically infeasible; and

(B) is consistent with the public interest, convenience, and necessity. The State commission shall act upon any petition filed under this paragraph within 180 days after receiving such petition. Pending such action, the State commission may suspend enforcement of the requirement or requirements to which the petition applies with respect to the petitioning carrier or carriers.

(g) CONTINUED ENFORCEMENT OF EXCHANGE ACCESS AND INTERCONNECTION REQUIREMENTS- On and after the date of enactment of the Telecommunications Act of 1996, each local exchange carrier, to the extent that it provides wireline services, shall provide exchange access, information access, and exchange services for such access to interexchange carriers and information service providers in accordance with the same equal access and nondiscriminatory interconnection restrictions and obligations (including receipt of compensation) that apply to such carrier on the date immediately preceding the date of enactment of the Telecommunications Act of 1996 under any court order, consent decree, or regulation, order, or policy of the Commission, until such restrictions and obligations are explicitly superseded by regulations prescribed by the Commission after such date of enactment. During the period beginning on such date of enactment and until such restrictions and obligations are so superseded, such restrictions and obligations shall be enforceable in the same manner as regulations of the Commission.

(h) DEFINITION OF INCUMBENT LOCAL EXCHANGE CARRIER-

(1) DEFINITION- For purposes of this section, the term incumbent local exchange carrier means, with respect to an area, the local exchange carrier that—

(A) on the date of enactment of the Telecommunications Act of 1996, provided telephone exchange service in such area; and

(B)(i) on such date of enactment, was deemed to be a member of the exchange carrier association pursuant to section 69.601(b) of the Commissions regulations (47 C.F.R. 69.601(b)); or

(ii) is a person or entity that, on or after such date of enactment, became a successor or assign of a member described in clause (i).

(2) TREATMENT OF COMPARABLE CARRIERS AS INCUMBENTS- The Commission may, by rule, provide for the treatment of a local exchange carrier (or class or category thereof) as an incumbent local exchange carrier for purposes of this section if—

(A) such carrier occupies a position in the market for telephone exchange service within an area that is comparable to the position occupied by a carrier described in paragraph (1);

(B) such carrier has substantially replaced an incumbent local exchange carrier described in paragraph (1); and

(C) such treatment is consistent with the public interest, convenience, and necessity and the purposes of this section.

(i) SAVINGS PROVISION- Nothing in this section shall be construed to limit or otherwise affect the Commissions authority under section 201.

SEC. 252. PROCEDURES FOR NEGOTIATION, ARBITRATION, AND APPROVAL OF AGREEMENTS.

(a) AGREEMENTS ARRIVED AT THROUGH NEGOTIATION-

(1) VOLUNTARY NEGOTIATIONS- Upon receiving a request for interconnection, services, or network elements pursuant to section 251, an incumbent local exchange carrier may negotiate and enter into a binding agreement with the requesting telecommunications carrier or carriers without regard to the standards set forth in subsections (b) and (c) of section 251. The agreement shall include a detailed schedule of itemized charges for interconnection and each service or network element included in the agreement. The agreement, including any interconnection agreement negotiated before the date of enactment of the

Telecommunications Act of 1996, shall be submitted to the State commission under subsection (e) of this section.

(2) MEDIATION- Any party negotiating an agreement under this section may, at any point in the negotiation, ask a State commission to participate in the negotiation and to mediate any differences arising in the course of the negotiation.

(b) AGREEMENTS ARRIVED AT THROUGH COMPULSORY ARBITRATION-

(1) ARBITRATION- During the period from the 135th to the 160th day (inclusive) after the date on which an incumbent local exchange carrier receives a request for negotiation under this section, the carrier or any other party to the negotiation may petition a State commission to arbitrate any open issues.

(2) DUTY OF PETITIONER-

(A) A party that petitions a State commission under paragraph (1) shall, at the same time as it submits the petition, provide the State commission all relevant documentation concerning—

(i) the unresolved issues;

(ii) the position of each of the parties with respect to those issues; and

(iii) any other issue discussed and resolved by the parties.

(B) A party petitioning a State commission under paragraph (1) shall provide a copy of the petition and any documentation to the other party or parties not later than the day on which the State commission receives the petition.

(3) OPPORTUNITY TO RESPOND- A non-petitioning party to a negotiation under this section may respond to the other partys petition and provide such additional information as it wishes within 25 days after the State commission receives the petition.

(4) ACTION BY STATE COMMISSION-

(A) The State commission shall limit its consideration of any petition under paragraph (1) (and any response thereto) to the issues set forth in the petition and in the response, if any, filed under paragraph (3).

(B) The State commission may require the petitioning party and the responding party to provide such information as may be necessary for the State commission to reach a decision on the unresolved issues. If any party refuses or fails unreasonably to respond on a timely basis to any reasonable request from the State commission, then the State commission may proceed on the basis of the best information available to it from whatever source derived.

(C) The State commission shall resolve each issue set forth in the petition and the response, if any, by imposing appropriate conditions as required to implement subsection

(c) upon the parties to the agreement, and shall conclude the resolution of any unresolved issues not later than 9 months after the date on which the local exchange carrier received the request under this section.

(5) REFUSAL TO NEGOTIATE- The refusal of any other party to the negotiation to participate further in the negotiations, to cooperate with the State commission in carrying out its function as an arbitrator, or to continue to negotiate in good faith in the presence, or with the assistance, of the State commission shall be considered a failure to negotiate in good faith.

(c) STANDARDS FOR ARBITRATION- In resolving by arbitration under subsection (b) any open issues and imposing conditions upon the parties to the agreement, a State commission shall—

(1) ensure that such resolution and conditions meet the requirements of section 251, including the regulations prescribed by the Commission pursuant to section 251;

(2) establish any rates for interconnection, services, or network elements according to subsection (d); and

(3) provide a schedule for implementation of the terms and conditions by the parties to the agreement.

(d) PRICING STANDARDS-

(1) INTERCONNECTION AND NETWORK ELEMENT CHARGES- Determinations by a State commission of the just and reasonable rate for the interconnection of facilities and equipment for purposes of subsection (c)(2) of section 251, and the just and reasonable rate for network elements for purposes of subsection (c)(3) of such section—

(A) shall be—

(i) based on the cost (determined without reference to a rate-of-return or other rate-based proceeding) of providing the interconnection or network element (whichever is applicable), and

(ii) nondiscriminatory, and

(B) may include a reasonable profit.

(2) CHARGES FOR TRANSPORT AND TERMINATION OF TRAFFIC-

(A) IN GENERAL- For the purposes of compliance by an incumbent local exchange carrier with section 251(b)(5), a State commission shall not consider the terms and conditions for reciprocal compensation to be just and reasonable unless—

(i) such terms and conditions provide for the mutual and reciprocal recovery by each carrier of costs associated with the transport and termination on each carriers network facilities of calls that originate on the network facilities of the other carrier; and

(ii) such terms and conditions determine such costs on the basis of a reasonable approximation of the additional costs of terminating such calls.

(B) RULES OF CONSTRUCTION- This paragraph shall not be construed—

(i) to preclude arrangements that afford the mutual recovery of costs through the offsetting of reciprocal obligations, including arrangements that waive mutual recovery (such as bill-and-keep arrangements); or

(ii) to authorize the Commission or any State commission to engage in any rate regulation proceeding to establish with particularity the additional costs of transporting or terminating calls, or to require carriers to maintain records with respect to the additional costs of such calls.

(3) WHOLESALE PRICES FOR TELECOMMUNICATIONS SERVICES- For the purposes of section 251(c)(4), a State commission shall determine wholesale rates on the basis of retail rates charged to subscribers for the telecommunications service requested, excluding the portion thereof attributable to any marketing, billing, collection, and other costs that will be avoided by the local exchange carrier.

(e) APPROVAL BY STATE COMMISSION-

(1) APPROVAL REQUIRED- Any interconnection agreement adopted by negotiation or arbitration shall be submitted for approval to the State commission. A State commission to which an agreement is submitted shall approve or reject the agreement, with written findings as to any deficiencies.

(2) GROUNDS FOR REJECTION- The State commission may only reject—

(A) an agreement (or any portion thereof) adopted by negotiation under subsection (a) if it finds that—

(i) the agreement (or portion thereof) discriminates against a telecommunications carrier not a party to the agreement; or

(ii) the implementation of such agreement or portion is not consistent with the public interest, convenience, and necessity; or

(B) an agreement (or any portion thereof) adopted by arbitration under subsection (b) if it finds that the agreement does not meet the requirements of section 251, including the regulations prescribed by the Commission pursuant to section 251, or the standards set forth in subsection (d) of this section.

(3) PRESERVATION OF AUTHORITY- Notwithstanding paragraph

(2), but subject to section 253, nothing in this section shall prohibit a State commission from establishing or enforcing other requirements of State law in its review of an agreement, including requiring compliance with intrastate telecommunications service quality standards or requirements.

(4) SCHEDULE FOR DECISION- If the State commission does not act to approve or reject the agreement within 90 days after submission by the parties of an agreement adopted by negotiation under subsection (a), or within 30 days after submission by the parties of an agreement adopted by arbitration under subsection (b), the agreement shall be deemed approved. No State court shall have jurisdiction to review the action of a State commission in approving or rejecting an agreement under this section.

(5) COMMISSION TO ACT IF STATE WILL NOT ACT- If a State commission fails to act to carry out its responsibility under this section in any proceeding or other matter under this section, then the Commission shall issue an order preempting the State commissions jurisdiction of that proceeding or matter within 90 days after being notified (or taking notice) of such failure, and shall assume the responsibility of the State commission under this section with respect to the proceeding or matter and act for the State commission.

(6) REVIEW OF STATE COMMISSION ACTIONS- In a case in which a State fails to act as described in paragraph (5), the proceeding by the Commission under such paragraph and any judicial review of the Commissions actions shall be the exclusive remedies for a State commissions failure to act. In any case in which a State commission makes a determination under this section, any party aggrieved by such determination may bring an action in an appropriate Federal district court to determine whether the agreement or statement meets the requirements of section 251 and this section.

(f) STATEMENTS OF GENERALLY AVAILABLE TERMS-

(1) IN GENERAL- A Bell operating company may prepare and file with a State commission a statement of the terms and conditions that such company generally offers within that State to comply with the requirements of section 251 and the regulations thereunder and the standards applicable under this section.

(2) STATE COMMISSION REVIEW- A State commission may not approve such statement unless such statement complies with subsection (d) of this section and section 251 and the regulations thereunder. Except as provided in section 253, nothing in this section shall prohibit a State commission from establishing or enforcing other requirements of State law in its review of such statement, including requiring compliance with intrastate telecommunications service quality standards or requirements.

(3) SCHEDULE FOR REVIEW- The State commission to which a statement is submitted shall, not later than 60 days after the date of such submission—

(A) complete the review of such statement under paragraph (2) (including any reconsideration thereof), unless the submitting carrier agrees to an extension of the period for such review; or

(B) permit such statement to take effect.

(4) AUTHORITY TO CONTINUE REVIEW- Paragraph (3) shall not preclude the State commission from continuing to review a statement that has been permitted to take effect under subparagraph (B) of such paragraph or from approving or disapproving such statement under paragraph (2).

(5) DUTY TO NEGOTIATE NOT AFFECTED- The submission or approval of a statement under this subsection shall not relieve a Bell operating company of its duty to negotiate the terms and conditions of an agreement under section 251.

(g) CONSOLIDATION OF STATE PROCEEDINGS- Where not inconsistent with the requirements of this Act, a State commission may, to the extent practical, consolidate proceedings under sections 214(e), 251(f), 253, and this section in order to reduce administrative burdens on telecommunications carriers, other parties to the proceedings, and the State commission in carrying out its responsibilities under this Act.

(h) FILING REQUIRED- A State commission shall make a copy of each agreement approved under subsection (e) and each statement approved under subsection (f) available for public inspection and copying within 10 days after the agreement or statement is approved. The State commission may charge a reasonable and nondiscriminatory fee to the parties to the agreement or to the party filing the statement to cover the costs of approving and filing such agreement or statement.

(i) AVAILABILITY TO OTHER TELECOMMUNICATIONS CARRIERS- A local exchange carrier shall make available any interconnection, service, or network element provided under an agreement approved under this section to which it is a party to any other requesting telecommunications carrier upon the same terms and conditions as those provided in the agreement.

(j) DEFINITION OF INCUMBENT LOCAL EXCHANGE CARRIER- For purposes of this section, the term incumbent local exchange carrier has the meaning provided in section 251(h).

SEC. 253. REMOVAL OF BARRIERS TO ENTRY.

(a) IN GENERAL- No State or local statute or regulation, or other State or local legal requirement, may prohibit or have the effect of prohibiting the ability of any entity to provide any interstate or intrastate telecommunications service.

(b) STATE REGULATORY AUTHORITY- Nothing in this section shall affect the ability of a State to impose, on a competitively neutral basis and consistent with section 254, requirements necessary to preserve and advance universal service, protect the public safety and welfare, ensure the continued quality of telecommunications services, and safeguard the rights of consumers.

(c) STATE AND LOCAL GOVERNMENT AUTHORITY- Nothing in this section affects the authority of a State or local government to manage the public rights-of-way or to require fair and reasonable compensation from telecommunications providers, on a competitively neutral and nondiscriminatory basis, for use of public rights-of-way on a nondiscriminatory basis, if the compensation required is publicly disclosed by such government.

(d) PREEMPTION- If, after notice and an opportunity for public comment, the Commission determines that a State or local government has permitted or imposed any statute, regulation, or legal requirement that violates subsection (a) or (b), the Commission shall preempt the enforcement of such statute, regulation, or legal requirement to the extent necessary to correct such violation or inconsistency.

(e) COMMERCIAL MOBILE SERVICE PROVIDERS- Nothing in this section shall affect the application of section 332(c)(3) to commercial mobile service providers.

(f) RURAL MARKETS- It shall not be a violation of this section for a State to require a telecommunications carrier that seeks to provide telephone exchange service or exchange access in a service area served by a rural telephone company to meet the requirements in section 214(e)(1) for designation as an eligible telecommunications carrier for that area before being permitted to provide such service. This subsection shall not apply—

(1) to a service area served by a rural telephone company that has obtained an exemption, suspension, or modification of section 251(c)(4) that effectively prevents a competitor from meeting the requirements of section 214(e)(1); and

(2) to a provider of commercial mobile services.

SEC. 254. UNIVERSAL SERVICE.

(a) PROCEDURES TO REVIEW UNIVERSAL SERVICE REQUIREMENTS-

(1) FEDERAL-STATE JOINT BOARD ON UNIVERSAL SERVICE- Within one month after the date of enactment of the Telecommunications Act of 1996, the Commission shall institute and refer to a Federal-State Joint Board under section 410(c) a proceeding to recommend changes to any of its regulations in order to implement sections 214(e) and this section, including the definition of the services that are supported by Federal universal service support mechanisms and a specific timetable for completion of such recommendations. In addition to the members of the Joint Board required under section 410(c), one member of such Joint Board shall be a State-appointed utility consumer advocate nominated by a national organization of State utility consumer advocates. The Joint Board shall, after notice and opportunity for public comment, make its recommendations to the Commission 9 months after the date of enactment of the Telecommunications Act of 1996.

(2) COMMISSION ACTION- The Commission shall initiate a single proceeding to implement the recommendations from the Joint Board required by paragraph (1) and shall complete such proceeding within 15 months after the date of enactment of the Telecommunications Act of 1996. The rules established by such proceeding shall include a definition of the services that are supported by Federal universal service support mechanisms and a specific timetable for implementation. Thereafter, the Commission shall complete any proceeding to implement subsequent recommendations from any Joint Board on universal service within one year after receiving such recommendations.

(b) UNIVERSAL SERVICE PRINCIPLES- The Joint Board and the Commission shall base policies for the preservation and advancement of universal service on the following principles:

(1) QUALITY AND RATES- Quality services should be available at just, reasonable, and affordable rates.

(2) ACCESS TO ADVANCED SERVICES- Access to advanced telecommunications and information services should be provided in all regions of the Nation.

(3) ACCESS IN RURAL AND HIGH COST AREAS- Consumers in all regions of the Nation, including low-income consumers and those in rural, insular, and high cost areas, should have access to telecommunications and information services, including interexchange services and advanced telecommunications and information services, that are reasonably comparable to those services provided in urban areas and that are available at rates that are reasonably comparable to rates charged for similar services in urban areas.

(4) EQUITABLE AND NONDISCRIMINATORY CONTRIBUTIONS- All providers of telecommunications services should make an equitable and nondiscriminatory contribution to the preservation and advancement of universal service.

(5) SPECIFIC AND PREDICTABLE SUPPORT MECHANISMS- There should be specific, predictable and sufficient Federal and State mechanisms to preserve and advance universal service.

(6) ACCESS TO ADVANCED TELECOMMUNICATIONS SERVICES FOR SCHOOLS, HEALTH CARE, AND LIBRARIES- Elementary and secondary schools and classrooms, health care providers, and libraries should have access to advanced telecommunications services as described in subsection (h).

(7) ADDITIONAL PRINCIPLES- Such other principles as the Joint Board and the Commission determine are necessary and appropriate for the protection of the public interest, convenience, and necessity and are consistent with this Act.

(c) DEFINITION-

(1) IN GENERAL- Universal service is an evolving level of telecommunications services that the Commission shall establish periodically under this section, taking into account advances in telecommunications and information technologies and services. The Joint Board in recommending, and the Commission in establishing, the definition of the services that are supported by Federal universal service support mechanisms shall consider the extent to which such telecommunications services—

(A) are essential to education, public health, or public safety;

(B) have, through the operation of market choices by customers, been subscribed to by a substantial majority of residential customers;

(C) are being deployed in public telecommunications networks by telecommunications carriers; and

(D) are consistent with the public interest, convenience, and necessity.

(2) ALTERATIONS AND MODIFICATIONS- The Joint Board may, from time to time, recommend to the Commission modifications in the definition of the services that are supported by Federal universal service support mechanisms.

(3) SPECIAL SERVICES- In addition to the services included in the definition of universal service under paragraph (1), the Commission may designate additional services for such support mechanisms for schools, libraries, and health care providers for the purposes of subsection (h).

(d) TELECOMMUNICATIONS CARRIER CONTRIBUTION- Every telecommunications carrier that provides interstate telecommunications services shall contribute, on an equitable and nondiscriminatory basis, to the specific, predictable, and sufficient mechanisms established by the Commission to preserve and advance universal service. The Commission may exempt a carrier or class of carriers from this requirement if the carriers telecommunications activities are limited to such an extent that the level of such carriers contribution to the preservation and advancement of universal service would be de minimis. Any other provider of interstate telecommunications may be required to contribute to the preservation and advancement of universal service if the public interest so requires.

(e) UNIVERSAL SERVICE SUPPORT- After the date on which Commission regulations implementing this section take effect, only an eligible telecommunications carrier designated under section 214(e) shall be eligible to receive specific Federal universal service support. A carrier that receives such support shall use that support only for the provision, maintenance, and upgrading of facilities and services for which the support is intended. Any such support should be explicit and sufficient to achieve the purposes of this section.

(f) STATE AUTHORITY- A State may adopt regulations not inconsistent with the Commissions rules to preserve and advance universal service. Every telecommunications carrier that provides intrastate telecommunications services shall contribute, on an equitable and nondiscriminatory basis, in a manner determined by the State to the preservation and advancement of universal service in that State. A State may adopt regulations to provide for additional definitions and standards to preserve and advance universal service within that State only to the extent that such regulations adopt additional specific, predictable, and sufficient mechanisms to support such definitions or standards that do not rely on or burden Federal universal service support mechanisms.

(g) INTEREXCHANGE AND INTERSTATE SERVICES- Within 6 months after the date of enactment of the Telecommunications Act of 1996, the Commission shall adopt rules to require that the rates charged by providers of interexchange telecommunications services to subscribers in rural and high cost areas shall be no higher than the rates charged by each such provider to its subscribers in urban areas. Such rules shall also require that a provider of interstate interexchange telecommunications services shall provide such services to its subscribers in each State at rates no higher than the rates charged to its subscribers in any other State.

(h) TELECOMMUNICATIONS SERVICES FOR CERTAIN PROVIDERS-

(1) IN GENERAL-

(A) HEALTH CARE PROVIDERS FOR RURAL AREAS- A telecommunications carrier shall, upon receiving a bona fide request, provide telecommunications services which are necessary for the provision of health care services in a State, including instruction relating to such services, to any public or nonprofit health care provider that serves persons who reside in rural areas in that State at rates that are reasonably comparable to rates charged for similar services in urban areas in that State. A telecommunications carrier providing service under this paragraph shall be entitled to have an amount equal to the difference, if any, between the rates for services provided to health care providers for rural areas in a State and the rates for similar services provided to other customers in comparable rural areas in that State treated as a service obligation as a part of its obligation to participate in the mechanisms to preserve and advance universal service.

(B) EDUCATIONAL PROVIDERS AND LIBRARIES- All telecommunications carriers serving a geographic area shall, upon a bona fide request for any of its services that are within the definition of universal service under subsection (c)(3), provide such services to elementary schools, secondary schools, and libraries for educational purposes at rates less than the amounts charged for similar services to other parties. The discount shall be an amount that the Commission, with respect to interstate services, and the States, with respect to intrastate services, determine is appropriate and necessary to ensure affordable access to and use of such services by such entities. A telecommunications carrier providing service under this paragraph shall—

(i) have an amount equal to the amount of the discount treated as an offset to its obligation to contribute to the mechanisms to preserve and advance universal service, or

(ii) notwithstanding the provisions of subsection

(e) of this section, receive reimbursement utilizing the support mechanisms to preserve and advance universal service.

(2) ADVANCED SERVICES- The Commission shall establish competitively neutral rules—

(A) to enhance, to the extent technically feasible and economically reasonable, access to advanced telecommunications and information services for all public and nonprofit elementary and secondary school classrooms, health care providers, and libraries; and

(B) to define the circumstances under which a telecommunications carrier may be required to connect its network to such public institutional telecommunications users.

(3) TERMS AND CONDITIONS- Telecommunications services and network capacity provided to a public institutional telecommunications user under this subsection may not be sold, resold, or otherwise transferred by such user in consideration for money or any other thing of value.

(4) ELIGIBILITY OF USERS- No entity listed in this subsection shall be entitled to preferential rates or treatment as required by this subsection, if such entity operates as a for-profit business, is a school described in paragraph (5)(A) with an endowment of more than $50,000,000, or is a library not eligible for participation in State-based plans for funds under title III of the Library Services and Construction Act (20 U.S.C. 335c et seq.).

(5) DEFINITIONS- For purposes of this subsection:

(A) ELEMENTARY AND SECONDARY SCHOOLS- The term elementary and secondary schools means elementary schools and secondary schools, as defined in paragraphs (14) and (25), respectively, of section 14101 of the Elementary and Secondary Education Act of 1965 (20 U.S.C. 8801).

(B) HEALTH CARE PROVIDER- The term health care provider means—

(i) post-secondary educational institutions offering health care instruction, teaching hospitals, and medical schools;

(ii) community health centers or health centers providing health care to migrants;

(iii) local health departments or agencies;

(iv) community mental health centers;

(v) not-for-profit hospitals;

(vi) rural health clinics; and

(vii) consortia of health care providers consisting of one or more entities described in clauses (i) through (vi).

(C) PUBLIC INSTITUTIONAL TELECOMMUNICATIONS USER- The term public institutional telecommunications user means an elementary or secondary school, a library, or a health care provider as those terms are defined in this paragraph.

(i) CONSUMER PROTECTION- The Commission and the States should ensure that universal service is available at rates that are just, reasonable, and affordable.

(j) LIFELINE ASSISTANCE- Nothing in this section shall affect the collection, distribution, or administration of the Lifeline Assistance Program provided for by the

Commission under regulations set forth in section 69.117 of title 47, Code of Federal Regulations, and other related sections of such title.

(k) SUBSIDY OF COMPETITIVE SERVICES PROHIBITED- A telecommunications carrier may not use services that are not competitive to subsidize services that are subject to competition. The Commission, with respect to interstate services, and the States, with respect to intrastate services, shall establish any necessary cost allocation rules, accounting safeguards, and guidelines to ensure that services included in the definition of universal service bear no more than a reasonable share of the joint and common costs of facilities used to provide those services.

SEC. 255. ACCESS BY PERSONS WITH DISABILITIES.

(a) DEFINITIONS- As used in this section—

(1) DISABILITY- The term disability has the meaning given to it by section 3(2)(A) of the Americans with Disabilities Act of 1990 (42 U.S.C. 12102(2)(A)).

(2) READILY ACHIEVABLE- The term readily achievable has the meaning given to it by section 301(9) of that Act (42 U.S.C. 12181(9)).

(b) MANUFACTURING- A manufacturer of telecommunications equipment or customer premises equipment shall ensure that the equipment is designed, developed, and fabricated to be accessible to and usable by individuals with disabilities, if readily achievable.

(c) TELECOMMUNICATIONS SERVICES- A provider of telecommunications service shall ensure that the service is accessible to and usable by individuals with disabilities, if readily achievable.

(d) COMPATIBILITY- Whenever the requirements of subsections (b) and (c) are not readily achievable, such a manufacturer or provider shall ensure that the equipment or service is compatible with existing peripheral devices or specialized customer premises equipment commonly used by individuals with disabilities to achieve access, if readily achievable.

(e) GUIDELINES- Within 18 months after the date of enactment of the Telecommunications Act of 1996, the Architectural and Transportation Barriers Compliance Board shall develop guidelines for accessibility of telecommunications equipment and customer premises equipment in conjunction with the Commission. The Board shall review and update the guidelines periodically.

(f) NO ADDITIONAL PRIVATE RIGHTS AUTHORIZED- Nothing in this section shall be construed to authorize any private right of action to enforce any requirement of this section or any regulation thereunder. The Commission shall have exclusive jurisdiction with respect to any complaint under this section.

SEC. 256. COORDINATION FOR INTERCONNECTIVITY.

(a) PURPOSE- It is the purpose of this section—

(1) to promote nondiscriminatory accessibility by the broadest number of users and vendors of communications products and services to public telecommunications networks used to provide telecommunications service through—

(A) coordinated public telecommunications network planning and design by telecommunications carriers and other providers of telecommunications service; and

(B) public telecommunications network interconnectivity, and interconnectivity of devices with such networks used to provide telecommunications service; and

(2) to ensure the ability of users and information providers to seamlessly and transparently transmit and receive information between and across telecommunications networks.

(b) COMMISSION FUNCTIONS- In carrying out the purposes of this section, the Commission—

(1) shall establish procedures for Commission oversight of coordinated network planning by telecommunications carriers and other providers of telecommunications service for the effective and efficient interconnection of public telecommunications networks used to provide telecommunications service; and

(2) may participate, in a manner consistent with its authority and practice prior to the date of enactment of this section, in the development by appropriate industry standards-setting organizations of public telecommunications network interconnectivity standards that promote access to—

(A) public telecommunications networks used to provide telecommunications service;

(B) network capabilities and services by individuals with disabilities; and

(C) information services by subscribers of rural telephone companies.

(c) COMMISSIONS AUTHORITY- Nothing in this section shall be construed as expanding or limiting any authority that the Commission may have under law in effect before the date of enactment of the Telecommunications Act of 1996.

(d) DEFINITION- As used in this section, the term public telecommunications network interconnectivity means the ability of two or more public telecommunications networks used to provide telecommunications service to communicate and exchange information without degeneration, and to interact in concert with one another.

SEC. 257. MARKET ENTRY BARRIERS PROCEEDING.

(a) ELIMINATION OF BARRIERS- Within 15 months after the date of enactment of the Telecommunications Act of 1996, the Commission shall complete a proceeding for the purpose of identifying and eliminating, by regulations pursuant to its authority under this Act (other than this section), market entry barriers for entrepreneurs and other small businesses in the provision and ownership of telecommunications services and information services, or in the provision of parts or services to providers of telecommunications services and information services.

(b) NATIONAL POLICY- In carrying out subsection (a), the Commission shall seek to promote the policies and purposes of this Act favoring diversity of media voices, vigorous economic competition, technological advancement, and promotion of the public interest, convenience, and necessity.

(c) PERIODIC REVIEW- Every 3 years following the completion of the proceeding required by subsection (a), the Commission shall review and report to Congress on—

(1) any regulations prescribed to eliminate barriers within its jurisdiction that are identified under subsection (a) and that can be prescribed consistent with the public interest, convenience, and necessity; and

(2) the statutory barriers identified under subsection (a) that the Commission recommends be eliminated, consistent with the public interest, convenience, and necessity.

SEC. 258. ILLEGAL CHANGES IN SUBSCRIBER CARRIER SELECTIONS.

(a) PROHIBITION- No telecommunications carrier shall submit or execute a change in a subscribers selection of a provider of telephone exchange service or telephone toll service except in accordance with such verification procedures as the Commission shall prescribe. Nothing in this section shall preclude any State commission from enforcing such procedures with respect to intrastate services.

(b) LIABILITY FOR CHARGES- Any telecommunications carrier that violates the verification procedures described in subsection (a) and that collects charges for telephone exchange service or telephone toll service from a subscriber shall be liable to the carrier previously selected by the subscriber in an amount equal to all charges paid by such subscriber after such violation, in accordance with such procedures as the Commission may prescribe. The remedies provided by this subsection are in addition to any other remedies available by law.

SEC. 259. INFRASTRUCTURE SHARING.

(a) REGULATIONS REQUIRED- The Commission shall prescribe, within one year after the date of enactment of the Telecommunications Act of 1996, regulations that require incumbent local exchange carriers (as defined in section 251(h)) to make available to any qualifying carrier such public switched network infrastructure, technology, information, and telecommunications facilities and functions as may be requested by such qualifying carrier for the purpose of enabling such qualifying carrier to provide telecommunications services, or to provide access to information services, in the service area in which such qualifying carrier has requested and obtained designation as an eligible telecommunications carrier under section 214(e).

(b) TERMS AND CONDITIONS OF REGULATIONS- The regulations prescribed by the Commission pursuant to this section shall—

(1) not require a local exchange carrier to which this section applies to take any action that is economically unreasonable or that is contrary to the public interest;

(2) permit, but shall not require, the joint ownership or operation of public switched network infrastructure and services by or among such local exchange carrier and a qualifying carrier;

(3) ensure that such local exchange carrier will not be treated by the Commission or any State as a common carrier for hire or as offering common carrier services with respect to any infrastructure, technology, information, facilities, or functions made available to a qualifying carrier in accordance with regulations issued pursuant to this section;

(4) ensure that such local exchange carrier makes such infrastructure, technology, information, facilities, or functions available to a qualifying carrier on just and reasonable terms and conditions that permit such qualifying carrier to fully benefit from the economies of scale and scope of such local exchange carrier, as determined in accordance with guidelines prescribed by the Commission in regulations issued pursuant to this section;

(5) establish conditions that promote cooperation between local exchange carriers to which this section applies and qualifying carriers;

(6) not require a local exchange carrier to which this section applies to engage in any infrastructure sharing agreement for any services or access which are to be provided or offered to consumers by the qualifying carrier in such local exchange carriers telephone exchange area; and

(7) require that such local exchange carrier file with the Commission or State for public inspection, any tariffs, contracts, or other arrangements showing the rates, terms, and conditions under which such carrier is making available public switched network infrastructure and functions under this section.

(c) INFORMATION CONCERNING DEPLOYMENT OF NEW SERVICES AND EQUIPMENT- A local exchange carrier to which this section applies that has entered into an infrastructure sharing agreement under this section shall provide to each party to such agreement timely information on the planned deployment of telecommunications services and equipment, including any software or upgrades of software integral to the use or operation of such telecommunications equipment.

(d) DEFINITION- For purposes of this section, the term qualifying carrier means a telecommunications carrier that—

(1) lacks economies of scale or scope, as determined in accordance with regulations prescribed by the Commission pursuant to this section; and

(2) offers telephone exchange service, exchange access, and any other service that is included in universal service, to all consumers without preference throughout the service area for which such carrier has been designated as an eligible telecommunications carrier under section 214(e).

SEC. 260. PROVISION OF TELEMESSAGING SERVICE.

(a) NONDISCRIMINATION SAFEGUARDS- Any local exchange carrier subject to the requirements of section 251(c) that provides telemessaging service—

(1) shall not subsidize its telemessaging service directly or indirectly from its telephone exchange service or its exchange access; and

(2) shall not prefer or discriminate in favor of its telemessaging service operations in its provision of telecommunications services.

(b) EXPEDITED CONSIDERATION OF COMPLAINTS- The Commission shall establish procedures for the receipt and review of complaints concerning violations of subsection (a) or the regulations thereunder that result in material financial harm to a provider of telemessaging service. Such procedures shall ensure that the Commission will make a final determination with respect to any such complaint within 120 days after receipt of the complaint. If the complaint contains an appropriate showing that the alleged violation occurred, the Commission shall, within 60 days after receipt of the complaint, order the local exchange carrier and any affiliates to cease engaging in such violation pending such final determination.

(c) DEFINITION- As used in this section, the term telemessaging service means voice mail and voice storage and retrieval services, any live operator services used to record, transcribe, or relay messages (other than telecommunications relay services), and any ancillary services offered in combination with these services.

SEC. 261. EFFECT ON OTHER REQUIREMENTS.

(a) COMMISSION REGULATIONS- Nothing in this part shall be construed to prohibit the Commission from enforcing regulations prescribed prior to the date of enactment of the Telecommunications Act of 1996 in fulfilling the requirements of this part, to the extent that such regulations are not inconsistent with the provisions of this part.

(b) EXISTING STATE REGULATIONS- Nothing in this part shall be construed to prohibit any State commission from enforcing regulations prescribed prior to the date of enactment of the Telecommunications Act of 1996, or from prescribing regulations after such date of enactment, in fulfilling the requirements of this part, if such regulations are not inconsistent with the provisions of this part.

(c) ADDITIONAL STATE REQUIREMENTS- Nothing in this part precludes a State from imposing requirements on a telecommunications carrier for intrastate services that are necessary to further competition in the provision of telephone exchange service or exchange access, as long as the States requirements are not inconsistent with this part or the Commissions regulations to implement this part..

(b) DESIGNATION OF PART I- Title II of the Act is further amended by inserting before the heading of section 201 the following new heading:

PART I--COMMON CARRIER REGULATION

(c) STYLISTIC CONSISTENCY- The Act is amended so that—

(1) the designation and heading of each title of the Act shall be in the form and typeface of the designation and heading of this title of this Act; and

(2) the designation and heading of each part of each title of the Act shall be in the form and typeface of the designation and heading of part I of title II of the Act, as amended by subsection (a).

SEC. 102. ELIGIBLE TELECOMMUNICATIONS CARRIERS.

(a) IN GENERAL- Section 214 (47 U.S.C. 214) is amended by adding at the end thereof the following new subsection:

(e) PROVISION OF UNIVERSAL SERVICE-

(1) ELIGIBLE TELECOMMUNICATIONS CARRIERS- A common carrier designated as an eligible telecommunications carrier under paragraph (2) or (3) shall be eligible to receive universal service support in accordance with section 254 and shall, throughout the service area for which the designation is received—

(A) offer the services that are supported by Federal universal service support mechanisms under section 254(c), either using its own facilities or a combination of its own facilities and resale of another carriers services (including the services offered by another eligible telecommunications carrier); and

(B) advertise the availability of such services and the charges therefor using media of general distribution.

(2) DESIGNATION OF ELIGIBLE TELECOMMUNICATIONS CARRIERS- A State commission shall upon its own motion or upon request designate a common carrier that meets the requirements of paragraph (1) as an eligible telecommunications carrier for a service area designated by the State commission. Upon request and consistent with the public interest, convenience, and necessity, the State commission may, in the case of an area served by a rural telephone company, and shall, in the case of all other areas, designate more than one common carrier as an eligible telecommunications carrier for a service area designated by the State commission, so long as each additional requesting carrier meets the requirements of paragraph (1). Before designating an additional eligible telecommunications carrier for an

area served by a rural telephone company, the State commission shall find that the designation is in the public interest.

(3) DESIGNATION OF ELIGIBLE TELECOMMUNICATIONS CARRIERS FOR UNSERVED AREAS- If no common carrier will provide the services that are supported by Federal universal service support mechanisms under section 254(c) to an unserved community or any portion thereof that requests such service, the Commission, with respect to interstate services, or a State commission, with respect to intrastate services, shall determine which common carrier or carriers are best able to provide such service to the requesting unserved community or portion thereof and shall order such carrier or carriers to provide such service for that unserved community or portion thereof. Any carrier or carriers ordered to provide such service under this paragraph shall meet the requirements of paragraph (1) and shall be designated as an eligible telecommunications carrier for that community or portion thereof.

(4) RELINQUISHMENT OF UNIVERSAL SERVICE- A State commission shall permit an eligible telecommunications carrier to relinquish its designation as such a carrier in any area served by more than one eligible telecommunications carrier. An eligible telecommunications carrier that seeks to relinquish its eligible telecommunications carrier designation for an area served by more than one eligible telecommunications carrier shall give advance notice to the State commission of such relinquishment. Prior to permitting a telecommunications carrier designated as an eligible telecommunications carrier to cease providing universal service in an area served by more than one eligible telecommunications carrier, the State commission shall require the remaining eligible telecommunications carrier or carriers to ensure that all customers served by the relinquishing carrier will continue to be served, and shall require sufficient notice to permit the purchase or construction of adequate facilities by any remaining eligible telecommunications carrier. The State commission shall establish a time, not to exceed one year after the State commission approves such relinquishment under this paragraph, within which such purchase or construction shall be completed.

(5) SERVICE AREA DEFINED- The term service area means a geographic area established by a State commission for the purpose of determining universal service obligations and support mechanisms. In the case of an area served by a rural telephone company, service area means such companys study area unless and until the Commission and the States, after taking into account recommendations of a Federal-State Joint Board instituted under section 410(c), establish a different definition of service area for such company..

SEC. 103. EXEMPT TELECOMMUNICATIONS COMPANIES.

The Public Utility Holding Company Act of 1935 (15 U.S.C. 79 and following) is amended by redesignating sections 34 and 35 as sections 35 and 36, respectively, and by inserting the following new section after section 33:

SEC. 34. EXEMPT TELECOMMUNICATIONS COMPANIES.

(a) DEFINITIONS- For purposes of this section—

(1) EXEMPT TELECOMMUNICATIONS COMPANY- The term exempt telecommunications company means any person determined by the Federal Communications Commission to be engaged directly or indirectly, wherever located, through one or more affiliates (as defined in section 2(a)(11)(B)), and exclusively in the business of providing---

(A) telecommunications services;

(B) information services;

(C) other services or products subject to the jurisdiction of the Federal Communications Commission; or

(D) products or services that are related or incidental to the provision of a product or service described in subparagraph (A), (B), or (C).

No person shall be deemed to be an exempt telecommunications company under this section unless such person has applied to the Federal Communications Commission for a determination under this paragraph. A person applying in good faith for such a determination shall be deemed an exempt telecommunications company under this section, with all of the exemptions provided by this section, until the Federal Communications Commission makes such determination. The Federal Communications Commission shall make such determination within 60 days of its receipt of any such application filed after the enactment of this section and shall notify the Commission whenever a determination is made under this paragraph that any person is an exempt telecommunications company. Not later than 12 months after the date of enactment of this section, the Federal Communications Commission shall promulgate rules implementing the provisions of this paragraph which shall be applicable to applications filed under this paragraph after the effective date of such rules.

(2) OTHER TERMS- For purposes of this section, the terms telecommunications services and information services shall have the same meanings as provided in the Communications Act of 1934.

(b) STATE CONSENT FOR SALE OF EXISTING RATE-BASED FACILITIES- If a rate or charge for the sale of electric energy or natural gas (other than any portion of a rate or charge which represents recovery of the cost of a wholesale rate or charge) for, or in connection with, assets of a public utility company that is an associate company or affiliate of a registered holding company was in effect under the laws of any State as of December 19, 1995, the public utility company owning such assets may not sell such assets to an exempt telecommunications company that is an associate company or affiliate unless State commissions having jurisdiction over such public utility company approve such sale. Nothing in this subsection shall preempt the otherwise applicable authority of any State to approve or disapprove the sale of such assets. The approval of the Commission under this Act shall not be required for the sale of assets as provided in this subsection.

(c) OWNERSHIP OF ETCS BY EXEMPT HOLDING COMPANIES- Notwithstanding any provision of this Act, a holding company that is exempt under section 3 of this Act shall be permitted, without condition or limitation under this Act, to acquire and maintain an interest in the business of one or more exempt telecommunications companies.

(d) OWNERSHIP OF ETCS BY REGISTERED HOLDING COMPANIES- Notwithstanding any provision of this Act, a registered holding company shall be permitted (without the need to apply for, or receive, approval from the Commission, and otherwise without condition under this Act) to acquire and hold the securities, or an interest in the business, of one or more exempt telecommunications companies.

(e) FINANCING AND OTHER RELATIONSHIPS BETWEEN ETCS AND REGISTERED HOLDING COMPANIES- The relationship between an exempt telecommunications company and a registered holding company, its affiliates and associate companies, shall remain subject to the jurisdiction of the Commission under this Act: [Italic->] Provided, [<-Italic] That—

(1) section 11 of this Act shall not prohibit the ownership of an interest in the business of one or more exempt telecommunications companies by a registered holding company (regardless of activities engaged in or where facilities owned or operated by such exempt telecommunications companies are located), and such ownership by a registered holding company shall be deemed consistent with the operation of an integrated public utility system;

(2) the ownership of an interest in the business of one or more exempt telecommunications companies by a registered holding company (regardless of activities engaged in or where facilities owned or operated by such exempt telecommunications companies are located) shall be considered as reasonably incidental, or economically necessary or appropriate, to the operations of an integrated public utility system;

(3) the Commission shall have no jurisdiction under this Act over, and there shall be no restriction or approval required under this Act with respect to (A) the issue or sale of a security by a registered holding company for purposes of financing the acquisition of an exempt telecommunications company, or (B) the guarantee of a security of an exempt telecommunications company by a registered holding company; and

(4) except for costs that should be fairly and equitably allocated among companies that are associate companies of a registered holding company, the Commission shall have no jurisdiction under this Act over the sales, service, and construction contracts between an exempt telecommunications company and a registered holding company, its affiliates and associate companies.

(f) REPORTING OBLIGATIONS CONCERNING INVESTMENTS AND ACTIVITIES OF REGISTERED PUBLIC-UTILITY HOLDING COMPANY SYSTEMS-

(1) OBLIGATIONS TO REPORT INFORMATION- Any registered holding company or subsidiary thereof that acquires or holds the securities, or an interest in the business, of an exempt telecommunications company shall file with the Commission such information as the Commission, by rule, may prescribe concerning—

(A) investments and activities by the registered holding company, or any subsidiary thereof, with respect to exempt telecommunications companies, and

(B) any activities of an exempt telecommunications company within the holding company system, that are reasonably likely to have a material impact on the financial or operational condition of the holding company system.

(2) AUTHORITY TO REQUIRE ADDITIONAL INFORMATION- If, based on reports provided to the Commission pursuant to paragraph (1) of this subsection or other available information, the Commission reasonably concludes that it has concerns regarding the financial or operational condition of any registered holding company or any subsidiary thereof (including an exempt telecommunications company), the Commission may require such registered holding company to make additional reports and provide additional information.

(3) AUTHORITY TO LIMIT DISCLOSURE OF INFORMATION- Notwithstanding any other provision of law, the Commission shall not be compelled to disclose any information required to be reported under this subsection. Nothing in this subsection shall authorize the Commission to withhold the information from Congress, or prevent the Commission from complying with a request for information from any other Federal or State department or agency requesting the information for purposes within the scope of its jurisdiction. For purposes of section 552 of title 5, United States Code, this subsection shall be considered a statute described in subsection (b)(3)(B) of such section 552.

(g) ASSUMPTION OF LIABILITIES- Any public utility company that is an associate company, or an affiliate, of a registered holding company and that is subject to the jurisdiction of a State commission with respect to its retail electric or gas rates shall not issue any security for the purpose of financing the acquisition, ownership, or operation of an exempt telecommunications company. Any public utility company that is an associate company, or an affiliate, of a registered holding company and that is subject to the jurisdiction of a State commission with respect to its retail electric or gas rates shall not assume any obligation or liability as guarantor, endorser, surety, or otherwise by the public utility company in respect of any security of an exempt telecommunications company.

(h) PLEDGING OR MORTGAGING OF ASSETS- Any public utility company that is an associate company, or affiliate, of a registered holding company and that is subject to the jurisdiction of a State commission with respect to its retail electric or gas rates shall not pledge, mortgage, or otherwise use as collateral any assets of the public utility company or assets of any subsidiary company thereof for the benefit of an exempt telecommunications company.

(i) PROTECTION AGAINST ABUSIVE AFFILIATE TRANSACTIONS- A public utility company may enter into a contract to purchase services or products described in subsection (a)(1) from an exempt telecommunications company that is an affiliate or associate company of the public utility company only if—

(1) every State commission having jurisdiction over the retail rates of such public utility company approves such contract; or

(2) such public utility company is not subject to State commission retail rate regulation and the purchased services or products—

(A) would not be resold to any affiliate or associate company; or

(B) would be resold to an affiliate or associate company and every State commission having jurisdiction over the retail rates of such affiliate or associate company makes the determination required by subparagraph (A). The requirements of this subsection shall not apply in any case in which the State or the State commission concerned publishes a notice that the State or State commission waives its authority under this subsection.

(j) NONPREEMPTION OF RATE AUTHORITY- Nothing in this Act shall preclude the Federal Energy Regulatory Commission or a State commission from exercising its jurisdiction under otherwise applicable law to determine whether a public utility company may recover in rates the costs of products or services purchased from or sold to an associate company or affiliate that is an exempt telecommunications company, regardless of whether such costs are incurred through the direct or indirect purchase or sale of products or services from such associate company or affiliate.

(k) RECIPROCAL ARRANGEMENTS PROHIBITED- Reciprocal arrangements among companies that are not affiliates or associate companies of each other that are entered into in order to avoid the provisions of this section are prohibited.

(l) BOOKS AND RECORDS- (1) Upon written order of a State commission, a State commission may examine the books, accounts, memoranda, contracts, and records of—

(A) a public utility company subject to its regulatory authority under State law;

(B) any exempt telecommunications company selling products or services to such public utility company or to an associate company of such public utility company; and

(C) any associate company or affiliate of an exempt telecommunications company which sells products or services to a public utility company referred to in subparagraph (A), wherever located, if such examination is required for the effective discharge of the State commissions regulatory responsibilities affecting the provision of electric or gas service in connection with the activities of such exempt telecommunications company.

(2) Where a State commission issues an order pursuant to paragraph (1), the State commission shall not publicly disclose trade secrets or sensitive commercial information.

(3) Any United States district court located in the State in which the State commission referred to in paragraph (1) is located shall have jurisdiction to enforce compliance with this subsection.

(4) Nothing in this section shall—

(A) preempt applicable State law concerning the provision of records and other information; or

(B) in any way limit rights to obtain records and other information under Federal law, contracts, or otherwise.

(m) INDEPENDENT AUDIT AUTHORITY FOR STATE COMMISSIONS-

(1) STATE MAY ORDER AUDIT- Any State commission with jurisdiction over a public utility company that—

(A) is an associate company of a registered holding company; and

(B) transacts business, directly or indirectly, with a subsidiary company, an affiliate or an associate company that is an exempt telecommunications company, may order an independent audit to be performed, no more frequently than on an annual basis, of all matters deemed relevant by the selected auditor that reasonably relate to retail rates: [Italic->] Provided [<-Italic] , That such matters relate, directly or indirectly, to transactions or transfers between the public utility company subject to its jurisdiction and such exempt telecommunications company.

(2) SELECTION OF FIRM TO CONDUCT AUDIT- (A) If a State commission orders an audit in accordance with paragraph (1), the public utility company and the State commission shall jointly select, within 60 days, a firm to perform the audit. The firm selected to perform the audit shall possess demonstrated qualifications relating to—

(i) competency, including adequate technical training and professional proficiency in each discipline necessary to carry out the audit; and

(ii) independence and objectivity, including that the firm be free from personal or external impairments to independence, and should assume an independent position with the State commission and auditee, making certain that the audit is based upon an impartial consideration of all pertinent facts and responsible opinions.

(B) The public utility company and the exempt telecommunications company shall cooperate fully with all reasonable requests necessary to perform the audit and the public utility company shall bear all costs of having the audit performed.

(3) AVAILABILITY OF AUDITORS REPORT- The auditors report shall be provided to the State commission not later than 6 months after the selection of the auditor, and provided to the public utility company not later than 60 days thereafter.

(n) APPLICABILITY OF TELECOMMUNICATIONS REGULATION- Nothing in this section shall affect the authority of the Federal Communications Commission under the Communications Act of 1934, or the authority of State commissions under State laws concerning the provision of telecommunications services, to regulate the activities of an exempt telecommunications company..

SEC. 104. NONDISCRIMINATION PRINCIPLE.

Section 1 (47 U.S.C. 151) is amended by inserting after to all the people of the United States the following: , without discrimination on the basis of race, color, religion, national origin, or sex,.

SUBTITLE B--SPECIAL PROVISIONS CONCERNING BELL OPERATING COMPANIES

SEC. 151. BELL OPERATING COMPANY PROVISIONS.

(a) ESTABLISHMENT OF PART III OF TITLE II- Title II is amended by adding at the end of part II (as added by section 101) the following new part:

PART III--SPECIAL PROVISIONS CONCERNING BELL OPERATING COMPANIES

SEC. 271. BELL OPERATING COMPANY ENTRY INTO INTERLATA SERVICES.

(a) GENERAL LIMITATION- Neither a Bell operating company, nor any affiliate of a Bell operating company, may provide interLATA services except as provided in this section.

(b) INTERLATA SERVICES TO WHICH THIS SECTION APPLIES-

(1) IN-REGION SERVICES- A Bell operating company, or any affiliate of that Bell operating company, may provide interLATA services originating in any of its in-region States (as defined in subsection (i)) if the Commission approves the application of such company for such State under subsection (d)(3).

(2) OUT-OF-REGION SERVICES- A Bell operating company, or any affiliate of that Bell operating company, may provide interLATA services originating outside its in-region States after the date of enactment of the Telecommunications Act of 1996, subject to subsection (j).

(3) INCIDENTAL INTERLATA SERVICES- A Bell operating company, or any affiliate of a Bell operating company, may provide incidental interLATA services (as defined in subsection (g)) originating in any State after the date of enactment of the Telecommunications Act of 1996.

(4) TERMINATION- Nothing in this section prohibits a Bell operating company or any of its affiliates from providing termination for interLATA services, subject to subsection (j).

(c) REQUIREMENTS FOR PROVIDING CERTAIN IN-REGION INTERLATA SERVICES-

(1) AGREEMENT OR STATEMENT- A Bell operating company meets the requirements of this paragraph if it meets the requirements of subparagraph (A) or subparagraph (B) of this paragraph for each State for which the authorization is sought.

(A) PRESENCE OF A FACILITIES-BASED COMPETITOR- A Bell operating company meets the requirements of this subparagraph if it has entered into one or more binding agreements that have been approved under section 252 specifying the terms and conditions under which the Bell operating company is providing access and interconnection to its network facilities for the network facilities of one or more unaffiliated competing providers of telephone exchange service (as defined in section 3(47)(A), but excluding exchange access) to residential and business subscribers. For the purpose of this subparagraph, such telephone exchange service may be offered by such competing providers either exclusively over their own telephone exchange service facilities or predominantly over their own telephone exchange service facilities in combination with the resale of the telecommunications services of another carrier. For the purpose of this subparagraph, services provided pursuant to subpart K of part 22 of the Commissions regulations (47 C.F.R. 22.901 et seq.) shall not be considered to be telephone exchange services.

(B) FAILURE TO REQUEST ACCESS- A Bell operating company meets the requirements of this subparagraph if, after 10 months after the date of enactment of the Telecommunications Act of 1996, no such provider has requested the access and interconnection described in subparagraph (A) before the date which is 3 months before the date the company makes its application under subsection (d)(1), and a statement of the terms and conditions that the company generally offers to provide such access and interconnection has been approved or permitted to take effect by the State commission under section 252(f). For purposes of this subparagraph, a Bell operating company shall be considered not to have received any request for access and interconnection if the State commission of such State certifies that the only provider or providers making such a request have (i) failed to negotiate in good faith as required by section 252, or (ii) violated the terms of an agreement approved under section 252 by the providers failure to comply, within a reasonable period of time, with the implementation schedule contained in such agreement.

(2) SPECIFIC INTERCONNECTION REQUIREMENTS-

(A) AGREEMENT REQUIRED- A Bell operating company meets the requirements of this paragraph if, within the State for which the authorization is sought—

(i)(I) such company is providing access and interconnection pursuant to one or more agreements described in paragraph (1)(A), or

(II) such company is generally offering access and interconnection pursuant to a statement described in paragraph (1)(B), and

(ii) such access and interconnection meets the requirements of subparagraph (B) of this paragraph.

(B) COMPETITIVE CHECKLIST- Access or interconnection provided or generally offered by a Bell operating company to other telecommunications carriers meets the requirements of this subparagraph if such access and interconnection includes each of the following:

(i) Interconnection in accordance with the requirements of sections 251(c)(2) and 252(d)(1).

(ii) Nondiscriminatory access to network elements in accordance with the requirements of sections 251(c)(3) and 252(d)(1).

(iii) Nondiscriminatory access to the poles, ducts, conduits, and rights-of-way owned or controlled by the Bell operating company at just and reasonable rates in accordance with the requirements of section 224.

(iv) Local loop transmission from the central office to the customers premises, unbundled from local switching or other services.

(v) Local transport from the trunk side of a wireline local exchange carrier switch unbundled from switching or other services.

(vi) Local switching unbundled from transport, local loop transmission, or other services.

(vii) Nondiscriminatory access to—

(I) 911 and E911 services;

(II) directory assistance services to allow the other carriers customers to obtain telephone numbers; and

(III) operator call completion services.

(viii) White pages directory listings for customers of the other carriers telephone exchange service.

(ix) Until the date by which telecommunications numbering administration guidelines, plan, or rules are established, nondiscriminatory access to telephone numbers for assignment to the other carriers telephone exchange service customers. After that date, compliance with such guidelines, plan, or rules.

(x) Nondiscriminatory access to databases and associated signaling necessary for call routing and completion.

(xi) Until the date by which the Commission issues regulations pursuant to section 251 to require number portability, interim telecommunications number portability through remote call forwarding, direct inward dialing trunks, or other comparable arrangements, with as little impairment of functioning, quality, reliability, and convenience as possible. After that date, full compliance with such regulations.

(xii) Nondiscriminatory access to such services or information as are necessary to allow the requesting carrier to implement local dialing parity in accordance with the requirements of section 251(b)(3).

(xiii) Reciprocal compensation arrangements in accordance with the requirements of section 252(d)(2).

(xiv) Telecommunications services are available for resale in accordance with the requirements of sections 251(c)(4) and 252(d)(3).

(d) ADMINISTRATIVE PROVISIONS-

(1) APPLICATION TO COMMISSION- On and after the date of enactment of the Telecommunications Act of 1996, a Bell operating company or its affiliate may apply to the Commission for authorization to provide interLATA services originating in any in-region State. The application shall identify each State for which the authorization is sought.

(2) CONSULTATION-

(A) CONSULTATION WITH THE ATTORNEY GENERAL- The Commission shall notify the Attorney General promptly of any application under paragraph (1). Before making any determination under this subsection, the Commission shall consult with the Attorney General, and if the Attorney General submits any comments in writing, such comments shall be included in the record of the Commissions decision. In consulting with and submitting comments to the Commission under this paragraph, the Attorney General shall provide to the Commission an evaluation of the application using any standard the Attorney General considers appropriate. The Commission shall give substantial weight to the Attorney Generals evaluation, but such evaluation shall not have any preclusive effect on any Commission decision under paragraph (3).

(B) CONSULTATION WITH STATE COMMISSIONS- Before making any determination under this subsection, the Commission shall consult with the State commission of any State that is the subject of the application in order to verify the compliance of the Bell operating company with the requirements of subsection (c).

(3) DETERMINATION- Not later than 90 days after receiving an application under paragraph (1), the Commission shall issue a written determination approving or denying the

authorization requested in the application for each State. The Commission shall not approve the authorization requested in an application submitted under paragraph (1) unless it finds that—

(A) the petitioning Bell operating company has met the requirements of subsection (c)(1) and—

(i) with respect to access and interconnection provided pursuant to subsection (c)(1)(A), has fully implemented the competitive checklist in subsection (c)(2)(B); or

(ii) with respect to access and interconnection generally offered pursuant to a statement under subsection (c)(1)(B), such statement offers all of the items included in the competitive checklist in subsection (c)(2)(B);

(B) the requested authorization will be carried out in accordance with the requirements of section 272; and

(C) the requested authorization is consistent with the public interest, convenience, and necessity. The Commission shall state the basis for its approval or denial of the application.

(4) LIMITATION ON COMMISSION- The Commission may not, by rule or otherwise, limit or extend the terms used in the competitive checklist set forth in subsection (c)(2)(B).

(5) PUBLICATION- Not later than 10 days after issuing a determination under paragraph (3), the Commission shall publish in the Federal Register a brief description of the determination.

(6) ENFORCEMENT OF CONDITIONS-

(A) COMMISSION AUTHORITY- If at any time after the approval of an application under paragraph (3), the Commission determines that a Bell operating company has ceased to meet any of the conditions required for such approval, the Commission may, after notice and opportunity for a hearing—

(i) issue an order to such company to correct the deficiency;

(ii) impose a penalty on such company pursuant to title V; or

(iii) suspend or revoke such approval.

(B) RECEIPT AND REVIEW OF COMPLAINTS- The Commission shall establish procedures for the review of complaints concerning failures by Bell operating companies to meet conditions required for approval under paragraph (3). Unless the parties otherwise agree, the Commission shall act on such complaint within 90 days.

(e) LIMITATIONS-

(1) JOINT MARKETING OF LOCAL AND LONG DISTANCE SERVICES- Until a Bell operating company is authorized pursuant to subsection (d) to provide interLATA services in an in-region State, or until 36 months have passed since the date of enactment of the Telecommunications Act of 1996, whichever is earlier, a telecommunications carrier that serves greater than 5 percent of the Nations presubscribed access lines may not jointly market in such State telephone exchange service obtained from such company pursuant to section 251(c)(4) with interLATA services offered by that telecommunications carrier.

(2) INTRALATA TOLL DIALING PARITY-

(A) PROVISION REQUIRED- A Bell operating company granted authority to provide interLATA services under subsection (d) shall provide intraLATA toll dialing parity throughout that State coincident with its exercise of that authority.

(B) LIMITATION- Except for single-LATA States and States that have issued an order by December 19, 1995, requiring a Bell operating company to implement intraLATA toll dialing parity, a State may not require a Bell operating company to implement intraLATA toll dialing parity in that State before a Bell operating company has been granted authority under this section to provide interLATA services originating in that State or before 3 years after the date of enactment of the Telecommunications Act of 1996, whichever is earlier. Nothing in this subparagraph precludes a State from issuing an order requiring intraLATA toll dialing parity in that State prior to either such date so long as such order does not take effect until after the earlier of either such dates.

(f) EXCEPTION FOR PREVIOUSLY AUTHORIZED ACTIVITIES- Neither subsection (a) nor section 273 shall prohibit a Bell operating company or affiliate from engaging, at any time after the date of enactment of the Telecommunications Act of 1996, in any activity to the extent authorized by, and subject to the terms and conditions contained in, an order entered by the United States District Court for the District of Columbia pursuant to section VII or VIII(C) of the AT&T Consent Decree if such order was entered on or before such date of enactment, to the extent such order is not reversed or vacated on appeal. Nothing in this subsection shall be construed to limit, or to impose terms or conditions on, an activity in which a Bell operating company is otherwise authorized to engage under any other provision of this section.

(g) DEFINITION OF INCIDENTAL INTERLATA SERVICES- For purposes of this section, the term incidental interLATA services means the interLATA provision by a Bell operating company or its affiliate—

(1)(A) of audio programming, video programming, or other programming services to subscribers to such services of such company or affiliate;

(B) of the capability for interaction by such subscribers to select or respond to such audio programming, video programming, or other programming services;

(C) to distributors of audio programming or video programming that such company or affiliate owns or controls, or is licensed by the copyright owner of such programming (or by an assignee of such owner) to distribute; or

(D) of alarm monitoring services;

(2) of two-way interactive video services or Internet services over dedicated facilities to or for elementary and secondary schools as defined in section 254(h)(5);

(3) of commercial mobile services in accordance with section 332(c) of this Act and with the regulations prescribed by the Commission pursuant to paragraph (8) of such section;

(4) of a service that permits a customer that is located in one LATA to retrieve stored information from, or file information for storage in, information storage facilities of such company that are located in another LATA;

(5) of signaling information used in connection with the provision of telephone exchange services or exchange access by a local exchange carrier; or

(6) of network control signaling information to, and receipt of such signaling information from, common carriers offering interLATA services at any location within the area in which such Bell operating company provides telephone exchange services or exchange access.

(h) LIMITATIONS- The provisions of subsection (g) are intended to be narrowly construed. The interLATA services provided under subparagraph (A), (B), or (C) of subsection (g)(1) are limited to those interLATA transmissions incidental to the provision by a Bell operating company or its affiliate of video, audio, and other programming services that the company or its affiliate is engaged in providing to the public. The Commission shall ensure that the provision of services authorized under subsection (g) by a Bell operating company or its affiliate will not adversely affect telephone exchange service ratepayers or competition in any telecommunications market.

(i) ADDITIONAL DEFINITIONS- As used in this section—

(1) IN-REGION STATE- The term in-region State means a State in which a Bell operating company or any of its affiliates was authorized to provide wireline telephone exchange service pursuant to the reorganization plan approved under the AT&T Consent Decree, as in effect on the day before the date of enactment of the Telecommunications Act of 1996.

(2) AUDIO PROGRAMMING SERVICES- The term audio programming services means programming provided by, or generally considered to be comparable to programming provided by, a radio broadcast station.

(3) VIDEO PROGRAMMING SERVICES; OTHER PROGRAMMING SERVICES- The terms video programming service and other programming services have the same meanings as such terms have under section 602 of this Act.

(j) CERTAIN SERVICE APPLICATIONS TREATED AS IN-REGION SERVICE APPLICATIONS- For purposes of this section, a Bell operating company application to provide 800 service, private line service, or their equivalents that—

(1) terminate in an in-region State of that Bell operating company, and

(2) allow the called party to determine the interLATA carrier, shall be considered an in-region service subject to the requirements of subsection (b)(1).

SEC. 272. SEPARATE AFFILIATE; SAFEGUARDS.

(a) SEPARATE AFFILIATE REQUIRED FOR COMPETITIVE ACTIVITIES-

(1) IN GENERAL- A Bell operating company (including any affiliate) which is a local exchange carrier that is subject to the requirements of section 251(c) may not provide any service described in paragraph (2) unless it provides that service through one or more affiliates that—

(A) are separate from any operating company entity that is subject to the requirements of section 251(c); and

(B) meet the requirements of subsection (b).

(2) SERVICES FOR WHICH A SEPARATE AFFILIATE IS REQUIRED- The services for which a separate affiliate is required by paragraph (1) are:

(A) Manufacturing activities (as defined in section 273(h)).

(B) Origination of interLATA telecommunications services, other than—

(i) incidental interLATA services described in paragraphs (1), (2), (3), (5), and (6) of section 271(g);

(ii) out-of-region services described in section 271(b)(2); or

(iii) previously authorized activities described in section 271(f).

(C) InterLATA information services, other than electronic publishing (as defined in section 274(h)) and alarm monitoring services (as defined in section 275(e)).

(b) STRUCTURAL AND TRANSACTIONAL REQUIREMENTS- The separate affiliate required by this section—

(1) shall operate independently from the Bell operating company;

(2) shall maintain books, records, and accounts in the manner prescribed by the Commission which shall be separate from the books, records, and accounts maintained by the Bell operating company of which it is an affiliate;

(3) shall have separate officers, directors, and employees from the Bell operating company of which it is an affiliate;

(4) may not obtain credit under any arrangement that would permit a creditor, upon default, to have recourse to the assets of the Bell operating company; and

(5) shall conduct all transactions with the Bell operating company of which it is an affiliate on an arms length basis with any such transactions reduced to writing and available for public inspection.

(c) NONDISCRIMINATION SAFEGUARDS- In its dealings with its affiliate described in subsection (a), a Bell operating company—

(1) may not discriminate between that company or affiliate and any other entity in the provision or procurement of goods, services, facilities, and information, or in the establishment of standards; and

(2) shall account for all transactions with an affiliate described in subsection (a) in accordance with accounting principles designated or approved by the Commission.

(d) BIENNIAL AUDIT-

(1) GENERAL REQUIREMENT- A company required to operate a separate affiliate under this section shall obtain and pay for a joint Federal/State audit every 2 years conducted by an independent auditor to determine whether such company has complied with this section and the regulations promulgated under this section, and particularly whether such company has complied with the separate accounting requirements under subsection (b).

(2) RESULTS SUBMITTED TO COMMISSION; STATE COMMISSIONS- The auditor described in paragraph (1) shall submit the results of the audit to the Commission and to the State commission of each State in which the company audited provides service, which shall make such results available for public inspection. Any party may submit comments on the final audit report.

(3) ACCESS TO DOCUMENTS- For purposes of conducting audits and reviews under this subsection—

(A) the independent auditor, the Commission, and the State commission shall have access to the financial accounts and records of each company and of its affiliates necessary to verify transactions conducted with that company that are relevant to the specific activities permitted under this section and that are necessary for the regulation of rates;

(B) the Commission and the State commission shall have access to the working papers and supporting materials of any auditor who performs an audit under this section; and

(C) the State commission shall implement appropriate procedures to ensure the protection of any proprietary information submitted to it under this section.

(e) FULFILLMENT OF CERTAIN REQUESTS- A Bell operating company and an affiliate that is subject to the requirements of section 251(c)—

(1) shall fulfill any requests from an unaffiliated entity for telephone exchange service and exchange access within a period no longer than the period in which it provides such telephone exchange service and exchange access to itself or to its affiliates;

(2) shall not provide any facilities, services, or information concerning its provision of exchange access to the affiliate described in subsection (a) unless such facilities, services, or information are made available to other providers of interLATA services in that market on the same terms and conditions;

(3) shall charge the affiliate described in subsection (a), or impute to itself (if using the access for its provision of its own services), an amount for access to its telephone exchange

service and exchange access that is no less than the amount charged to any unaffiliated interexchange carriers for such service; and

(4) may provide any interLATA or intraLATA facilities or services to its interLATA affiliate if such services or facilities are made available to all carriers at the same rates and on the same terms and conditions, and so long as the costs are appropriately allocated.

(f) SUNSET-

(1) MANUFACTURING AND LONG DISTANCE- The provisions of this section (other than subsection (e)) shall cease to apply with respect to the manufacturing activities or the interLATA telecommunications services of a Bell operating company 3 years after the date such Bell operating company or any Bell operating company affiliate is authorized to provide interLATA telecommunications services under section 271(d), unless the Commission extends such 3-year period by rule or order.

(2) INTERLATA INFORMATION SERVICES- The provisions of this section (other than subsection (e)) shall cease to apply with respect to the interLATA information services of a Bell operating company 4 years after the date of enactment of the Telecommunications Act of 1996, unless the Commission extends such 4-year period by rule or order.

(3) PRESERVATION OF EXISTING AUTHORITY- Nothing in this subsection shall be construed to limit the authority of the Commission under any other section of this Act to prescribe safeguards consistent with the public interest, convenience, and necessity.

(g) JOINT MARKETING-

(1) AFFILIATE SALES OF TELEPHONE EXCHANGE SERVICES- A Bell operating company affiliate required by this section may not market or sell telephone exchange services provided by the Bell operating company unless that company permits other entities offering the same or similar service to market and sell its telephone exchange services.

(2) BELL OPERATING COMPANY SALES OF AFFILIATE SERVICES- A Bell operating company may not market or sell interLATA service provided by an affiliate required by this section within any of its in-region States until such company is authorized to provide interLATA services in such State under section 271(d).

(3) RULE OF CONSTRUCTION- The joint marketing and sale of services permitted under this subsection shall not be considered to violate the nondiscrimination provisions of subsection (c).

(h) TRANSITION- With respect to any activity in which a Bell operating company is engaged on the date of enactment of the Telecommunications Act of 1996, such company shall have one year from such date of enactment to comply with the requirements of this section.

SEC. 273. MANUFACTURING BY BELL OPERATING COMPANIES.

(a) AUTHORIZATION- A Bell operating company may manufacture and provide telecommunications equipment, and manufacture customer premises equipment, if the Commission authorizes that Bell operating company or any Bell operating company affiliate to provide interLATA services under section 271(d), subject to the requirements of this section and the regulations prescribed thereunder, except that neither a Bell operating company nor any of its affiliates may engage in such manufacturing in conjunction with a Bell operating company not so affiliated or any of its affiliates.

(b) COLLABORATION; RESEARCH AND ROYALTY AGREEMENTS-

(1) COLLABORATION- Subsection (a) shall not prohibit a Bell operating company from engaging in close collaboration with any manufacturer of customer premises equipment or telecommunications equipment during the design and development of hardware, software, or combinations thereof related to such equipment.

(2) CERTAIN RESEARCH ARRANGEMENTS; ROYALTY AGREEMENTS- Subsection (a) shall not prohibit a Bell operating company from—

(A) engaging in research activities related to manufacturing, and

(B) entering into royalty agreements with manufacturers of telecommunications equipment.

(c) INFORMATION REQUIREMENTS-

(1) INFORMATION ON PROTOCOLS AND TECHNICAL REQUIREMENTS- Each Bell operating company shall, in accordance with regulations prescribed by the Commission, maintain and file with the Commission full and complete information with respect to the protocols and technical requirements for connection with and use of its telephone exchange service facilities. Each such company shall report promptly to the Commission any material changes or planned changes to such protocols and requirements, and the schedule for implementation of such changes or planned changes.

(2) DISCLOSURE OF INFORMATION- A Bell operating company shall not disclose any information required to be filed under paragraph (1) unless that information has been filed promptly, as required by regulation by the Commission.

(3) ACCESS BY COMPETITORS TO INFORMATION- The Commission may prescribe such additional regulations under this subsection as may be necessary to ensure that manufacturers have access to the information with respect to the protocols and technical requirements for connection with and use of telephone exchange service facilities that a Bell operating company makes available to any manufacturing affiliate or any unaffiliated manufacturer.

(4) PLANNING INFORMATION- Each Bell operating company shall provide, to interconnecting carriers providing telephone exchange service, timely information on the planned deployment of telecommunications equipment.

(d) MANUFACTURING LIMITATIONS FOR STANDARD-SETTING ORGANIZATIONS-

(1) APPLICATION TO BELL COMMUNICATIONS RESEARCH OR MANUFACTURERS- Bell Communications Research, Inc., or any successor entity or affiliate—

(A) shall not be considered a Bell operating company or a successor or assign of a Bell operating company at such time as it is no longer an affiliate of any Bell operating company; and

(B) notwithstanding paragraph (3), shall not engage in manufacturing telecommunications equipment or customer premises equipment as long as it is an affiliate of more than 1 otherwise unaffiliated Bell operating company or successor or assign of any such company. Nothing in this subsection prohibits Bell Communications Research, Inc., or any successor entity, from engaging in any activity in which it is lawfully engaged on the date of enactment of the Telecommunications Act of 1996. Nothing provided in this subsection shall render Bell Communications Research, Inc., or any successor entity, a common carrier under title II of this Act. Nothing in this subsection restricts any manufacturer from engaging in any activity in which it is lawfully engaged on the date of enactment of the Telecommunications Act of 1996.

(2) PROPRIETARY INFORMATION- Any entity which establishes standards for telecommunications equipment or customer premises equipment, or generic network requirements for such equipment, or certifies telecommunications equipment or customer premises equipment, shall be prohibited from releasing or otherwise using any proprietary information, designated as such by its owner, in its possession as a result of such activity, for any purpose other than purposes authorized in writing by the owner of such information, even after such entity ceases to be so engaged.

(3) MANUFACTURING SAFEGUARDS- (A) Except as prohibited in paragraph (1), and subject to paragraph (6), any entity which certifies telecommunications equipment or customer premises equipment manufactured by an unaffiliated entity shall only manufacture a particular class of telecommunications equipment or customer premises equipment for which it is undertaking or has undertaken, during the previous 18 months, certification activity for such class of equipment through a separate affiliate.

(B) Such separate affiliate shall—

(i) maintain books, records, and accounts separate from those of the entity that certifies such equipment, consistent with generally acceptable accounting principles;

(ii) not engage in any joint manufacturing activities with such entity; and

(iii) have segregated facilities and separate employees with such entity.

(C) Such entity that certifies such equipment shall—

(i) not discriminate in favor of its manufacturing affiliate in the establishment of standards, generic requirements, or product certification;

(ii) not disclose to the manufacturing affiliate any proprietary information that has been received at any time from an unaffiliated manufacturer, unless authorized in writing by the owner of the information; and

(iii) not permit any employee engaged in product certification for telecommunications equipment or customer premises equipment to engage jointly in sales or marketing of any such equipment with the affiliated manufacturer.

(4) STANDARD-SETTING ENTITIES- Any entity that is not an accredited standards development organization and that establishes industry-wide standards for telecommunications equipment or customer premises equipment, or industry-wide generic network requirements for such equipment, or that certifies telecommunications equipment or customer premises equipment manufactured by an unaffiliated entity, shall—

(A) establish and publish any industry-wide standard for, industry-wide generic requirement for, or any substantial modification of an existing industry-wide standard or industry-wide generic requirement for, telecommunications equipment or customer premises equipment only in compliance with the following procedure—

(i) such entity shall issue a public notice of its consideration of a proposed industry-wide standard or industry-wide generic requirement;

(ii) such entity shall issue a public invitation to interested industry parties to fund and participate in such efforts on a reasonable and nondiscriminatory basis, administered in such a manner as not to unreasonably exclude any interested industry party;

(iii) such entity shall publish a text for comment by such parties as have agreed to participate in the process pursuant to clause (ii), provide such parties a full opportunity to submit comments, and respond to comments from such parties;

(iv) such entity shall publish a final text of the industry-wide standard or industry-wide generic requirement, including the comments in their entirety, of any funding party which requests to have its comments so published; and

(v) such entity shall attempt, prior to publishing a text for comment, to agree with the funding parties as a group on a mutually satisfactory dispute resolution process which such parties shall utilize as their sole recourse in the event of a dispute on technical issues as to which there is disagreement between any funding party and the entity conducting such activities, except that if no dispute resolution process is agreed to by all the parties, a funding party may utilize the dispute resolution procedures established pursuant to paragraph (5) of this subsection;

(B) engage in product certification for telecommunications equipment or customer premises equipment manufactured by unaffiliated entities only if—

(i) such activity is performed pursuant to published criteria;

(ii) such activity is performed pursuant to auditable criteria; and

(iii) such activity is performed pursuant to available industry-accepted testing methods and standards, where applicable, unless otherwise agreed upon by the parties funding and performing such activity;

(C) not undertake any actions to monopolize or attempt to monopolize the market for such services; and

(D) not preferentially treat its own telecommunications equipment or customer premises equipment, or that of its affiliate, over that of any other entity in establishing and publishing industry-wide standards or industry-wide generic requirements for, and in certification of, telecommunications equipment and customer premises equipment.

(5) ALTERNATE DISPUTE RESOLUTION- Within 90 days after the date of enactment of the Telecommunications Act of 1996, the Commission shall prescribe a dispute resolution process to be utilized in the event that a dispute resolution process is not agreed upon by all the parties when establishing and publishing any industry-wide standard or industry-wide generic requirement for telecommunications equipment or customer premises equipment, pursuant to paragraph (4)(A)(v). The Commission shall not establish itself as a party to the dispute resolution process. Such dispute resolution process shall permit any funding party to resolve a dispute with the entity conducting the activity that significantly affects such funding partys interests, in an open, nondiscriminatory, and unbiased fashion, within 30 days after the filing of such dispute. Such disputes may be filed within 15 days after the date the funding party receives a response to its comments from the entity conducting the activity. The Commission shall establish penalties to be assessed for delays caused by referral of frivolous disputes to the dispute resolution process.

(6) SUNSET- The requirements of paragraphs (3) and (4) shall terminate for the particular relevant activity when the Commission determines that there are alternative sources of industry-wide standards, industry-wide generic requirements, or product certification for a particular class of telecommunications equipment or customer premises equipment available in the United States. Alternative sources shall be deemed to exist when such sources provide commercially viable alternatives that are providing such services to customers. The Commission shall act on any application for such a determination within 90 days after receipt of such application, and shall receive public comment on such application.

(7) ADMINISTRATION AND ENFORCEMENT AUTHORITY- For the purposes of administering this subsection and the regulations prescribed thereunder, the Commission shall

have the same remedial authority as the Commission has in administering and enforcing the provisions of this title with respect to any common carrier subject to this Act.

(8) DEFINITIONS- For purposes of this subsection:

(A) The term affiliate shall have the same meaning as in section 3 of this Act, except that, for purposes of paragraph (1)(B)—

(i) an aggregate voting equity interest in Bell Communications Research, Inc., of at least 5 percent of its total voting equity, owned directly or indirectly by more than 1 otherwise unaffiliated Bell operating company, shall constitute an affiliate relationship; and

(ii) a voting equity interest in Bell Communications Research, Inc., by any otherwise unaffiliated Bell operating company of less than 1 percent of Bell Communications Researchs total voting equity shall not be considered to be an equity interest under this paragraph.

(B) The term generic requirement means a description of acceptable product attributes for use by local exchange carriers in establishing product specifications for the purchase of telecommunications equipment, customer premises equipment, and software integral thereto.

(C) The term industry-wide means activities funded by or performed on behalf of local exchange carriers for use in providing wireline telephone exchange service whose combined total of deployed access lines in the United States constitutes at least 30 percent of all access lines deployed by telecommunications carriers in the United States as of the date of enactment of the Telecommunications Act of 1996.

(D) The term certification means any technical process whereby a party determines whether a product, for use by more than one local exchange carrier, conforms with the specified requirements pertaining to such product.

(E) The term accredited standards development organization means an entity composed of industry members which has been accredited by an institution vested with the responsibility for standards accreditation by the industry.

(e) BELL OPERATING COMPANY EQUIPMENT PROCUREMENT AND SALES-

(1) NONDISCRIMINATION STANDARDS FOR MANUFACTURING- In the procurement or awarding of supply contracts for telecommunications equipment, a Bell operating company, or any entity acting on its behalf, for the duration of the requirement for a separate subsidiary including manufacturing under this Act—

(A) shall consider such equipment, produced or supplied by unrelated persons; and

(B) may not discriminate in favor of equipment produced or supplied by an affiliate or related person.

(2) PROCUREMENT STANDARDS- Each Bell operating company or any entity acting on its behalf shall make procurement decisions and award all supply contracts for equipment, services, and software on the basis of an objective assessment of price, quality, delivery, and other commercial factors.

(3) NETWORK PLANNING AND DESIGN- A Bell operating company shall, to the extent consistent with the antitrust laws, engage in joint network planning and design with local exchange carriers operating in the same area of interest. No participant in such planning shall be allowed to delay the introduction of new technology or the deployment of facilities to provide telecommunications services, and agreement with such other carriers shall not be required as a prerequisite for such introduction or deployment.

(4) SALES RESTRICTIONS- Neither a Bell operating company engaged in manufacturing nor a manufacturing affiliate of such a company shall restrict sales to any local

exchange carrier of telecommunications equipment, including software integral to the operation of such equipment and related upgrades.

(5) PROTECTION OF PROPRIETARY INFORMATION- A Bell operating company and any entity it owns or otherwise controls shall protect the proprietary information submitted for procurement decisions from release not specifically authorized by the owner of such information.

(f) ADMINISTRATION AND ENFORCEMENT AUTHORITY- For the purposes of administering and enforcing the provisions of this section and the regulations prescribed thereunder, the Commission shall have the same authority, power, and functions with respect to any Bell operating company or any affiliate thereof as the Commission has in administering and enforcing the provisions of this title with respect to any common carrier subject to this Act.

(g) ADDITIONAL RULES AND REGULATIONS- The Commission may prescribe such additional rules and regulations as the Commission determines are necessary to carry out the provisions of this section, and otherwise to prevent discrimination and cross-subsidization in a Bell operating companys dealings with its affiliate and with third parties.

(h) DEFINITION- As used in this section, the term manufacturing has the same meaning as such term has under the AT&T Consent Decree.

SEC. 274. ELECTRONIC PUBLISHING BY BELL OPERATING COMPANIES.

(a) LIMITATIONS- No Bell operating company or any affiliate may engage in the provision of electronic publishing that is disseminated by means of such Bell operating companys or any of its affiliates basic telephone service, except that nothing in this section shall prohibit a separated affiliate or electronic publishing joint venture operated in accordance with this section from engaging in the provision of electronic publishing.

(b) SEPARATED AFFILIATE OR ELECTRONIC PUBLISHING JOINT VENTURE REQUIREMENTS- A separated affiliate or electronic publishing joint venture shall be operated independently from the Bell operating company. Such separated affiliate or joint venture and the Bell operating company with which it is affiliated shall—

(1) maintain separate books, records, and accounts and prepare separate financial statements;

(2) not incur debt in a manner that would permit a creditor of the separated affiliate or joint venture upon default to have recourse to the assets of the Bell operating company;

(3) carry out transactions (A) in a manner consistent with such independence, (B) pursuant to written contracts or tariffs that are filed with the Commission and made publicly available, and (C) in a manner that is auditable in accordance with generally accepted auditing standards;

(4) value any assets that are transferred directly or indirectly from the Bell operating company to a separated affiliate or joint venture, and record any transactions by which such assets are transferred, in accordance with such regulations as may be prescribed by the Commission or a State commission to prevent improper cross subsidies;

(5) between a separated affiliate and a Bell operating company—

(A) have no officers, directors, and employees in common after the effective date of this section; and

(B) own no property in common;

(6) not use for the marketing of any product or service of the separated affiliate or joint venture, the name, trademarks, or service marks of an existing Bell operating company except for names, trademarks, or service marks that are owned by the entity that owns or controls the Bell operating company;

(7) not permit the Bell operating company-- (A) to perform hiring or training of personnel on behalf of a separated affiliate; (B) to perform the purchasing, installation, or maintenance of equipment on behalf of a separated affiliate, except for telephone service that it provides under tariff or contract subject to the provisions of this section; or (C) to perform research and development on behalf of a separated affiliate;

(8) each have performed annually a compliance review—

(A) that is conducted by an independent entity for the purpose of determining compliance during the preceding calendar year with any provision of this section; and

(B) the results of which are maintained by the separated affiliate or joint venture and the Bell operating company for a period of 5 years subject to review by any lawful authority; and

(9) within 90 days of receiving a review described in paragraph (8), file a report of any exceptions and corrective action with the Commission and allow any person to inspect and copy such report subject to reasonable safeguards to protect any proprietary information contained in such report from being used for purposes other than to enforce or pursue remedies under this section.

(c) JOINT MARKETING-

(1) IN GENERAL- Except as provided in paragraph (2)—

(A) a Bell operating company shall not carry out any promotion, marketing, sales, or advertising for or in conjunction with a separated affiliate; and

(B) a Bell operating company shall not carry out any promotion, marketing, sales, or advertising for or in conjunction with an affiliate that is related to the provision of electronic publishing.

(2) PERMISSIBLE JOINT ACTIVITIES-

(A) JOINT TELEMARKETING- A Bell operating company may provide inbound telemarketing or referral services related to the provision of electronic publishing for a separated affiliate, electronic publishing joint venture, affiliate, or unaffiliated electronic publisher: [Italic->] P rovided, [<-Italic] That if such services are provided to a separated affiliate, electronic publishing joint venture, or affiliate, such services shall be made available to all electronic publishers on request, on nondiscriminatory terms.

(B) TEAMING ARRANGEMENTS- A Bell operating company may engage in nondiscriminatory teaming or business arrangements to engage in electronic publishing with any separated affiliate or with any other electronic publisher if (i) the Bell operating company only provides facilities, services, and basic telephone service information as authorized by this section, and (ii) the Bell operating company does not own such teaming or business arrangement.

(C) ELECTRONIC PUBLISHING JOINT VENTURES- A Bell operating company or affiliate may participate on a nonexclusive basis in electronic publishing joint ventures with entities that are not a Bell operating company, affiliate, or separated affiliate to provide electronic publishing services, if the Bell operating company or affiliate has not more than a 50 percent direct or indirect equity interest (or the equivalent thereof) or the right to more than 50 percent of the gross revenues under a revenue sharing or royalty agreement in any electronic publishing joint venture. Officers and employees of a Bell operating company or affiliate participating in an electronic publishing joint venture may not have more than 50 percent of the voting control over the electronic publishing joint venture. In the case of joint ventures with small, local electronic publishers, the Commission for good cause shown may authorize the Bell operating company or affiliate to have a larger equity interest, revenue share, or voting control but not to exceed 80 percent. A Bell operating company participating in an electronic publishing joint venture may provide promotion, marketing, sales, or advertising personnel and services to such joint venture.

(d) BELL OPERATING COMPANY REQUIREMENT- A Bell operating company under common ownership or control with a separated affiliate or electronic publishing joint venture shall provide network access and interconnections for basic telephone service to electronic publishers at just and reasonable rates that are tariffed (so long as rates for such services are subject to regulation) and that are not higher on a per-unit basis than those charged for such services to any other electronic publisher or any separated affiliate engaged in electronic publishing.

(e) PRIVATE RIGHT OF ACTION-

(1) DAMAGES- Any person claiming that any act or practice of any Bell operating company, affiliate, or separated affiliate constitutes a violation of this section may file a complaint with the Commission or bring suit as provided in section 207 of this Act, and such Bell operating company, affiliate, or separated affiliate shall be liable as provided in section 206 of this Act; except that damages may not be awarded for a violation that is discovered by a compliance review as required by subsection (b)(7) of this section and corrected within 90 days.

(2) CEASE AND DESIST ORDERS- In addition to the provisions of paragraph (1), any person claiming that any act or practice of any Bell operating company, affiliate, or separated affiliate constitutes a violation of this section may make application to the Commission for an order to cease and desist such violation or may make application in any district court of the United States of competent jurisdiction for an order enjoining such acts or practices or for an order compelling compliance with such requirement.

(f) SEPARATED AFFILIATE REPORTING REQUIREMENT- Any separated affiliate under this section shall file with the Commission annual reports in a form substantially equivalent to the Form 10-K required by regulations of the Securities and Exchange Commission.

(g) EFFECTIVE DATES-

(1) TRANSITION- Any electronic publishing service being offered to the public by a Bell operating company or affiliate on the date of enactment of the Telecommunications Act of 1996 shall have one year from such date of enactment to comply with the requirements of this section.

(2) SUNSET- The provisions of this section shall not apply to conduct occurring after 4 years after the date of enactment of the Telecommunications Act of 1996.

(h) DEFINITION OF ELECTRONIC PUBLISHING-

(1) IN GENERAL- The term electronic publishing means the dissemination, provision, publication, or sale to an unaffiliated entity or person, of any one or more of the following: news (including sports); entertainment (other than interactive games); business, financial, legal, consumer, or credit materials; editorials, columns, or features; advertising; photos or images; archival or research material; legal notices or public records; scientific, educational,

instructional, technical, professional, trade, or other literary materials; or other like or similar information.

(2) EXCEPTIONS- The term electronic publishing shall not include the following services:

(A) Information access, as that term is defined by the AT&T Consent Decree.

(B) The transmission of information as a common carrier.

(C) The transmission of information as part of a gateway to an information service that does not involve the generation or alteration of the content of information, including data transmission, address translation, protocol conversion, billing management, introductory information content, and navigational systems that enable users to access electronic publishing services, which do not affect the presentation of such electronic publishing services to users.

(D) Voice storage and retrieval services, including voice messaging and electronic mail services.

(E) Data processing or transaction processing services that do not involve the generation or alteration of the content of information.

(F) Electronic billing or advertising of a Bell operating companys regulated telecommunications services.

(G) Language translation or data format conversion.

(H) The provision of information necessary for the management, control, or operation of a telephone company telecommunications system.

(I) The provision of directory assistance that provides names, addresses, and telephone numbers and does not include advertising.

(J) Caller identification services.

(K) Repair and provisioning databases and credit card and billing validation for telephone company operations.

(L) 911-E and other emergency assistance databases.

(M) Any other network service of a type that is like or similar to these network services and that does not involve the generation or alteration of the content of information.

(N) Any upgrades to these network services that do not involve the generation or alteration of the content of information.

(O) Video programming or full motion video entertainment on demand.

(i) ADDITIONAL DEFINITIONS- As used in this section—

(1) The term affiliate means any entity that, directly or indirectly, owns or controls, is owned or controlled by, or is under common ownership or control with, a Bell operating company. Such term shall not include a separated affiliate.

(2) The term basic telephone service means any wireline telephone exchange service, or wireline telephone exchange service facility, provided by a Bell operating company in a telephone exchange area, except that such term does not include—

(A) a competitive wireline telephone exchange service provided in a telephone exchange area where another entity provides a wireline telephone exchange service that was provided on January 1, 1984, or

(B) a commercial mobile service.

(3) The term basic telephone service information means network and customer information of a Bell operating company and other information acquired by a Bell operating company as a result of its engaging in the provision of basic telephone service.

(4) The term control has the meaning that it has in 17 C.F.R. 240.12b-2, the regulations promulgated by the Securities and Exchange Commission pursuant to the Securities Exchange Act of 1934 (15 U.S.C. 78a et seq.) or any successor provision to such section.

(5) The term electronic publishing joint venture means a joint venture owned by a Bell operating company or affiliate that engages in the provision of electronic publishing which is disseminated by means of such Bell operating companys or any of its affiliates basic telephone service.

(6) The term entity means any organization, and includes corporations, partnerships, sole proprietorships, associations, and joint ventures.

(7) The term inbound telemarketing means the marketing of property, goods, or services by telephone to a customer or potential customer who initiated the call.

(8) The term own with respect to an entity means to have a direct or indirect equity interest (or the equivalent thereof) of more than 10 percent of an entity, or the right to more than 10 percent of the gross revenues of an entity under a revenue sharing or royalty agreement.

(9) The term separated affiliate means a corporation under common ownership or control with a Bell operating company that does not own or control a Bell operating company and is not owned or controlled by a Bell operating company and that engages in the provision of electronic publishing which is disseminated by means of such Bell operating companys or any of its affiliates basic telephone service.

(10) The term Bell operating company has the meaning provided in section 3, except that such term includes any entity or corporation that is owned or controlled by such a company (as so defined) but does not include an electronic publishing joint venture owned by such an entity or corporation.

SEC. 275. ALARM MONITORING SERVICES.

(a) DELAYED ENTRY INTO ALARM MONITORING-

(1) PROHIBITION- No Bell operating company or affiliate thereof shall engage in the provision of alarm monitoring services before the date which is 5 years after the date of enactment of the Telecommunications Act of 1996.

(2) EXISTING ACTIVITIES- Paragraph (1) does not prohibit or limit the provision, directly or through an affiliate, of alarm monitoring services by a Bell operating company that was engaged in providing alarm monitoring services as of November 30, 1995, directly or through an affiliate. Such Bell operating company or affiliate may not acquire any equity interest in, or obtain financial control of, any unaffiliated alarm monitoring service entity after November 30, 1995, and until 5 years after the date of enactment of the Telecommunications Act of 1996, except that this sentence shall not prohibit an exchange of customers for the customers of an unaffiliated alarm monitoring service entity.

(b) NONDISCRIMINATION- An incumbent local exchange carrier (as defined in section 251(h)) engaged in the provision of alarm monitoring services shall—

(1) provide nonaffiliated entities, upon reasonable request, with the network services it provides to its own alarm monitoring operations, on nondiscriminatory terms and conditions; and

(2) not subsidize its alarm monitoring services either directly or indirectly from telephone exchange service operations.

(c) EXPEDITED CONSIDERATION OF COMPLAINTS- The Commission shall establish procedures for the receipt and review of complaints concerning violations of subsection (b) or the regulations thereunder that result in material financial harm to a provider of alarm monitoring service. Such procedures shall ensure that the Commission will make a final determination with respect to any such complaint within 120 days after receipt of the complaint. If the complaint contains an appropriate showing that the alleged violation occurred, as determined by the Commission in accordance with such regulations, the Commission shall, within 60 days after receipt of the complaint, order the incumbent local exchange carrier (as defined in section 251(h)) and its affiliates to cease engaging in such violation pending such final determination.

(d) USE OF DATA- A local exchange carrier may not record or use in any fashion the occurrence or contents of calls received by providers of alarm monitoring services for the purposes of marketing such services on behalf of such local exchange carrier, or any other entity. Any regulations necessary to enforce this subsection shall be issued initially within 6 months after the date of enactment of the Telecommunications Act of 1996.

(e) DEFINITION OF ALARM MONITORING SERVICE- The term alarm monitoring service means a service that uses a device located at a residence, place of business, or other fixed premises—

(1) to receive signals from other devices located at or about such premises regarding a possible threat at such premises to life, safety, or property, from burglary, fire, vandalism, bodily injury, or other emergency, and

(2) to transmit a signal regarding such threat by means of transmission facilities of a local exchange carrier or one of its affiliates to a remote monitoring center to alert a person at such center of the need to inform the customer or another person or police, fire, rescue, security, or public safety personnel of such threat, but does not include a service that uses a medical monitoring device attached to an individual for the automatic surveillance of an ongoing medical condition.

SEC. 276. PROVISION OF PAYPHONE SERVICE.

(a) NONDISCRIMINATION SAFEGUARDS- After the effective date of the rules prescribed pursuant to subsection (b), any Bell operating company that provides payphone service—

(1) shall not subsidize its payphone service directly or indirectly from its telephone exchange service operations or its exchange access operations; and

(2) shall not prefer or discriminate in favor of its payphone service.

(b) REGULATIONS-

(1) CONTENTS OF REGULATIONS- In order to promote competition among payphone service providers and promote the widespread deployment of payphone services to the benefit of the general public, within 9 months after the date of enactment of the Telecommunications Act of 1996, the Commission shall take all actions necessary (including any reconsideration) to prescribe regulations that—

(A) establish a per call compensation plan to ensure that all payphone service providers are fairly compensated for each and every completed intrastate and interstate call using their payphone, except that emergency calls and telecommunications relay service calls for hearing disabled individuals shall not be subject to such compensation;

(B) discontinue the intrastate and interstate carrier access charge payphone service elements and payments in effect on such date of enactment, and all intrastate and interstate payphone subsidies from basic exchange and exchange access revenues, in favor of a compensation plan as specified in subparagraph (A);

(C) prescribe a set of nonstructural safeguards for Bell operating company payphone service to implement the provisions of paragraphs (1) and (2) of subsection (a), which safeguards shall, at a minimum, include the nonstructural safeguards equal to those adopted in the Computer Inquiry-III (CC Docket No. 90-623) proceeding;

(D) provide for Bell operating company payphone service providers to have the same right that independent payphone providers have to negotiate with the location provider on the location providers selecting and contracting with, and, subject to the terms of any agreement with the location provider, to select and contract with, the carriers that carry interLATA calls from their payphones, unless the Commission determines in the rulemaking pursuant to this section that it is not in the public interest; and

(E) provide for all payphone service providers to have the right to negotiate with the location provider on the location providers selecting and contracting with, and, subject to the terms of any agreement with the location provider, to select and contract with, the carriers that carry intraLATA calls from their payphones.

(2) PUBLIC INTEREST TELEPHONES- In the rulemaking conducted pursuant to paragraph (1), the Commission shall determine whether public interest payphones, which are provided in the interest of public health, safety, and welfare, in locations where there would otherwise not be a payphone, should be maintained, and if so, ensure that such public interest payphones are supported fairly and equitably.

(3) EXISTING CONTRACTS- Nothing in this section shall affect any existing contracts between location providers and payphone service providers or interLATA or intraLATA carriers that are in force and effect as of the date of enactment of the Telecommunications Act of 1996.

(c) STATE PREEMPTION- To the extent that any State requirements are inconsistent with the Commissions regulations, the Commissions regulations on such matters shall preempt such State requirements.

(d) DEFINITION- As used in this section, the term payphone service means the provision of public or semi-public pay telephones, the provision of inmate telephone service in correctional institutions, and any ancillary services..

(b) REVIEW OF ENTRY DECISIONS- Section 402(b) (47 U.S.C. 402(b)) is amended—

(1) in paragraph (6), by striking (3), and (4) and inserting (3), (4), and (9); and

(2) by adding at the end the following new paragraph: (9) By any applicant for authority to provide interLATA services under section 271 of this Act whose application is denied by the Commission..

TITLE II--BROADCAST SERVICES

SEC. 201. BROADCAST SPECTRUM FLEXIBILITY.

Title III is amended by inserting after section 335 (47 U.S.C. 335) the following new section: SEC. 336. BROADCAST SPECTRUM FLEXIBILITY.

(a) COMMISSION ACTION- If the Commission determines to issue additional licenses for advanced television services, the Commission—

(1) should limit the initial eligibility for such licenses to persons that, as of the date of such issuance, are licensed to operate a television broadcast station or hold a permit to construct such a station (or both); and

(2) shall adopt regulations that allow the holders of such licenses to offer such ancillary or supplementary services on designated frequencies as may be consistent with the public interest, convenience, and necessity.

(b) CONTENTS OF REGULATIONS- In prescribing the regulations required by subsection (a), the Commission shall—

(1) only permit such licensee or permittee to offer ancillary or supplementary services if the use of a designated frequency for such services is consistent with the technology or method designated by the Commission for the provision of advanced television services;

(2) limit the broadcasting of ancillary or supplementary services on designated frequencies so as to avoid derogation of any advanced television services, including high definition television broadcasts, that the Commission may require using such frequencies;

(3) apply to any other ancillary or supplementary service such of the Commissions regulations as are applicable to the offering of analogous services by any other person, except that no ancillary or supplementary service shall have any rights to carriage under section 614 or 615 or be deemed a multichannel video programming distributor for purposes of section 628;

(4) adopt such technical and other requirements as may be necessary or appropriate to assure the quality of the signal used to provide advanced television services, and may adopt regulations that stipulate the minimum number of hours per day that such signal must be transmitted; and

(5) prescribe such other regulations as may be necessary for the protection of the public interest, convenience, and necessity.

(c) RECOVERY OF LICENSE- If the Commission grants a license for advanced television services to a person that, as of the date of such issuance, is licensed to operate a television broadcast station or holds a permit to construct such a station (or both), the Commission shall, as a condition of such license, require that either the additional license or the original license held by the licensee be surrendered to the Commission for reallocation or reassignment (or both) pursuant to Commission regulation.

(d) PUBLIC INTEREST REQUIREMENT- Nothing in this section shall be construed as relieving a television broadcasting station from its obligation to serve the public interest, convenience, and necessity. In the Commissions review of any application for renewal of a broadcast license for a television station that provides ancillary or supplementary services, the television licensee shall establish that all of its program services on the existing or advanced television spectrum are in the public interest. Any violation of the Commission rules applicable to ancillary or supplementary services shall reflect upon the licensees qualifications for renewal of its license.

(e) FEES-

(1) SERVICES TO WHICH FEES APPLY- If the regulations prescribed pursuant to subsection (a) permit a licensee to offer ancillary or supplementary services on a designated frequency—

(A) for which the payment of a subscription fee is required in order to receive such services, or

(B) for which the licensee directly or indirectly receives compensation from a third party in return for transmitting material furnished by such third party (other than commercial advertisements used to support broadcasting for which a subscription fee is not required), the Commission shall establish a program to assess and collect from the licensee for such designated frequency an annual fee or other schedule or method of payment that promotes the objectives described in subparagraphs (A) and (B) of paragraph (2).

(2) COLLECTION OF FEES- The program required by paragraph (1) shall—

(A) be designed (i) to recover for the public a portion of the value of the public spectrum resource made available for such commercial use, and (ii) to avoid unjust enrichment through the method employed to permit such uses of that resource;

(B) recover for the public an amount that, to the extent feasible, equals but does not exceed (over the term of the license) the amount that would have been recovered had such services been licensed pursuant to the provisions of section 309(j) of this Act and the Commissions regulations thereunder; and

(C) be adjusted by the Commission from time to time in order to continue to comply with the requirements of this paragraph.

(3) TREATMENT OF REVENUES-

(A) GENERAL RULE- Except as provided in subparagraph (B), all proceeds obtained pursuant to the regulations required by this subsection shall be deposited in the Treasury in accordance with chapter 33 of title 31, United States Code.

(B) RETENTION OF REVENUES- Notwithstanding subparagraph (A), the salaries and expenses account of the Commission shall retain as an offsetting collection such sums as may be necessary from such proceeds for the costs of developing and implementing the program required by this section and regulating and supervising advanced television services. Such offsetting collections shall be available for obligation subject to the terms and conditions of the receiving appropriations account, and shall be deposited in such accounts on a quarterly basis.

(4) REPORT- Within 5 years after the date of enactment of the Telecommunications Act of 1996, the Commission shall report to the Congress on the implementation of the program required by this subsection, and shall annually thereafter advise the Congress on the amounts collected pursuant to such program.

(f) EVALUATION- Within 10 years after the date the Commission first issues additional licenses for advanced television services, the Commission shall conduct an evaluation of the advanced television services program. Such evaluation shall include—

(1) an assessment of the willingness of consumers to purchase the television receivers necessary to receive broadcasts of advanced television services;

(2) an assessment of alternative uses, including public safety use, of the frequencies used for such broadcasts; and

(3) the extent to which the Commission has been or will be able to reduce the amount of spectrum assigned to licensees.

(g) DEFINITIONS- As used in this section:

(1) ADVANCED TELEVISION SERVICES- The term advanced television services means television services provided using digital or other advanced technology as further defined in the opinion, report, and order of the Commission entitled Advanced Television

Systems and Their Impact Upon the Existing Television Broadcast Service, MM Docket 87-268, adopted September 17, 1992, and successor proceedings.

(2) DESIGNATED FREQUENCIES- The term designated frequency means each of the frequencies designated by the Commission for licenses for advanced television services.

(3) HIGH DEFINITION TELEVISION- The term high definition television refers to systems that offer approximately twice the vertical and horizontal resolution of receivers generally available on the date of enactment of the Telecommunications Act of 1996, as further defined in the proceedings described in paragraph (1) of this subsection..

SEC. 202. BROADCAST OWNERSHIP.

(a) NATIONAL RADIO STATION OWNERSHIP RULE CHANGES REQUIRED- The Commission shall modify section 73.3555 of its regulations (47 C.F.R. 73.3555) by eliminating any provisions limiting the number of AM or FM broadcast stations which may be owned or controlled by one entity nationally.

(b) LOCAL RADIO DIVERSITY-

(1) APPLICABLE CAPS- The Commission shall revise section 73.3555(a) of its regulations (47 C.F.R. 73.3555) to provide that—

(A) in a radio market with 45 or more commercial radio stations, a party may own, operate, or control up to 8 commercial radio stations, not more than 5 of which are in the same service (AM or FM);

(B) in a radio market with between 30 and 44 (inclusive) commercial radio stations, a party may own, operate, or control up to 7 commercial radio stations, not more than 4 of which are in the same service (AM or FM);

(C) in a radio market with between 15 and 29 (inclusive) commercial radio stations, a party may own, operate, or control up to 6 commercial radio stations, not more than 4 of which are in the same service (AM or FM); and

(D) in a radio market with 14 or fewer commercial radio stations, a party may own, operate, or control up to 5 commercial radio stations, not more than 3 of which are in the same service (AM or FM), except that a party may not own, operate, or control more than 50 percent of the stations in such market.

(2) EXCEPTION- Notwithstanding any limitation authorized by this subsection, the Commission may permit a person or entity to own, operate, or control, or have a cognizable interest in, radio broadcast stations if the Commission determines that such ownership, operation, control, or interest will result in an increase in the number of radio broadcast stations in operation.

(c) TELEVISION OWNERSHIP LIMITATIONS-

(1) NATIONAL OWNERSHIP LIMITATIONS- The Commission shall modify its rules for multiple ownership set forth in section 73.3555 of its regulations (47 C.F.R. 73.3555)—

(A) by eliminating the restrictions on the number of television stations that a person or entity may directly or indirectly own, operate, or control, or have a cognizable interest in, nationwide; and

(B) by increasing the national audience reach limitation for television stations to 35 percent.

(2) LOCAL OWNERSHIP LIMITATIONS- The Commission shall conduct a rulemaking proceeding to determine whether to retain, modify, or eliminate its limitations on the number of television stations that a person or entity may own, operate, or control, or have a cognizable interest in, within the same television market.

(d) RELAXATION OF ONE-TO-A-MARKET- With respect to its enforcement of its one-to-a-market ownership rules under section 73.3555 of its regulations, the Commission shall extend its waiver policy to any of the top 50 markets, consistent with the public interest, convenience, and necessity.

(e) DUAL NETWORK CHANGES- The Commission shall revise section 73.658(g) of its regulations (47 C.F.R. 658(g)) to permit a television broadcast station to affiliate with a person or entity that maintains 2 or more networks of television broadcast stations unless such dual or multiple networks are composed of—

(1) two or more persons or entities that, on the date of enactment of the Telecommunications Act of 1996, are networks as defined in section 73.3613(a)(1) of the Commissions regulations (47 C.F.R. 73.3613(a)(1)); or

(2) any network described in paragraph (1) and an English-language program distribution service that, on such date, provides 4 or more hours of programming per week on a national basis pursuant to network affiliation arrangements with local television broadcast stations in markets reaching more than 75 percent of television homes (as measured by a national ratings service).

(f) CABLE CROSS OWNERSHIP-

(1) ELIMINATION OF RESTRICTIONS- The Commission shall revise section 76.501 of its regulations (47 C.F.R. 76.501) to permit a person or entity to own or control a network of broadcast stations and a cable system.

(2) SAFEGUARDS AGAINST DISCRIMINATION- The Commission shall revise such regulations if necessary to ensure carriage, channel positioning, and nondiscriminatory treatment of nonaffiliated broadcast stations by a cable system described in paragraph (1).

(g) LOCAL MARKETING AGREEMENTS- Nothing in this section shall be construed to prohibit the origination, continuation, or renewal of any television local marketing agreement that is in compliance with the regulations of the Commission.

(h) FURTHER COMMISSION REVIEW- The Commission shall review its rules adopted pursuant to this section and all of its ownership rules biennially as part of its regulatory reform review under section 11 of the Communications Act of 1934 and shall determine whether any of such rules are necessary in the public interest as the result of competition. The Commission shall repeal or modify any regulation it determines to be no longer in the public interest.

(i) ELIMINATION OF STATUTORY RESTRICTION- Section 613(a) (47 U.S.C. 533(a)) is amended—

(1) by striking paragraph (1);

(2) by redesignating paragraph (2) as subsection (a);

(3) by redesignating subparagraphs (A) and (B) as paragraphs (1) and (2), respectively;

(4) by striking and at the end of paragraph (1) (as so redesignated);

(5) by striking the period at the end of paragraph (2) (as so redesignated) and inserting ; and; and

(6) by adding at the end the following new paragraph:

(3) shall not apply the requirements of this subsection to any cable operator in any franchise area in which a cable operator is subject to effective competition as determined under section 623(l)..

SEC. 203. TERM OF LICENSES.

Section 307(c) (47 U.S.C. 307(c)) is amended to read as follows:

(c) TERMS OF LICENSES-

(1) INITIAL AND RENEWAL LICENSES- Each license granted for the operation of a broadcasting station shall be for a term of not to exceed 8 years. Upon application therefor, a renewal of such license may be granted from time to time for a term of not to exceed 8 years from the date of expiration of the preceding license, if the Commission finds that public interest, convenience, and necessity would be served thereby. Consistent with the foregoing provisions of this subsection, the Commission may by rule prescribe the period or periods for which licenses shall be granted and renewed for particular classes of stations, but the Commission may not adopt or follow any rule which would preclude it, in any case involving a station of a particular class, from granting or renewing a license for a shorter period than that prescribed for stations of such class if, in its judgment, the public interest, convenience, or necessity would be served by such action.

(2) MATERIALS IN APPLICATION- In order to expedite action on applications for renewal of broadcasting station licenses and in order to avoid needless expense to applicants for such renewals, the Commission shall not require any such applicant to file any information which previously has been furnished to the Commission or which is not directly material to the considerations that affect the granting or denial of such application, but the Commission may require any new or additional facts it deems necessary to make its findings.

(3) CONTINUATION PENDING DECISION- Pending any hearing and final decision on such an application and the disposition of any petition for rehearing pursuant to section 405, the Commission shall continue such license in effect.

SEC. 204. BROADCAST LICENSE RENEWAL PROCEDURES.

(a) RENEWAL PROCEDURES-

(1) AMENDMENT- Section 309 (47 U.S.C. 309) is amended by adding at the end thereof the following new subsection:

(k) BROADCAST STATION RENEWAL PROCEDURES-

(1) STANDARDS FOR RENEWAL- If the licensee of a broadcast station submits an application to the Commission for renewal of such license, the Commission shall grant the application if it finds, with respect to that station, during the preceding term of its license—

(A) the station has served the public interest, convenience, and necessity;

(B) there have been no serious violations by the licensee of this Act or the rules and regulations of the Commission; and

(C) there have been no other violations by the licensee of this Act or the rules and regulations of the Commission which, taken together, would constitute a pattern of abuse.

(2) CONSEQUENCE OF FAILURE TO MEET STANDARD- If any licensee of a broadcast station fails to meet the requirements of this subsection, the Commission may deny the application for renewal in accordance with paragraph (3), or grant such application on terms and conditions as are appropriate, including renewal for a term less than the maximum otherwise permitted.

(3) STANDARDS FOR DENIAL- If the Commission determines, after notice and opportunity for a hearing as provided in subsection (e), that a licensee has failed to meet the requirements specified in paragraph (1) and that no mitigating factors justify the imposition of lesser sanctions, the Commission shall—

(A) issue an order denying the renewal application filed by such licensee under section 308; and

(B) only thereafter accept and consider such applications for a construction permit as may be filed under section 308 specifying the channel or broadcasting facilities of the former licensee.

(4) COMPETITOR CONSIDERATION PROHIBITED- In making the determinations specified in paragraph (1) or (2), the Commission shall not consider whether the public interest, convenience, and necessity might be served by the grant of a license to a person other than the renewal applicant..

(2) CONFORMING AMENDMENT- Section 309(d) (47 U.S.C. 309(d)) is amended by inserting after with subsection (a) each place it appears the following: (or subsection (k) in the case of renewal of any broadcast station license).

(b) SUMMARY OF COMPLAINTS ON VIOLENT PROGRAMMING- Section 308 (47 U.S.C. 308) is amended by adding at the end the following new subsection: (d) SUMMARY OF COMPLAINTS- Each applicant for the renewal of a commercial or noncommercial television license shall attach as an exhibit to the application a summary of written comments and suggestions received from the public and maintained by the licensee (in accordance with Commission regulations) that comment on the applicants programming, if any, and that are characterized by the commentor as constituting violent programming..

(c) EFFECTIVE DATE- The amendments made by this section apply to applications filed after May 1, 1995. SEC. 205. DIRECT BROADCAST SATELLITE SERVICE.

(a) DBS SIGNAL SECURITY- Section 705(e)(4) (47 U.S.C. 605(e)(4)) is amended by inserting or direct-to-home satellite services, after programming,.

(b) FCC JURISDICTION OVER DIRECT-TO-HOME SATELLITE SERVICES- Section 303 (47 U.S.C. 303) is amended by adding at the end thereof the following new subsection:

(v) Have exclusive jurisdiction to regulate the provision of direct-to-home satellite services. As used in this subsection, the term direct-to-home satellite services means the distribution or broadcasting of programming or services by satellite directly to the subscribers premises without the use of ground receiving or distribution equipment, except at the subscribers premises or in the uplink process to the satellite.

SEC. 206. AUTOMATED SHIP DISTRESS AND SAFETY SYSTEMS.

Part II of title III is amended by inserting after section 364 (47 U.S.C. 362) the following new section: SEC. 365. AUTOMATED SHIP DISTRESS AND SAFETY SYSTEMS.

Notwithstanding any provision of this Act or any other provision of law or regulation, a ship documented under the laws of the United States operating in accordance with the Global Maritime Distress and Safety System provisions of the Safety of Life at Sea Convention shall not be required to be equipped with a radio telegraphy station operated by one or more radio officers or operators. This section shall take effect for each vessel upon a determination by the United States Coast Guard that such vessel has the equipment required to implement the Global Maritime Distress and Safety System installed and operating in good working condition.

SEC. 207. RESTRICTIONS ON OVER-THE-AIR RECEPTION DEVICES.

Within 180 days after the date of enactment of this Act, the Commission shall, pursuant to section 303 of the Communications Act of 1934, promulgate regulations to prohibit restrictions that impair a viewers ability to receive video programming services through devices designed for over-the-air reception of television broadcast signals, multichannel multipoint distribution service, or direct broadcast satellite services.

TITLE III--CABLE SERVICES

SEC. 301. CABLE ACT REFORM.

(a) DEFINITIONS-

(1) DEFINITION OF CABLE SERVICE- Section 602(6)(B) (47 U.S.C. 522(6)(B)) is amended by inserting or use after the selection.

(2) CHANGE IN DEFINITION OF CABLE SYSTEM- Section 602(7) (47 U.S.C. 522(7)) is amended by striking (B) a facility that serves only subscribers in 1 or more multiple unit dwellings under common ownership, control, or management, unless such facility or facilities uses any public right-of-way; and inserting (B) a facility that serves subscribers without using any public right-of-way;.

(b) RATE DEREGULATION-

(1) UPPER TIER REGULATION- Section 623(c) (47 U.S.C. 543(c)) is amended—

(A) in paragraph (1)(B), by striking subscriber, franchising authority, or other relevant State or local government entity and inserting franchising authority (in accordance with paragraph (3));

(B) in paragraph (1)(C), by striking such complaint and inserting the first complaint filed with the franchising authority under paragraph (3); and

(C) by striking paragraph (3) and inserting the following:

(3) REVIEW OF RATE CHANGES- The Commission shall review any complaint submitted by a franchising authority after the date of enactment of the Telecommunications Act of 1996 concerning an increase in rates for cable programming services and issue a final order within 90 days after it receives such a complaint, unless the parties agree to extend the period for such review. A franchising authority may not file a complaint under this paragraph unless, within 90 days after such increase becomes effective it receives subscriber complaints.

(4) SUNSET OF UPPER TIER RATE REGULATION- This subsection shall not apply to cable programming services provided after March 31, 1999..

(2) SUNSET OF UNIFORM RATE STRUCTURE IN MARKETS WITH EFFECTIVE COMPETITION- Section 623(d) (47 U.S.C. 543(d)) is amended by adding at the end thereof the following: This subsection does not apply to (1) a cable operator with respect to the provision of cable service over its cable system in any geographic area in which the video programming services offered by the operator in that area are subject to effective competition, or (2) any video programming offered on a per channel or per program basis. Bulk discounts to multiple dwelling units shall not be subject to this subsection, except that a cable operator of a cable system that is not subject to effective competition may not charge predatory prices to a multiple dwelling unit. Upon a prima facie showing by a complainant that there are

reasonable grounds to believe that the discounted price is predatory, the cable system shall have the burden of showing that its discounted price is not predatory..

(3) EFFECTIVE COMPETITION- Section 623(l)(1) (47 U.S.C. 543(l)(1)) is amended—

(A) by striking or at the end of subparagraph (B);

(B) by striking the period at the end of subparagraph (C) and inserting ; or; and

(C) by adding at the end the following:

(D) a local exchange carrier or its affiliate (or any multichannel video programming distributor using the facilities of such carrier or its affiliate) offers video programming services directly to subscribers by any means (other than direct-to-home satellite services) in the franchise area of an unaffiliated cable operator which is providing cable service in that franchise area, but only if the video programming services so offered in that area are comparable to the video programming services provided by the unaffiliated cable operator in that area..

(c) GREATER DEREGULATION FOR SMALLER CABLE COMPANIES- Section 623 (47 U.S.C 543) is amended by adding at the end thereof the following:

(m) SPECIAL RULES FOR SMALL COMPANIES-

(1) IN GENERAL- Subsections (a), (b), and (c) do not apply to a small cable operator with respect to—

(A) cable programming services, or

(B) a basic service tier that was the only service tier subject to regulation as of December 31, 1994, in any franchise area in which that operator services 50,000 or fewer subscribers.

(2) DEFINITION OF SMALL CABLE OPERATOR- For purposes of this subsection, the term small cable operator means a cable operator that, directly or through an affiliate, serves in the aggregate fewer than 1 percent of all subscribers in the United States and is not affiliated with any entity or entities whose gross annual revenues in the aggregate exceed $250,000,000..

(d) MARKET DETERMINATIONS-

(1) MARKET DETERMINATIONS; EXPEDITED DECISIONMAKING- Section 614(h)(1)(C) (47 U.S.C. 534(h)(1)(C)) is amended—

(A) by striking in the manner provided in section 73.3555(d)(3)(i) of title 47, Code of Federal Regulations, as in effect on May 1, 1991, in clause (i) and inserting by the Commission by regulation or order using, where available, commercial publications which delineate television markets based on viewing patterns,; and

(B) by striking clause (iv) and inserting the following:

(iv) Within 120 days after the date on which a request is filed under this subparagraph (or 120 days after the date of enactment of the Telecommunications Act of 1996, if later), the Commission shall grant or deny the request..

(2) APPLICATION TO PENDING REQUESTS- The amendment made by paragraph (1) shall apply to—

(A) any request pending under section 614(h)(1)(C) of the Communications Act of 1934 (47 U.S.C. 534(h)(1)(C)) on the date of enactment of this Act; and

(B) any request filed under that section after that date.

(e) TECHNICAL STANDARDS- Section 624(e) (47 U.S.C. 544(e)) is amended by striking the last two sentences and inserting the following: No State or franchising authority may prohibit, condition, or restrict a cable systems use of any type of subscriber equipment or any transmission technology..

(f) CABLE EQUIPMENT COMPATIBILITY- Section 624A (47 U.S.C. 544A) is amended—

(1) in subsection (a) by striking and at the end of paragraph (2), by striking the period at the end of paragraph (3) and inserting ; and; and by adding at the end the following new paragraph:

(4) compatibility among televisions, video cassette recorders, and cable systems can be assured with narrow technical standards that mandate a minimum degree of common design and operation, leaving all features, functions, protocols, and other product and service options for selection through open competition in the market.;

(2) in subsection (c)(1)—

(A) by redesignating subparagraphs (A) and (B) as subparagraphs (B) and (C), respectively; and

(B) by inserting before such redesignated subparagraph

(B) the following new subparagraph:

(A) the need to maximize open competition in the market for all features, functions, protocols, and other product and service options of converter boxes and other cable converters unrelated to the descrambling or decryption of cable television signals;; and

(3) in subsection (c)(2)—

(A) by redesignating subparagraphs (D) and (E) as subparagraphs (E) and (F), respectively; and

(B) by inserting after subparagraph (C) the following new subparagraph:

(D) to ensure that any standards or regulations developed under the authority of this section to ensure compatibility between televisions, video cassette recorders, and cable systems do not affect features, functions, protocols, and other product and service options other than those specified in paragraph (1)(B), including telecommunications interface equipment, home automation communications, and computer network services;.

(g) SUBSCRIBER NOTICE- Section 632 (47 U.S.C. 552) is amended—

(1) by redesignating subsection (c) as subsection (d); and

(2) by inserting after subsection (b) the following new subsection:

(c) SUBSCRIBER NOTICE- A cable operator may provide notice of service and rate changes to subscribers using any reasonable written means at its sole discretion. Notwithstanding section 623(b)(6) or any other provision of this Act, a cable operator shall not be required to provide prior notice of any rate change that is the result of a regulatory fee, franchise fee, or any other fee, tax, assessment, or charge of any kind imposed by any Federal agency, State, or franchising authority on the transaction between the operator and the subscriber..

(h) PROGRAM ACCESS- Section 628 (47 U.S.C. 548) is amended by adding at the end the following:

(j) COMMON CARRIERS- Any provision that applies to a cable operator under this section shall apply to a common carrier or its affiliate that provides video programming by any means directly to subscribers. Any such provision that applies to a satellite cable programming vendor in which a cable operator has an attributable interest shall apply to any satellite cable programming vendor in which such common carrier has an attributable interest. For the purposes of this subsection, two or fewer common officers or directors shall not by itself establish an attributable interest by a common carrier in a satellite cable programming vendor (or its parent company)..

(i) ANTITRAFFICKING- Section 617 (47 U.S.C. 537) is amended—

(1) by striking subsections (a) through (d); and

(2) in subsection (e), by striking (e) and all that follows through a franchising authority and inserting A franchising authority.

(j) AGGREGATION OF EQUIPMENT COSTS- Section 623(a) (47 U.S.C. 543(a)) is amended by adding at the end the following new paragraph:

(7) AGGREGATION OF EQUIPMENT COSTS-

(A) IN GENERAL- The Commission shall allow cable operators, pursuant to any rules promulgated under subsection (b)(3), to aggregate, on a franchise, system, regional, or company level, their equipment costs into broad categories, such as converter boxes, regardless of the varying levels of functionality of the equipment within each such broad category. Such aggregation shall not be permitted with respect to equipment used by subscribers who receive only a rate regulated basic service tier.

(B) REVISION TO COMMISSION RULES; FORMS- Within 120 days of the date of enactment of the Telecommunications Act of 1996, the Commission shall issue revisions to the appropriate rules and forms necessary to implement subparagraph (A)..

(k) TREATMENT OF PRIOR YEAR LOSSES-

(1) AMENDMENT- Section 623 (48 U.S.C. 543) is amended by adding at the end thereof the following:

(n) TREATMENT OF PRIOR YEAR LOSSES- Notwithstanding any other provision of this section or of section 612, losses associated with a cable system (including losses associated with the grant or award of a franchise) that were incurred prior to September 4, 1992, with respect to a cable system that is owned and operated by the original franchisee of such system shall not be disallowed, in whole or in part, in the determination of whether the rates for any tier of service or any type of equipment that is subject to regulation under this section are lawful..

(2) EFFECTIVE DATE- The amendment made by paragraph (1) shall take effect on the date of enactment of this Act and shall be applicable to any rate proposal filed on or after September 4, 1993, upon which no final action has been taken by December 1, 1995.

SEC. 302. CABLE SERVICE PROVIDED BY TELEPHONE COMPANIES.

(a) PROVISIONS FOR REGULATION OF CABLE SERVICE PROVIDED BY TELEPHONE COMPANIES- Title VI (47 U.S.C. 521 et seq.) is amended by adding at the end the following new part:

PART V--VIDEO PROGRAMMING SERVICES PROVIDED BY TELEPHONE COMPANIES

SEC. 651. REGULATORY TREATMENT OF VIDEO PROGRAMMING SERVICES.

(a) LIMITATIONS ON CABLE REGULATION-

(1) RADIO-BASED SYSTEMS- To the extent that a common carrier (or any other person) is providing video programming to subscribers using radio communication, such carrier (or other person) shall be subject to the requirements of title III and section 652, but shall not otherwise be subject to the requirements of this title.

(2) COMMON CARRIAGE OF VIDEO TRAFFIC- To the extent that a common carrier is providing transmission of video programming on a common carrier basis, such carrier shall be subject to the requirements of title II and section 652, but shall not otherwise be subject to the requirements of this title. This paragraph shall not affect the treatment under section 602(7)(C) of a facility of a common carrier as a cable system.

(3) CABLE SYSTEMS AND OPEN VIDEO SYSTEMS- To the extent that a common carrier is providing video programming to its subscribers in any manner other than that described in paragraphs (1) and (2)—

(A) such carrier shall be subject to the requirements of this title, unless such programming is provided by means of an open video system for which the Commission has approved a certification under section 653; or

(B) if such programming is provided by means of an open video system for which the Commission has approved a certification under section 653, such carrier shall be subject to the requirements of this part, but shall be subject to parts I through IV of this title only as provided in 653(c).

(4) ELECTION TO OPERATE AS OPEN VIDEO SYSTEM- A common carrier that is providing video programming in a manner described in paragraph (1) or (2), or a combination thereof, may elect to provide such programming by means of an open video system that complies with section 653. If the Commission approves such carriers certification under section 653, such carrier shall be subject to the requirements of this part, but shall be subject to parts I through IV of this title only as provided in 653(c).

(b) LIMITATIONS ON INTERCONNECTION OBLIGATIONS- A local exchange carrier that provides cable service through an open video system or a cable system shall not be required, pursuant to title II of this Act, to make capacity available on a nondiscriminatory basis to any other person for the provision of cable service directly to subscribers.

(c) ADDITIONAL REGULATORY RELIEF- A common carrier shall not be required to obtain a certificate under section 214 with respect to the establishment or operation of a system for the delivery of video programming. SEC. 652. PROHIBITION ON BUY OUTS.

(a) ACQUISITIONS BY CARRIERS- No local exchange carrier or any affiliate of such carrier owned by, operated by, controlled by, or under common control with such carrier may purchase or otherwise acquire directly or indirectly more than a 10 percent financial interest, or any management interest, in any cable operator providing cable service within the local exchange carriers telephone service area.

(b) ACQUISITIONS BY CABLE OPERATORS- No cable operator or affiliate of a cable operator that is owned by, operated by, controlled by, or under common ownership with such cable operator may purchase or otherwise acquire, directly or indirectly, more than a 10 percent financial interest, or any management interest, in any local exchange carrier providing telephone exchange service within such cable operators franchise area.

(c) JOINT VENTURES- A local exchange carrier and a cable operator whose telephone service area and cable franchise area, respectively, are in the same market may not enter into any joint venture or partnership to provide video programming directly to subscribers or to provide telecommunications services within such market.

(d) EXCEPTIONS-

(1) RURAL SYSTEMS- Notwithstanding subsections (a), (b), and (c) of this section, a local exchange carrier (with respect to a cable system located in its telephone service area) and a cable operator (with respect to the facilities of a local exchange carrier used to provide

telephone exchange service in its cable franchise area) may obtain a controlling interest in, management interest in, or enter into a joint venture or partnership with the operator of such system or facilities for the use of such system or facilities to the extent that—

(A) such system or facilities only serve incorporated or unincorporated—

(i) places or territories that have fewer than 35,000 inhabitants; and

(ii) are outside an urbanized area, as defined by the Bureau of the Census; and

(B) in the case of a local exchange carrier, such system, in the aggregate with any other system in which such carrier has an interest, serves less than 10 percent of the households in the telephone service area of such carrier.

(2) JOINT USE- Notwithstanding subsection (c), a local exchange carrier may obtain, with the concurrence of the cable operator on the rates, terms, and conditions, the use of that part of the transmission facilities of a cable system extending from the last multi-user terminal to the premises of the end user, if such use is reasonably limited in scope and duration, as determined by the Commission.

(3) ACQUISITIONS IN COMPETITIVE MARKETS- Notwithstanding subsections (a) and (c), a local exchange carrier may obtain a controlling interest in, or form a joint venture or other partnership with, or provide financing to, a cable system (hereinafter in this paragraph referred to as the subject cable system), if—

(A) the subject cable system operates in a television market that is not in the top 25 markets, and such market has more than 1 cable system operator, and the subject cable system is not the cable system with the most subscribers in such television market;

(B) the subject cable system and the cable system with the most subscribers in such television market held on May 1, 1995, cable television franchises from the largest municipality in the television market and the boundaries of such franchises were identical on such date;

(C) the subject cable system is not owned by or under common ownership or control of any one of the 50 cable system operators with the most subscribers as such operators existed on May 1, 1995; and

(D) the system with the most subscribers in the television market is owned by or under common ownership or control of any one of the 10 largest cable system operators as such operators existed on May 1, 1995. (4) EXEMPT CABLE SYSTEMS- Subsection (a) does not apply to any cable system if—

(A) the cable system serves no more than 17,000 cable subscribers, of which no less than 8,000 live within an urban area, and no less than 6,000 live within a nonurbanized area as of June 1, 1995;

(B) the cable system is not owned by, or under common ownership or control with, any of the 50 largest cable system operators in existence on June 1, 1995; and

(C) the cable system operates in a television market that was not in the top 100 television markets as of June 1, 1995.

(5) SMALL CABLE SYSTEMS IN NONURBAN AREAS- Notwithstanding subsections (a) and (c), a local exchange carrier with less than $100,000,000 in annual operating revenues (or any affiliate of such carrier owned by, operated by, controlled by, or under common control with such carrier) may purchase or otherwise acquire more than a 10 percent financial interest in, or any management interest in, or enter into a joint venture or partnership with, any cable system within the local exchange carriers telephone service area that serves no

more than 20,000 cable subscribers, if no more than 12,000 of those subscribers live within an urbanized area, as defined by the Bureau of the Census.

(6) WAIVERS- The Commission may waive the restrictions of subsections (a), (b), or (c) only if—

(A) the Commission determines that, because of the nature of the market served by the affected cable system or facilities used to provide telephone exchange service—

(i) the affected cable operator or local exchange carrier would be subjected to undue economic distress by the enforcement of such provisions;

(ii) the system or facilities would not be economically viable if such provisions were enforced; or

(iii) the anticompetitive effects of the proposed transaction are clearly outweighed in the public interest by the probable effect of the transaction in meeting the convenience and needs of the community to be served; and

(B) the local franchising authority approves of such waiver.

(e) DEFINITION OF TELEPHONE SERVICE AREA- For purposes of this section, the term telephone service area when used in connection with a common carrier subject in whole or in part to title II of this Act means the area within which such carrier provided telephone exchange service as of January 1, 1993, but if any common carrier after such date transfers its telephone exchange service facilities to another common carrier, the area to which such facilities provide telephone exchange service shall be treated as part of the telephone service area of the acquiring common carrier and not of the selling common carrier.

SEC. 653. ESTABLISHMENT OF OPEN VIDEO SYSTEMS.

(a) OPEN VIDEO SYSTEMS-

(1) CERTIFICATES OF COMPLIANCE- A local exchange carrier may provide cable service to its cable service subscribers in its telephone service area through an open video system that complies with this section. To the extent permitted by such regulations as the Commission may prescribe consistent with the public interest, convenience, and necessity, an operator of a cable system or any other person may provide video programming through an open video system that complies with this section. An operator of an open video system shall qualify for reduced regulatory burdens under subsection (c) of this section if the operator of such system certifies to the Commission that such carrier complies with the Commissions regulations under subsection (b) and the Commission approves such certification. The Commission shall publish notice of the receipt of any such certification and shall act to approve or disapprove any such certification within 10 days after receipt of such certification.

2) DISPUTE RESOLUTION- The Commission shall have the authority to resolve disputes under this section and the regulations prescribed thereunder. Any such dispute shall be resolved within 180 days after notice of such dispute is submitted to the Commission. At that time or subsequently in a separate damages proceeding, the Commission may, in the case of any violation of this section, require carriage, award damages to any person denied carriage, or any combination of such sanctions. Any aggrieved party may seek any other remedy available under this Act.

(b) COMMISSION ACTIONS-

(1) REGULATIONS REQUIRED- Within 6 months after the date of enactment of the Telecommunications Act of 1996, the Commission shall complete all actions necessary (including any reconsideration) to prescribe regulations that—

(A) except as required pursuant to section 611, 614, or 615, prohibit an operator of an open video system from discriminating among video programming providers with regard to carriage on its open video system, and ensure that the rates, terms, and conditions for such carriage are just and reasonable, and are not unjustly or unreasonably discriminatory;

(B) if demand exceeds the channel capacity of the open video system, prohibit an operator of an open video system and its affiliates from selecting the video programming services for carriage on more than one-third of the activated channel capacity on such system, but nothing in this subparagraph shall be construed to limit the number of channels that the carrier and its affiliates may offer to provide directly to subscribers;

(C) permit an operator of an open video system to carry on only one channel any video programming service that is offered by more than one video programming provider (including the local exchange carriers video programming affiliate): [Italic->] Provided, [<-Italic] That subscribers have ready and immediate access to any such video programming service;

(D) extend to the distribution of video programming over open video systems the Commissions regulations concerning sports exclusivity (47 C.F.R. 76.67), network nonduplication (47 C.F.R. 76.92 et seq.), and syndicated exclusivity (47 C.F.R. 76.151 et seq.); and

(E)(i) prohibit an operator of an open video system from unreasonably discriminating in favor of the operator or its affiliates with regard to material or information (including advertising) provided by the operator to subscribers for the purposes of selecting programming on the open video system, or in the way such material or information is presented to subscribers;

(ii) require an operator of an open video system to ensure that video programming providers or copyright holders (or both) are able suitably and uniquely to identify their programming services to subscribers;

(iii) if such identification is transmitted as part of the programming signal, require the carrier to transmit such identification without change or alteration; and

(iv) prohibit an operator of an open video system from omitting television broadcast stations or other unaffiliated video programming services carried on such system from any navigational device, guide, or menu.

(2) CONSUMER ACCESS- Subject to the requirements of paragraph (1) and the regulations thereunder, nothing in this section prohibits a common carrier or its affiliate from negotiating mutually agreeable terms and conditions with over-the-air broadcast stations and other unaffiliated video programming providers to allow consumer access to their signals on any level or screen of any gateway, menu, or other program guide, whether provided by the carrier or its affiliate.

(c) REDUCED REGULATORY BURDENS FOR OPEN VIDEO SYSTEMS-

(1) IN GENERAL- Any provision that applies to a cable operator under—

(A) sections 613 (other than subsection (a) thereof), 616, 623(f), 628, 631, and 634 of this title, shall apply,

(B) sections 611, 614, and 615 of this title, and section 325 of title III, shall apply in accordance with the regulations prescribed under paragraph (2), and

(C) sections 612 and 617, and parts III and IV (other than sections 623(f), 628, 631, and 634), of this title shall not apply, to any operator of an open video system for which the Commission has approved a certification under this section.

(2) IMPLEMENTATION-

(A) COMMISSION ACTION- In the rulemaking proceeding to prescribe the regulations required by subsection (b)(1), the Commission shall, to the extent possible, impose obligations that are no greater or lesser than the obligations contained in the provisions described in paragraph (1)(B) of this subsection. The Commission shall complete all action (including any reconsideration) to prescribe such regulations no later than 6 months after the date of enactment of the Telecommunications Act of 1996.

(B) FEES- An operator of an open video system under this part may be subject to the payment of fees on the gross revenues of the operator for the provision of cable service imposed by a local franchising authority or other governmental entity, in lieu of the franchise fees permitted under section 622. The rate at which such fees are imposed shall not exceed the rate at which franchise fees are imposed on any cable operator transmitting video programming in the franchise area, as determined in accordance with regulations prescribed by the Commission. An operator of an open video system may designate that portion of a subscribers bill attributable to the fee under this subparagraph as a separate item on the bill.

(3) REGULATORY STREAMLINING- With respect to the establishment and operation of an open video system, the requirements of this section shall apply in lieu of, and not in addition to, the requirements of title II.

(4) TREATMENT AS CABLE OPERATOR- Nothing in this Act precludes a video programming provider making use of an open video system from being treated as an operator of a cable system for purposes of section 111 of title 17, United States Code.

(d) DEFINITION OF TELEPHONE SERVICE AREA- For purposes of this section, the term telephone service area when used in connection with a common carrier subject in whole or in part to title II of this Act means the area within which such carrier is offering telephone exchange service..

(b) CONFORMING AND TECHNICAL AMENDMENTS-

(1) REPEAL- Subsection (b) of section 613 (47 U.S.C. 533(b)) is repealed.

(2) DEFINITIONS- Section 602 (47 U.S.C. 531) is amended—

(A) in paragraph (7), by striking , or (D) and inserting the following: , unless the extent of such use is solely to provide interactive on-demand services; (D) an open video system that complies with section 653 of this title; or (E);

(B) by redesignating paragraphs (12) through (19) as paragraphs (13) through (20), respectively; and

(C) by inserting after paragraph (11) the following new paragraph:

(12) the term interactive on-demand services means a service providing video programming to subscribers over switched networks on an on-demand, point-to-point basis, but does not include services providing video programming prescheduled by the programming provider;.

(3) TERMINATION OF VIDEO-DIALTONE REGULATIONS- The Commissions regulations and policies with respect to video dialtone requirements issued in CC Docket No. 87-266 shall cease to be effective on the date of enactment of this Act. This paragraph shall not be construed to require the termination of any video-dialtone system that the Commission has approved before the date of enactment of this Act.

SEC. 303. PREEMPTION OF FRANCHISING AUTHORITY REGULATION OF TELECOMMUNICATIONS SERVICES.

(a) PROVISION OF TELECOMMUNICATIONS SERVICES BY A CABLE OPERATOR- Section 621(b) (47 U.S.C. 541(b)) is amended by adding at the end thereof the following new paragraph:

(3)(A) If a cable operator or affiliate thereof is engaged in the provision of telecommunications services—

(i) such cable operator or affiliate shall not be required to obtain a franchise under this title for the provision of telecommunications services; and

(ii) the provisions of this title shall not apply to such cable operator or affiliate for the provision of telecommunications services.

(B) A franchising authority may not impose any requirement under this title that has the purpose or effect of prohibiting, limiting, restricting, or conditioning the provision of a telecommunications service by a cable operator or an affiliate thereof.

(C) A franchising authority may not order a cable operator or affiliate thereof—

(i) to discontinue the provision of a telecommunications service, or

(ii) to discontinue the operation of a cable system, to the extent such cable system is used for the provision of a telecommunications service, by reason of the failure of such cable operator or affiliate thereof to obtain a franchise or franchise renewal under this title with respect to the provision of such telecommunications service.

(D) Except as otherwise permitted by sections 611 and 612, a franchising authority may not require a cable operator to provide any telecommunications service or facilities, other than institutional networks, as a condition of the initial grant of a franchise, a franchise renewal, or a transfer of a franchise..

(b) FRANCHISE FEES- Section 622(b) (47 U.S.C. 542(b)) is amended by inserting to provide cable services immediately before the period at the end of the first sentence thereof.

SEC. 304. COMPETITIVE AVAILABILITY OF NAVIGATION DEVICES.

Part III of title VI is amended by inserting after section 628 (47 U.S.C. 548) the following new section: SEC. 629. COMPETITIVE AVAILABILITY OF NAVIGATION DEVICES.

(a) COMMERCIAL CONSUMER AVAILABILITY OF EQUIPMENT USED TO ACCESS SERVICES PROVIDED BY MULTICHANNEL VIDEO PROGRAMMING DISTRIBUTORS- The Commission shall, in consultation with appropriate industry standard-setting organizations, adopt regulations to assure the commercial availability, to consumers of multichannel video programming and other services offered over multichannel video programming systems, of converter boxes, interactive communications equipment, and other equipment used by consumers to access multichannel video programming and other services offered over multichannel video programming systems, from manufacturers, retailers, and other vendors not affiliated with any multichannel video programming distributor. Such regulations shall not prohibit any multichannel video programming distributor from also offering converter boxes, interactive communications equipment, and other equipment used by consumers to access multichannel video programming and other services offered over multichannel video programming systems, to consumers, if the system operators charges to consumers for such devices and equipment are separately stated and not subsidized by charges for any such service.

(b) PROTECTION OF SYSTEM SECURITY- The Commission shall not prescribe regulations under subsection (a) which would jeopardize security of multichannel video programming and other services offered over multichannel video programming systems, or impede the legal rights of a provider of such services to prevent theft of service.

(c) WAIVER- The Commission shall waive a regulation adopted under subsection (a) for a limited time upon an appropriate showing by a provider of multichannel video programming and other services offered over multichannel video programming systems, or an equipment provider, that such waiver is necessary to assist the development or introduction of a new or improved multichannel video programming or other service offered over multichannel video programming systems, technology, or products. Upon an appropriate showing, the Commission shall grant any such waiver request within 90 days of any application filed under this subsection, and such waiver shall be effective for all service providers and products in that category and for all providers of services and products.

(d) AVOIDANCE OF REDUNDANT REGULATIONS-

(1) COMMERCIAL AVAILABILITY DETERMINATIONS- Determinations made or regulations prescribed by the Commission with respect to commercial availability to consumers of converter boxes, interactive communications equipment, and other equipment used by consumers to access multichannel video programming and other services offered over multichannel video programming systems, before the date of enactment of the Telecommunications Act of 1996 shall fulfill the requirements of this section.

(2) REGULATIONS- Nothing in this section affects section 64.702(e) of the Commissions regulations (47 C.F.R. 64.702(e)) or other Commission regulations governing interconnection and competitive provision of customer premises equipment used in connection with basic common carrier communications services.

(e) SUNSET- The regulations adopted under this section shall cease to apply when the Commission determines that—

(1) the market for the multichannel video programming distributors is fully competitive;

(2) the market for converter boxes, and interactive communications equipment, used in conjunction with that service is fully competitive; and

(3) elimination of the regulations would promote competition and the public interest.

(f) COMMISSIONS AUTHORITY- Nothing in this section shall be construed as expanding or limiting any authority that the Commission may have under law in effect before the date of enactment of the Telecommunications Act of 1996.

SEC. 305. VIDEO PROGRAMMING ACCESSIBILITY.

Title VII is amended by inserting after section 712 (47 U.S.C. 612) the following new section: SEC. 713. VIDEO PROGRAMMING ACCESSIBILITY.

(a) COMMISSION INQUIRY- Within 180 days after the date of enactment of the Telecommunications Act of 1996, the Federal Communications Commission shall complete an inquiry to ascertain the level at which video programming is closed captioned. Such inquiry shall examine the extent to which existing or previously published programming is closed captioned, the size of the video programming provider or programming owner providing closed captioning, the size of the market served, the relative audience shares achieved, or any other related factors. The Commission shall submit to the Congress a report on the results of such inquiry.

(b) ACCOUNTABILITY CRITERIA- Within 18 months after such date of enactment, the Commission shall prescribe such regulations as are necessary to implement this section. Such regulations shall ensure that—

(1) video programming first published or exhibited after the effective date of such regulations is fully accessible through the provision of closed captions, except as provided in subsection (d); and

(2) video programming providers or owners maximize the accessibility of video programming first published or exhibited prior to the effective date of such regulations through the provision of closed captions, except as provided in subsection (d).

(c) DEADLINES FOR CAPTIONING- Such regulations shall include an appropriate schedule of deadlines for the provision of closed captioning of video programming.

(d) EXEMPTIONS- Notwithstanding subsection (b)—

(1) the Commission may exempt by regulation programs, classes of programs, or services for which the Commission has determined that the provision of closed captioning would be economically burdensome to the provider or owner of such programming;

(2) a provider of video programming or the owner of any program carried by the provider shall not be obligated to supply closed captions if such action would be inconsistent with contracts in effect on the date of enactment of the Telecommunications Act of 1996, except that nothing in this section shall be construed to relieve a video programming provider of its obligations to provide services required by Federal law; and

(3) a provider of video programming or program owner may petition the Commission for an exemption from the requirements of this section, and the Commission may grant such petition upon a showing that the requirements contained in this section would result in an undue burden.

(e) UNDUE BURDEN- The term undue burden means significant difficulty or expense. In determining whether the closed captions necessary to comply with the requirements of this paragraph would result in an undue economic burden, the factors to be considered include—

(1) the nature and cost of the closed captions for the programming;

(2) the impact on the operation of the provider or program owner;

(3) the financial resources of the provider or program owner; and

(4) the type of operations of the provider or program owner.

(f) VIDEO DESCRIPTIONS INQUIRY- Within 6 months after the date of enactment of the Telecommunications Act of 1996, the Commission shall commence an inquiry to examine the use of video descriptions on video programming in order to ensure the accessibility of video programming to persons with visual impairments, and report to Congress on its findings. The Commissions report shall assess appropriate methods and schedules for phasing video descriptions into the marketplace, technical and quality standards for video descriptions, a definition of programming for which video descriptions would apply, and other technical and legal issues that the Commission deems appropriate.

(g) VIDEO DESCRIPTION- For purposes of this section, video description means the insertion of audio narrated descriptions of a television programs key visual elements into natural pauses between the programs dialogue.

(h) PRIVATE RIGHTS OF ACTIONS PROHIBITED- Nothing in this section shall be construed to authorize any private right of action to enforce any requirement of this section or any regulation thereunder. The Commission shall have exclusive jurisdiction with respect to any complaint under this section..

TITLE IV--REGULATORY REFORM

SEC. 401. REGULATORY FORBEARANCE.

Title I is amended by inserting after section 9 (47 U.S.C. 159) the following new section:

SEC. 10. COMPETITION IN PROVISION OF TELECOMMUNICATIONS SERVICE.

(a) REGULATORY FLEXIBILITY- Notwithstanding section 332(c)(1)(A) of this Act, the Commission shall forbear from applying any regulation or any provision of this Act to a telecommunications carrier or telecommunications service, or class of telecommunications carriers or telecommunications services, in any or some of its or their geographic markets, if the Commission determines that—

(1) enforcement of such regulation or provision is not necessary to ensure that the charges, practices, classifications, or regulations by, for, or in connection with that telecommunications carrier or telecommunications service are just and reasonable and are not unjustly or unreasonably discriminatory;

(2) enforcement of such regulation or provision is not necessary for the protection of consumers; and

(3) forbearance from applying such provision or regulation is consistent with the public interest.

(b) COMPETITIVE EFFECT TO BE WEIGHED- In making the determination under subsection (a)(3), the Commission shall consider whether forbearance from enforcing the provision or regulation will promote competitive market conditions, including the extent to which such forbearance will enhance competition among providers of telecommunications services. If the Commission determines that such forbearance will promote competition among providers of telecommunications services, that determination may be the basis for a Commission finding that forbearance is in the public interest.

(c) PETITION FOR FORBEARANCE- Any telecommunications carrier, or class of telecommunications carriers, may submit a petition to the Commission requesting that the Commission exercise the authority granted under this section with respect to that carrier or those carriers, or any service offered by that carrier or carriers. Any such petition shall be deemed granted if the Commission does not deny the petition for failure to meet the requirements for forbearance under subsection (a) within one year after the Commission receives it, unless the one-year period is extended by the Commission. The Commission may extend the initial one-year period by an additional 90 days if the Commission finds that an extension is necessary to meet the requirements of subsection (a). The Commission may grant or deny a petition in whole or in part and shall explain its decision in writing.

(d) LIMITATION- Except as provided in section 251(f), the Commission may not forbear from applying the requirements of section 251(c) or 271 under subsection (a) of this section until it determines that those requirements have been fully implemented.

(e) STATE ENFORCEMENT AFTER COMMISSION FORBEARANCE- A State commission may not continue to apply or enforce any provision of this Act that the Commission has determined to forbear from applying under subsection (a).

SEC. 402. BIENNIAL REVIEW OF REGULATIONS; REGULATORY RELIEF.

(a) BIENNIAL REVIEW- Title I is amended by inserting after section 10 (as added by section 401) the following new section: SEC. 11. REGULATORY REFORM.

(a) BIENNIAL REVIEW OF REGULATIONS- In every even-numbered year (beginning with 1998), the Commission—

(1) shall review all regulations issued under this Act in effect at the time of the review that apply to the operations or activities of any provider of telecommunications service; and

(2) shall determine whether any such regulation is no longer necessary in the public interest as the result of meaningful economic competition between providers of such service.

(b) EFFECT OF DETERMINATION- The Commission shall repeal or modify any regulation it determines to be no longer necessary in the public interest..

(b) REGULATORY RELIEF-

(1) Streamlined procedures for changes in charges, classifications, regulations, or practices-

(A) Section 204(a) (47 U.S.C. 204(a)) is amended—

(i) by striking 12 months the first place it appears in paragraph (2)(A) and inserting 5 months;

(ii) by striking effective, and all that follows in paragraph (2)(A) and inserting effective.; and

(iii) by adding at the end thereof the following:

(3) A local exchange carrier may file with the Commission a new or revised charge, classification, regulation, or practice on a streamlined basis. Any such charge, classification, regulation, or practice shall be deemed lawful and shall be effective 7 days (in the case of a reduction in rates) or 15 days (in the case of an increase in rates) after the date on which it is filed with the Commission unless the Commission takes action under paragraph (1) before the end of that 7-day or 15-day period, as is appropriate..

(B) Section 208(b) (47 U.S.C. 208(b)) is amended—

(i) by striking 12 months the first place it appears in paragraph (1) and inserting 5 months; and

(ii) by striking filed, and all that follows in paragraph (1) and inserting filed..

(2) EXTENSIONS OF LINES UNDER SECTION 214; ARMIS REPORTS- The Commission shall permit any common carrier—

(A) to be exempt from the requirements of section 214 of the Communications Act of 1934 for the extension of any line; and

(B) to file cost allocation manuals and ARMIS reports annually, to the extent such carrier is required to file such manuals or reports.

(3) FORBEARANCE AUTHORITY NOT LIMITED- Nothing in this subsection shall be construed to limit the authority of the Commission to waive, modify, or forbear from applying any of the requirements to which reference is made in paragraph (1) under any other provision of this Act or other law.

(4) EFFECTIVE DATE OF AMENDMENTS- The amendments made by paragraph (1) of this subsection shall apply with respect to any charge, classification, regulation, or practice filed on or after one year after the date of enactment of this Act.

(c) CLASSIFICATION OF CARRIERS- In classifying carriers according to section 32.11 of its regulations (47 C.F.R. 32.11) and in establishing reporting requirements pursuant to part 43 of its regulations (47 C.F.R. part 43) and section 64.903 of its regulations (47 C.F.R. 64.903), the Commission shall adjust the revenue requirements to account for inflation as of the release date of the Commissions Report and Order in CC Docket No. 91-141, and annually thereafter. This subsection shall take effect on the date of enactment of this Act.

SEC. 403. ELIMINATION OF UNNECESSARY COMMISSION REGULATIONS AND FUNCTIONS.

(a) MODIFICATION OF AMATEUR RADIO EXAMINATION PROCEDURES- Section 4(f)(4) (47 U.S.C. 154(f)(4)) is amended—

(1) in subparagraph (A)—

(A) by inserting or administering after for purposes of preparing;

(B) by inserting of after than the class; and

(C) by inserting or administered after for which the examination is being prepared;

(2) by striking subparagraph (B);

(3) in subparagraph (H), by striking (A), (B), and (C) and inserting (A) and (B);

(4) in subparagraph (J)—

(A) by striking or (B); and

(B) by striking the last sentence; and

(5) by redesignating subparagraphs (C) through (J) as subparagraphs (B) through (I), respectively.

(b) AUTHORITY TO DESIGNATE ENTITIES TO INSPECT- Section 4(f)(3) (47 U.S.C. 154(f)(3)) is amended by inserting before the period at the end the following: : and [Italic->] Provided further, [<-Italic] That, in the alternative, an entity designated by the Commission may make the inspections referred to in this paragraph.

(c) EXPEDITING INSTRUCTIONAL TELEVISION FIXED SERVICE PROCESSING- Section 5(c)(1) (47 U.S.C. 155(c)(1)) is amended by striking the last sentence and inserting the following: Except for cases involving the authorization of service in the instructional television fixed service, or as otherwise provided in this Act, nothing in this paragraph shall authorize the Commission to provide for the conduct, by any person or persons other than persons referred to in paragraph (2) or (3) of section 556(b) of title 5, United States Code, of any hearing to which such section applies..

(d) REPEAL SETTING OF DEPRECIATION RATES- The first sentence of section 220(b) (47 U.S.C. 220(b)) is amended by striking shall prescribe for such carriers and inserting may prescribe, for such carriers as it determines to be appropriate,.

(e) USE OF INDEPENDENT AUDITORS- Section 220(c) (47 U.S.C. 220(c)) is amended by adding at the end thereof the following: The Commission may obtain the services of any person licensed to provide public accounting services under the law of any State to assist with, or conduct, audits under this section. While so employed or engaged in conducting an audit for the Commission under this section, any such person shall have the powers granted the Commission under this subsection and shall be subject to subsection (f) in the same manner as if that person were an employee of the Commission..

(f) DELEGATION OF EQUIPMENT TESTING AND CERTIFICATION TO PRIVATE LABORATORIES- Section 302 (47 U.S.C. 302) is amended by adding at the end the following:

(e) The Commission may—

(1) authorize the use of private organizations for testing and certifying the compliance of devices or home electronic equipment and systems with regulations promulgated under this section;

(2) accept as prima facie evidence of such compliance the certification by any such organization; and

(3) establish such qualifications and standards as it deems appropriate for such private organizations, testing, and certification..

(g) MAKING LICENSE MODIFICATION UNIFORM- Section 303(f) (47 U.S.C. 303(f)) is amended by striking unless, after a public hearing, and inserting unless.

(h) ELIMINATE FCC JURISDICTION OVER GOVERNMENT-OWNED SHIP RADIO STATIONS-

(1) Section 305 (47 U.S.C. 305) is amended by striking subsection (b) and redesignating subsections (c) and (d) as (b) and (c), respectively.

(2) Section 382(2) (47 U.S.C. 382(2)) is amended by striking except a vessel of the United States Maritime Administration, the Inland and Coastwise Waterways Service, or the Panama Canal Company,.

(i) PERMIT OPERATION OF DOMESTIC SHIP AND AIRCRAFT RADIOS WITHOUT LICENSE- Section 307(e) (47 U.S.C. 307(e)) is amended to read as follows:

(e)(1) Notwithstanding any license requirement established in this Act, if the Commission determines that such authorization serves the public interest, convenience, and necessity, the Commission may by rule authorize the operation of radio stations without individual licenses in the following radio services: (A) the citizens band radio service; (B) the radio control service; (C) the aviation radio service for aircraft stations operated on domestic flights when such aircraft are not otherwise required to carry a radio station; and (D) the maritime radio service for ship stations navigated on domestic voyages when such ships are not otherwise required to carry a radio station.

(2) Any radio station operator who is authorized by the Commission to operate without an individual license shall comply with all other provisions of this Act and with rules prescribed by the Commission under this Act.

(3) For purposes of this subsection, the terms citizens band radio service, radio control service, aircraft station and ship station shall have the meanings given them by the Commission by rule..

(j) EXPEDITED LICENSING FOR FIXED MICROWAVE SERVICE- Section 309(b)(2) (47 U.S.C. 309(b)(2)) is amended by striking subparagraph (A) and redesignating subparagraphs (B) through (G) as subparagraphs (A) through (F), respectively.

(k) FOREIGN DIRECTORS- Section 310(b) (47 U.S.C. 310(b)) is amended—

(1) in paragraph (3), by striking of which any officer or director is an alien or; and

(2) in paragraph (4), by striking of which any officer or more than one-fourth of the directors are aliens, or.

(l) LIMITATION ON SILENT STATION AUTHORIZATIONS- Section 312 (47 U.S.C. 312) is amended by adding at the end the following:

(g) If a broadcasting station fails to transmit broadcast signals for any consecutive 12-month period, then the station license granted for the operation of that broadcast station expires at the end of that period, notwithstanding any provision, term, or condition of the license to the contrary..

(m) MODIFICATION OF CONSTRUCTION PERMIT REQUIREMENT- Section 319(d) is amended by striking the last two sentences and inserting the following: With respect to any broadcasting station, the Commission shall not have any authority to waive the requirement of a permit for construction, except that the Commission may by regulation determine that a permit shall not be required for minor changes in the facilities of authorized broadcast stations. With respect to any other station or class of stations, the Commission shall not waive the requirement for a construction permit unless the Commission determines that the public interest, convenience, and necessity would be served by such a waiver..

(n) CONDUCT OF INSPECTIONS- Section 362(b) (47 U.S.C. 362(b)) is amended to read as follows:

(b) Every ship of the United States that is subject to this part shall have the equipment and apparatus prescribed therein inspected at least once each year by the Commission or an entity designated by the Commission. If, after such inspection, the Commission is satisfied that all relevant provisions of this Act and the station license have been complied with, the fact shall be so certified on the station license by the Commission. The Commission shall make such additional inspections at frequent intervals as the Commission determines may be necessary to ensure compliance with the requirements of this Act. The Commission may, upon a finding that the public interest could be served thereby—

(1) waive the annual inspection required under this section for a period of up to 90 days for the sole purpose of enabling a vessel to complete its voyage and proceed to a port in the United States where an inspection can be held; or

(2) waive the annual inspection required under this section for a vessel that is in compliance with the radio provisions of the Safety Convention and that is operating solely in waters beyond the jurisdiction of the United States: [Italic->] Provided, [<-Italic] That such inspection shall be performed within 30 days of such vessels return to the United States..

(o) INSPECTION BY OTHER ENTITIES- Section 385 (47 U.S.C. 385) is amended—

(1) by inserting or an entity designated by the Commission after The Commission; and

(2) by adding at the end thereof the following: In accordance with such other provisions of law as apply to Government contracts, the Commission may enter into contracts with any person for the purpose of carrying out such inspections and certifying compliance with those requirements, and may, as part of any such contract, allow any such person to accept reimbursement from the license holder for travel and expense costs of any employee conducting an inspection or certification..

TITLE V--OBSCENITY AND VIOLENCE SUBTITLE A--OBSCENE, HARASSING, AND WRONGFUL UTILIZATION OF TELECOMMUNICATIONS FACILITIES

SEC. 501. SHORT TITLE.

This title may be cited as the Communications Decency Act of 1996. SEC. 502. OBSCENE OR HARASSING USE OF TELECOMMUNICATIONS FACILITIES UNDER THE COMMUNICATIONS ACT OF 1934.

Section 223 (47 U.S.C. 223) is amended—

(1) by striking subsection (a) and inserting in lieu thereof:

(a) Whoever-- (1) in interstate or foreign communications—

(A) by means of a telecommunications device knowingly—

(i) makes, creates, or solicits, and

(ii) initiates the transmission of, any comment, request, suggestion, proposal, image, or other communication which is obscene, lewd, lascivious, filthy, or indecent, with intent to annoy, abuse, threaten, or harass another person;

(B) by means of a telecommunications device knowingly—

(i) makes, creates, or solicits, and

(ii) initiates the transmission of, any comment, request, suggestion, proposal, image, or other communication which is obscene or indecent, knowing that the recipient of the communication is under 18 years of age, regardless of whether the maker of such communication placed the call or initiated the communication;

(C) makes a telephone call or utilizes a telecommunications device, whether or not conversation or communication ensues, without disclosing his identity and with intent to annoy, abuse, threaten, or harass any person at the called number or who receives the communications;

(D) makes or causes the telephone of another repeatedly or continuously to ring, with intent to harass any person at the called number; or

(E) makes repeated telephone calls or repeatedly initiates communication with a telecommunications device, during which conversation or communication ensues, solely to harass any person at the called number or who receives the communication; or

(2) knowingly permits any telecommunications facility under his control to be used for any activity prohibited by paragraph (1) with the intent that it be used for such activity, shall be fined under title 18, United States Code, or imprisoned not more than two years, or both.; and (2) by adding at the end the following new subsections:

(d) Whoever—

(1) in interstate or foreign communications knowingly—

(A) uses an interactive computer service to send to a specific person or persons under 18 years of age, or

(B) uses any interactive computer service to display in a manner available to a person under 18 years of age, any comment, request, suggestion, proposal, image, or other communication that, in context, depicts or describes, in terms patently offensive as measured by contemporary community standards, sexual or excretory activities or organs, regardless of whether the user of such service placed the call or initiated the communication; or

(2) knowingly permits any telecommunications facility under such persons control to be used for an activity prohibited by paragraph (1) with the intent that it be used for such activity, shall be fined under title 18, United States Code, or imprisoned not more than two years, or both. (e) In addition to any other defenses available by law:

(1) No person shall be held to have violated subsection (a) or (d) solely for providing access or connection to or from a facility, system, or network not under that persons control, including transmission, downloading, intermediate storage, access software, or other related capabilities that are incidental to providing such access or connection that does not include the creation of the content of the communication.

(2) The defenses provided by paragraph (1) of this subsection shall not be applicable to a person who is a conspirator with an entity actively involved in the creation or knowing distribution of communications that violate this section, or who knowingly advertises the availability of such communications.

(3) The defenses provided in paragraph (1) of this subsection shall not be applicable to a person who provides access or connection to a facility, system, or network engaged in the violation of this section that is owned or controlled by such person.

(4) No employer shall be held liable under this section for the actions of an employee or agent unless the employees or agents conduct is within the scope of his or her employment or

agency and the employer (A) having knowledge of such conduct, authorizes or ratifies such conduct, or (B) recklessly disregards such conduct.

(5) It is a defense to a prosecution under subsection (a)(1)(B) or (d), or under subsection (a)(2) with respect to the use of a facility for an activity under subsection (a)(1)(B) that a person—

(A) has taken, in good faith, reasonable, effective, and appropriate actions under the circumstances to restrict or prevent access by minors to a communication specified in such subsections, which may involve any appropriate measures to restrict minors from such communications, including any method which is feasible under available technology; or

(B) has restricted access to such communication by requiring use of a verified credit card, debit account, adult access code, or adult personal identification number.

(6) The Commission may describe measures which are reasonable, effective, and appropriate to restrict access to prohibited communications under subsection (d). Nothing in this section authorizes the Commission to enforce, or is intended to provide the Commission with the authority to approve, sanction, or permit, the use of such measures. The Commission shall have no enforcement authority over the failure to utilize such measures. The Commission shall not endorse specific products relating to such measures. The use of such measures shall be admitted as evidence of good faith efforts for purposes of paragraph (5) in any action arising under subsection (d). Nothing in this section shall be construed to treat interactive computer services as common carriers or telecommunications carriers.

(f)(1) No cause of action may be brought in any court or administrative agency against any person on account of any activity that is not in violation of any law punishable by criminal or civil penalty, and that the person has taken in good faith to implement a defense authorized under this section or otherwise to restrict or prevent the transmission of, or access to, a communication specified in this section.

(2) No State or local government may impose any liability for commercial activities or actions by commercial entities, nonprofit libraries, or institutions of higher education in connection with an activity or action described in subsection (a)(2) or (d) that is inconsistent with the treatment of those activities or actions under this section: [Italic->] Provided, however [<-Italic] , That nothing herein shall preclude any State or local government from enacting and enforcing complementary oversight, liability, and regulatory systems, procedures, and requirements, so long as such systems, procedures, and requirements govern only intrastate services and do not result in the imposition of inconsistent rights, duties or obligations on the provision of interstate services. Nothing in this subsection shall preclude any State or local government from governing conduct not covered by this section.

(g) Nothing in subsection (a), (d), (e), or (f) or in the defenses to prosecution under subsection (a) or (d) shall be construed to affect or limit the application or enforcement of any other Federal law.

(h) For purposes of this section—

(1) The use of the term telecommunications device in this section—

(A) shall not impose new obligations on broadcasting station licensees and cable operators covered by obscenity and indecency provisions elsewhere in this Act; and

(B) does not include an interactive computer service.

(2) The term interactive computer service has the meaning provided in section 230(e)(2).

(3) The term access software means software (including client or server software) or enabling tools that do not create or provide the content of the communication but that allow a user to do any one or more of the following:

(A) filter, screen, allow, or disallow content;

(B) pick, choose, analyze, or digest content; or

(C) transmit, receive, display, forward, cache, search, subset, organize, reorganize, or translate content.

(4) The term institution of higher education has the meaning provided in section 1201 of the Higher Education Act of 1965 (20 U.S.C. 1141).

(5) The term library means a library eligible for participation in State-based plans for funds under title III of the Library Services and Construction Act (20 U.S.C. 355e et seq.).

SEC. 503. OBSCENE PROGRAMMING ON CABLE TELEVISION.

Section 639 (47 U.S.C. 559) is amended by striking not more than $10,000 and inserting under title 18, United States Code,.

SEC. 504. SCRAMBLING OF CABLE CHANNELS FOR NONSUBSCRIBERS.

Part IV of title VI (47 U.S.C. 551 et seq.) is amended by adding at the end the following: SEC. 640. SCRAMBLING OF CABLE CHANNELS FOR NONSUBSCRIBERS.

(a) SUBSCRIBER REQUEST- Upon request by a cable service subscriber, a cable operator shall, without charge, fully scramble or otherwise fully block the audio and video programming of each channel carrying such programming so that one not a subscriber does not receive it.

(b) DEFINITION- As used in this section, the term scramble means to rearrange the content of the signal of the programming so that the programming cannot be viewed or heard in an understandable manner.

SEC. 505. SCRAMBLING OF SEXUALLY EXPLICIT ADULT VIDEO SERVICE PROGRAMMING.

(a) REQUIREMENT- Part IV of title VI (47 U.S.C. 551 et seq.), as amended by this Act, is further amended by adding at the end the following: SEC. 641. SCRAMBLING OF SEXUALLY EXPLICIT ADULT VIDEO SERVICE PROGRAMMING.

(a) REQUIREMENT- In providing sexually explicit adult programming or other programming that is indecent on any channel of its service primarily dedicated to sexually-oriented programming, a multichannel video programming distributor shall fully scramble or otherwise fully block the video and audio portion of such channel so that one not a subscriber to such channel or programming does not receive it.

(b) IMPLEMENTATION- Until a multichannel video programming distributor complies with the requirement set forth in subsection (a), the distributor shall limit the access of children to the programming referred to in that subsection by not providing such programming during the hours of the day (as determined by the Commission) when a significant number of children are likely to view it.

(c) DEFINITION- As used in this section, the term scramble means to rearrange the content of the signal of the programming so that the programming cannot be viewed or heard in an understandable manner..

(b) EFFECTIVE DATE- The amendment made by subsection (a) shall take effect 30 days after the date of enactment of this Act.

SEC. 506. CABLE OPERATOR REFUSAL TO CARRY CERTAIN PROGRAMS.

(a) PUBLIC, EDUCATIONAL, AND GOVERNMENTAL CHANNELS- Section 611(e) (47 U.S.C. 531(e)) is amended by inserting before the period the following: , except a cable operator may refuse to transmit any public access program or portion of a public access program which contains obscenity, indecency, or nudity.

(b) CABLE CHANNELS FOR COMMERCIAL USE- Section 612(c)(2) (47 U.S.C. 532(c)(2)) is amended by striking an operator and inserting a cable operator may refuse to transmit any leased access program or portion of a leased access program which contains obscenity, indecency, or nudity and.

SEC. 507. CLARIFICATION OF CURRENT LAWS REGARDING COMMUNICATION OF OBSCENE MATERIALS THROUGH THE USE OF COMPUTERS.

(a) IMPORTATION OR TRANSPORTATION- Section 1462 of title 18, United States Code, is amended—

(1) in the first undesignated paragraph, by inserting or interactive computer service (as defined in section 230(e)(2) of the Communications Act of 1934) after carrier; and

(2) in the second undesignated paragraph—

(A) by inserting or receives, after takes;

(B) by inserting or interactive computer service (as defined in section 230(e)(2) of the Communications Act of 1934) after common carrier; and

(C) by inserting or importation after carriage.

(b) TRANSPORTATION FOR PURPOSES OF SALE OR DISTRIBUTION- The first undesignated paragraph of section 1465 of title 18, United States Code, is amended—

(1) by striking transports in and inserting transports or travels in, or uses a facility or means of,;

(2) by inserting or an interactive computer service (as defined in section 230(e)(2) of the Communications Act of 1934) in or affecting such commerce after foreign commerce the first place it appears;

(3) by striking , or knowingly travels in and all that follows through obscene material in interstate or foreign commerce, and inserting of.

(c) INTERPRETATION- The amendments made by this section are clarifying and shall not be interpreted to limit or repeal any prohibition contained in sections 1462 and 1465 of title 18, United States Code, before such amendment, under the rule established in United States v. Alpers, 338 U.S. 680 (1950). SEC. 508. COERCION AND ENTICEMENT OF MINORS. Section 2422 of title 18, United States Code, is amended—

(1) by inserting (a) before Whoever knowingly; and

(2) by adding at the end the following:

(b) Whoever, using any facility or means of interstate or foreign commerce, including the mail, or within the special maritime and territorial jurisdiction of the United States, knowingly persuades, induces, entices, or coerces any individual who has not attained the age of 18 years to engage in prostitution or any sexual act for which any person may be criminally prosecuted, or attempts to do so, shall be fined under this title or imprisoned not more than 10 years, or both.

SEC. 509. ONLINE FAMILY EMPOWERMENT.

Title II of the Communications Act of 1934 (47 U.S.C. 201 et seq.) is amended by adding at the end the following new section: SEC. 230. PROTECTION FOR PRIVATE BLOCKING AND SCREENING OF OFFENSIVE MATERIAL.

(a) FINDINGS- The Congress finds the following:

(1) The rapidly developing array of Internet and other interactive computer services available to individual Americans represent an extraordinary advance in the availability of educational and informational resources to our citizens.

(2) These services offer users a great degree of control over the information that they receive, as well as the potential for even greater control in the future as technology develops.

(3) The Internet and other interactive computer services offer a forum for a true diversity of political discourse, unique opportunities for cultural development, and myriad avenues for intellectual activity.

(4) The Internet and other interactive computer services have flourished, to the benefit of all Americans, with a minimum of government regulation.

(5) Increasingly Americans are relying on interactive media for a variety of political, educational, cultural, and entertainment services.

(b) POLICY- It is the policy of the United States—

(1) to promote the continued development of the Internet and other interactive computer services and other interactive media;

(2) to preserve the vibrant and competitive free market that presently exists for the Internet and other interactive computer services, unfettered by Federal or State regulation;

(3) to encourage the development of technologies which maximize user control over what information is received by individuals, families, and schools who use the Internet and other interactive computer services;

(4) to remove disincentives for the development and utilization of blocking and filtering technologies that empower parents to restrict their childrens access to objectionable or inappropriate online material; and

(5) to ensure vigorous enforcement of Federal criminal laws to deter and punish trafficking in obscenity, stalking, and harassment by means of computer.

(c) PROTECTION FOR GOOD SAMARITAN BLOCKING AND SCREENING OF OFFENSIVE MATERIAL-

(1) TREATMENT OF PUBLISHER OR SPEAKER- No provider or user of an interactive computer service shall be treated as the publisher or speaker of any information provided by another information content provider.

(2) CIVIL LIABILITY- No provider or user of an interactive computer service shall be held liable on account of—

(A) any action voluntarily taken in good faith to restrict access to or availability of material that the provider or user considers to be obscene, lewd, lascivious, filthy, excessively violent, harassing, or otherwise objectionable, whether or not such material is constitutionally protected; or

(B) any action taken to enable or make available to information content providers or others the technical means to restrict access to material described in paragraph (1).

(d) EFFECT ON OTHER LAWS-

(1) NO EFFECT ON CRIMINAL LAW- Nothing in this section shall be construed to impair the enforcement of section 223 of this Act, chapter 71 (relating to obscenity) or 110 (relating to sexual exploitation of children) of title 18, United States Code, or any other Federal criminal statute.

(2) NO EFFECT ON INTELLECTUAL PROPERTY LAW- Nothing in this section shall be construed to limit or expand any law pertaining to intellectual property.

(3) STATE LAW- Nothing in this section shall be construed to prevent any State from enforcing any State law that is consistent with this section. No cause of action may be brought and no liability may be imposed under any State or local law that is inconsistent with this section.

(4) NO EFFECT ON COMMUNICATIONS PRIVACY LAW- Nothing in this section shall be construed to limit the application of the Electronic Communications Privacy Act of 1986 or any of the amendments made by such Act, or any similar State law.

(e) DEFINITIONS- As used in this section:

(1) INTERNET- The term Internet means the international computer network of both Federal and non-Federal interoperable packet switched data networks.

(2) INTERACTIVE COMPUTER SERVICE- The term interactive computer service means any information service, system, or access software provider that provides or enables computer access by multiple users to a computer server, including specifically a service or system that provides access to the Internet and such systems operated or services offered by libraries or educational institutions.

(3) INFORMATION CONTENT PROVIDER- The term information content provider means any person or entity that is responsible, in whole or in part, for the creation or development of information provided through the Internet or any other interactive computer service.

(4) ACCESS SOFTWARE PROVIDER- The term access software provider means a provider of software (including client or server software), or enabling tools that do any one or more of the following:

(A) filter, screen, allow, or disallow content;

(B) pick, choose, analyze, or digest content; or

(C) transmit, receive, display, forward, cache, search, subset, organize, reorganize, or translate content..

SUBTITLE B--VIOLENCE

SEC. 551. PARENTAL CHOICE IN TELEVISION PROGRAMMING.

(a) FINDINGS- The Congress makes the following findings:

(1) Television influences childrens perception of the values and behavior that are common and acceptable in society.

(2) Television station operators, cable television system operators, and video programmers should follow practices in connection with video programming that take into consideration that television broadcast and cable programming has established a uniquely pervasive presence in the lives of American children.

(3) The average American child is exposed to 25 hours of television each week and some children are exposed to as much as 11 hours of television a day.

(4) Studies have shown that children exposed to violent video programming at a young age have a higher tendency for violent and aggressive behavior later in life than children not so exposed, and that children exposed to violent video programming are prone to assume that acts of violence are acceptable behavior.

(5) Children in the United States are, on average, exposed to an estimated 8,000 murders and 100,000 acts of violence on television by the time the child completes elementary school.

(6) Studies indicate that children are affected by the pervasiveness and casual treatment of sexual material on television, eroding the ability of parents to develop responsible attitudes and behavior in their children.

(7) Parents express grave concern over violent and sexual video programming and strongly support technology that would give them greater control to block video programming in the home that they consider harmful to their children.

(8) There is a compelling governmental interest in empowering parents to limit the negative influences of video programming that is harmful to children.

(9) Providing parents with timely information about the nature of upcoming video programming and with the technological tools that allow them easily to block violent, sexual, or other programming that they believe harmful to their children is a nonintrusive and narrowly tailored means of achieving that compelling governmental interest.

(b) ESTABLISHMENT OF TELEVISION RATING CODE-

(1) AMENDMENT- Section 303 (47 U.S.C. 303) is amended by adding at the end the following:

(w) Prescribe—

(1) on the basis of recommendations from an advisory committee established by the Commission in accordance with section 551(b)(2) of the Telecommunications Act of 1996, guidelines and recommended procedures for the identification and rating of video programming that contains sexual, violent, or other indecent material about which parents should be informed before it is displayed to children: [Italic->] Provided, [<-Italic] That nothing in this paragraph shall be construed to authorize any rating of video programming on the basis of its political or religious content; and

(2) with respect to any video programming that has been rated, and in consultation with the television industry, rules requiring distributors of such video programming to transmit such rating to permit parents to block the display of video programming that they have determined is inappropriate for their children..

(2) ADVISORY COMMITTEE REQUIREMENTS- In establishing an advisory committee for purposes of the amendment made by paragraph (1) of this subsection, the Commission shall—

(A) ensure that such committee is composed of parents, television broadcasters, television programming producers, cable operators, appropriate public interest groups, and other interested individuals from the private sector and is fairly balanced in terms of political affiliation, the points of view represented, and the functions to be performed by the committee;

(B) provide to the committee such staff and resources as may be necessary to permit it to perform its functions efficiently and promptly; and

(C) require the committee to submit a final report of its recommendations within one year after the date of the appointment of the initial members.

(c) REQUIREMENT FOR MANUFACTURE OF TELEVISIONS THAT BLOCK PROGRAMS- Section 303 (47 U.S.C. 303), as amended by subsection (a), is further amended by adding at the end the following:

(x) Require, in the case of an apparatus designed to receive television signals that are shipped in interstate commerce or manufactured in the United States and that have a picture screen 13 inches or greater in size (measured diagonally), that such apparatus be equipped with a feature designed to enable viewers to block display of all programs with a common rating, except as otherwise permitted by regulations pursuant to section 330(c)(4)..

(d) SHIPPING OF TELEVISIONS THAT BLOCK PROGRAMS-

(1) REGULATIONS- Section 330 (47 U.S.C. 330) is amended—

(A) by redesignating subsection (c) as subsection (d); and

(B) by adding after subsection (b) the following new subsection (c):

(c)(1) Except as provided in paragraph (2), no person shall ship in interstate commerce or manufacture in the United States any apparatus described in section 303(x) of this Act except in accordance with rules prescribed by the Commission pursuant to the authority granted by that section.

(2) This subsection shall not apply to carriers transporting apparatus referred to in paragraph (1) without trading in it.

(3) The rules prescribed by the Commission under this subsection shall provide for the oversight by the Commission of the adoption of standards by industry for blocking technology. Such rules shall require that all such apparatus be able to receive the rating signals which have been transmitted by way of line 21 of the vertical blanking interval and which conform to the signal and blocking specifications established by industry under the supervision of the Commission.

(4) As new video technology is developed, the Commission shall take such action as the Commission determines appropriate to ensure that blocking service continues to be available to consumers. If the Commission determines that an alternative blocking technology exists that—

(A) enables parents to block programming based on identifying programs without ratings,

(B) is available to consumers at a cost which is comparable to the cost of technology that allows parents to block programming based on common ratings, and

(C) will allow parents to block a broad range of programs on a multichannel system as effectively and as easily as technology that allows parents to block programming based on common ratings, the Commission shall amend the rules prescribed pursuant to section 303(x) to require that the apparatus described in such section be equipped with either the blocking technology described in such section or the alternative blocking technology described in this paragraph..

(2) CONFORMING AMENDMENT- Section 330(d), as redesignated by subsection (d)(1)(A), is amended by striking section 303(s), and section 303(u) and inserting in lieu thereof and sections 303(s), 303(u), and 303(x).

(e) APPLICABILITY AND EFFECTIVE DATES-

(1) APPLICABILITY OF RATING PROVISION- The amendment made by subsection (b) of this section shall take effect 1 year after the date of enactment of this Act, but only if the Commission determines, in consultation with appropriate public interest groups and interested individuals from the private sector, that distributors of video programming have not, by such date—

(A) established voluntary rules for rating video programming that contains sexual, violent, or other indecent material about which parents should be informed before it is displayed to children, and such rules are acceptable to the Commission; and

(B) agreed voluntarily to broadcast signals that contain ratings of such programming.

(2) EFFECTIVE DATE OF MANUFACTURING PROVISION- In prescribing regulations to implement the amendment made by subsection (c), the Federal Communications Commission shall, after consultation with the television manufacturing industry, specify the effective date for the applicability of the requirement to the apparatus covered by such amendment, which date shall not be less than two years after the date of enactment of this Act.

SEC. 552. TECHNOLOGY FUND.

It is the policy of the United States to encourage broadcast television, cable, satellite, syndication, other video programming distributors, and relevant related industries (in consultation with appropriate public interest groups and interested individuals from the private sector) to—

(1) establish a technology fund to encourage television and electronics equipment manufacturers to facilitate the development of technology which would empower parents to block programming they deem inappropriate for their children and to encourage the availability thereof to low income parents;

(2) report to the viewing public on the status of the development of affordable, easy to use blocking technology; and

(3) establish and promote effective procedures, standards, systems, advisories, or other mechanisms for ensuring that users have easy and complete access to the information necessary to effectively utilize blocking technology and to encourage the availability thereof to low income parents.

SUBTITLE C--JUDICIAL REVIEW

SEC. 561. EXPEDITED REVIEW.

(a) THREE-JUDGE DISTRICT COURT HEARING- Notwithstanding any other provision of law, any civil action challenging the constitutionality, on its face, of this title or any amendment made by this title, or any provision thereof, shall be heard by a district court of 3 judges convened pursuant to the provisions of section 2284 of title 28, United States Code.

(b) APPELLATE REVIEW- Notwithstanding any other provision of law, an interlocutory or final judgment, decree, or order of the court of 3 judges in an action under subsection (a) holding this title or an amendment made by this title, or any provision thereof, unconstitutional shall be reviewable as a matter of right by direct appeal to the Supreme Court. Any such appeal shall be filed not more than 20 days after entry of such judgment, decree, or order.

TITLE VI--EFFECT ON OTHER LAWS

SEC. 601. APPLICABILITY OF CONSENT DECREES AND OTHER LAW.

(a) APPLICABILITY OF AMENDMENTS TO FUTURE CONDUCT-

(1) AT&T CONSENT DECREE- Any conduct or activity that was, before the date of enactment of this Act, subject to any restriction or obligation imposed by the AT&T Consent Decree shall, on and after such date, be subject to the restrictions and obligations imposed by the Communications Act of 1934 as amended by this Act and shall not be subject to the restrictions and the obligations imposed by such Consent Decree.

(2) GTE CONSENT DECREE- Any conduct or activity that was, before the date of enactment of this Act, subject to any restriction or obligation imposed by the GTE Consent Decree shall, on and after such date, be subject to the restrictions and obligations imposed by the Communications Act of 1934 as amended by this Act and shall not be subject to the restrictions and the obligations imposed by such Consent Decree.

(3) MCCAW CONSENT DECREE- Any conduct or activity that was, before the date of enactment of this Act, subject to any restriction or obligation imposed by the McCaw Consent Decree shall, on and after such date, be subject to the restrictions and obligations imposed by the Communications Act of 1934 as amended by this Act and subsection (d) of this section and shall not be subject to the restrictions and the obligations imposed by such Consent Decree.

(b) ANTITRUST LAWS-

(1) SAVINGS CLAUSE- Except as provided in paragraphs (2) and (3), nothing in this Act or the amendments made by this Act shall be construed to modify, impair, or supersede the applicability of any of the antitrust laws.

(2) REPEAL- Subsection (a) of section 221 (47 U.S.C. 221(a)) is repealed.

(3) CLAYTON ACT- Section 7 of the Clayton Act (15 U.S.C. 18) is amended in the last paragraph by striking Federal Communications Commission,.

(c) FEDERAL, STATE, AND LOCAL LAW-

(1) NO IMPLIED EFFECT- This Act and the amendments made by this Act shall not be construed to modify, impair, or supersede Federal, State, or local law unless expressly so provided in such Act or amendments.

(2) STATE TAX SAVINGS PROVISION- Notwithstanding paragraph (1), nothing in this Act or the amendments made by this Act shall be construed to modify, impair, or supersede, or authorize the modification, impairment, or supersession of, any State or local law pertaining to taxation, except as provided in sections 622 and 653(c) of the Communications Act of 1934 and section 602 of this Act.

(d) COMMERCIAL MOBILE SERVICE JOINT MARKETING- Notwithstanding section 22.903 of the Commissions regulations (47 C.F.R. 22.903) or any other Commission regulation, a Bell operating company or any other company may, except as provided in sections 271(e)(1) and 272 of the Communications Act of 1934 as amended by this Act as they relate to wireline service, jointly market and sell commercial mobile services in conjunction with telephone exchange service, exchange access, intraLATA telecommunications service, interLATA telecommunications service, and information services.

(e) DEFINITIONS- As used in this section:

(1) AT&T CONSENT DECREE- The term AT&T Consent Decree means the order entered August 24, 1982, in the antitrust action styled United States v. Western Electric, Civil Action No. 82-0192, in the United States District Court for the District of Columbia, and includes any judgment or order with respect to such action entered on or after August 24, 1982..

(2) GTE CONSENT DECREE- The term GTE Consent Decree means the order entered December 21, 1984, as restated January 11, 1985, in the action styled United States v. GTE Corp., Civil Action No. 83-1298, in the United States District Court for the District of Columbia, and any judgment or order with respect to such action entered on or after December 21, 1984.

(3) MCCAW CONSENT DECREE- The term McCaw Consent Decree means the proposed consent decree filed on July 15, 1994, in the antitrust action styled United States v. AT&T Corp. and McCaw Cellular Communications, Inc., Civil Action No. 94-01555, in the United States District Court for the District of Columbia. Such term includes any stipulation that the parties will abide by the terms of such proposed consent decree until it is entered and any order entering such proposed consent decree.

(4) ANTITRUST LAWS- The term antitrust laws has the meaning given it in subsection (a) of the first section of the Clayton Act (15 U.S.C. 12(a)), except that such term includes the Act of June 19, 1936 (49 Stat. 1526; 15 U.S.C. 13 et seq.), commonly known as the Robinson-Patman Act, and section 5 of the Federal Trade Commission Act (15 U.S.C. 45) to the extent that such section 5 applies to unfair methods of competition.

SEC. 602. PREEMPTION OF LOCAL TAXATION WITH RESPECT TO DIRECT-TO-HOME SERVICES.

(a) PREEMPTION- A provider of direct-to-home satellite service shall be exempt from the collection or remittance, or both, of any tax or fee imposed by any local taxing jurisdiction on direct-to-home satellite service.

(b) DEFINITIONS- For the purposes of this section—

(1) DIRECT-TO-HOME SATELLITE SERVICE- The term direct-to-home satellite service means only programming transmitted or broadcast by satellite directly to the subscribers premises without the use of ground receiving or distribution equipment, except at the subscribers premises or in the uplink process to the satellite.

(2) PROVIDER OF DIRECT-TO-HOME SATELLITE SERVICE- For purposes of this section, a provider of direct-to-home satellite service means a person who transmits, broadcasts, sells, or distributes direct-to-home satellite service.

(3) LOCAL TAXING JURISDICTION- The term local taxing jurisdiction means any municipality, city, county, township, parish, transportation district, or assessment jurisdiction, or any other local jurisdiction in the territorial jurisdiction of the United States with the authority to impose a tax or fee, but does not include a State.

(4) STATE- The term State means any of the several States, the District of Columbia, or any territory or possession of the United States.

(5) TAX OR FEE- The terms tax and fee mean any local sales tax, local use tax, local intangible tax, local income tax, business license tax, utility tax, privilege tax, gross receipts tax, excise tax, franchise fees, local telecommunications tax, or any other tax, license, or fee that is imposed for the privilege of doing business, regulating, or raising revenue for a local taxing jurisdiction.

(c) PRESERVATION OF STATE AUTHORITY- This section shall not be construed to prevent taxation of a provider of direct-to-home satellite service by a State or to prevent a local taxing jurisdiction from receiving revenue derived from a tax or fee imposed and collected by a State.

TITLE VII--MISCELLANEOUS PROVISIONS

SEC. 701. PREVENTION OF UNFAIR BILLING PRACTICES FOR INFORMATION OR SERVICES PROVIDED OVER TOLL-FREE TELEPHONE CALLS.

(a) PREVENTION OF UNFAIR BILLING PRACTICES-

(1) IN GENERAL- Section 228(c) (47 U.S.C. 228(c)) is amended—

(A) by striking out subparagraph (C) of paragraph (7) and inserting in lieu thereof the following:

(C) the calling party being charged for information conveyed during the call unless—

(i) the calling party has a written agreement (including an agreement transmitted through electronic medium) that meets the requirements of paragraph (8); or

(ii) the calling party is charged for the information in accordance with paragraph (9); or;

(B)(i) by striking or at the end of subparagraph (C) of such paragraph;

(ii) by striking the period at the end of subparagraph

(D) of such paragraph and inserting a semicolon and or; and

(iii) by adding at the end thereof the following:

(E) the calling party being assessed, by virtue of being asked to connect or otherwise transfer to a pay-per-call service, a charge for the call.; and

(C) by adding at the end the following new paragraphs:

(8) SUBSCRIPTION AGREEMENTS FOR BILLING FOR INFORMATION PROVIDED VIA TOLL-FREE CALLS-

(A) IN GENERAL- For purposes of paragraph (7)(C)(i), a written subscription does not meet the requirements of this paragraph unless the agreement specifies the material terms and conditions under which the information is offered and includes—

(i) the rate at which charges are assessed for the information;

(ii) the information providers name;

(iii) the information providers business address;

(iv) the information providers regular business telephone number;

(v) the information providers agreement to notify the subscriber at least one billing cycle in advance of all future changes in the rates charged for the information; and

(vi) the subscribers choice of payment method, which may be by direct remit, debit, prepaid account, phone bill, or credit or calling card.

(B) BILLING ARRANGEMENTS- If a subscriber elects, pursuant to subparagraph (A)(vi), to pay by means of a phone bill—

(i) the agreement shall clearly explain that the subscriber will be assessed for calls made to the information service from the subscribers phone line;

(ii) the phone bill shall include, in prominent type, the following disclaimer: Common carriers may not disconnect local or long distance telephone service for failure to pay disputed charges for information services.; and

(iii) the phone bill shall clearly list the 800 number dialed.

(C) USE OF PINS TO PREVENT UNAUTHORIZED USE- A written agreement does not meet the requirements of this paragraph unless it—

(i) includes a unique personal identification number or other subscriber-specific identifier and requires a subscriber to use this number or identifier to obtain access to the information provided and includes instructions on its use; and

(ii) assures that any charges for services accessed by use of the subscribers personal identification number or subscriber-specific identifier be assessed to subscribers source of payment elected pursuant to subparagraph (A)(vi).

(D) EXCEPTIONS- Notwithstanding paragraph (7)(C), a written agreement that meets the requirements of this paragraph is not required—

(i) for calls utilizing telecommunications devices for the deaf;

(ii) for directory services provided by a common carrier or its affiliate or by a local exchange carrier or its affiliate; or

(iii) for any purchase of goods or of services that are not information services.

(E) TERMINATION OF SERVICE- On receipt by a common carrier of a complaint by any person that an information provider is in violation of the provisions of this section, a carrier shall—

(i) promptly investigate the complaint; and

(ii) if the carrier reasonably determines that the complaint is valid, it may terminate the provision of service to an information provider unless the provider supplies evidence of a written agreement that meets the requirements of this section.

(F) TREATMENT OF REMEDIES- The remedies provided in this paragraph are in addition to any other remedies that are available under title V of this Act.

(9) CHARGES BY CREDIT, PREPAID, DEBIT, CHARGE, OR CALLING CARD IN ABSENCE OF AGREEMENT- For purposes of paragraph (7)(C)(ii), a calling party is not charged in accordance with this paragraph unless the calling party is charged by means of a credit, prepaid, debit, charge, or calling card and the information service provider includes in response to each call an introductory disclosure message that—

(A) clearly states that there is a charge for the call;

(B) clearly states the services total cost per minute and any other fees for the service or for any service to which the caller may be transferred;

(C) explains that the charges must be billed on either a credit, prepaid, debit, charge, or calling card;

(D) asks the caller for the card number;

(E) clearly states that charges for the call begin at the end of the introductory message; and

(F) clearly states that the caller can hang up at or before the end of the introductory message without incurring any charge whatsoever.

(10) BYPASS OF INTRODUCTORY DISCLOSURE MESSAGE- The requirements of paragraph (9) shall not apply to calls from repeat callers using a bypass mechanism to avoid listening to the introductory message: [Italic->] Provided, [<-Italic] That information providers shall disable such a bypass mechanism after the institution of any price increase and

for a period of time determined to be sufficient by the Federal Trade Commission to give callers adequate and sufficient notice of a price increase.

(11) DEFINITION OF CALLING CARD- As used in this subsection, the term calling card means an identifying number or code unique to the individual, that is issued to the individual by a common carrier and enables the individual to be charged by means of a phone bill for charges incurred independent of where the call originates..

(2) REGULATIONS- The Federal Communications Commission shall revise its regulations to comply with the amendment made by paragraph (1) not later than 180 days after the date of enactment of this Act.

(3) EFFECTIVE DATE- The amendments made by paragraph (1) shall take effect on the date of enactment of this Act.

(b) CLARIFICATION OF PAY-PER-CALL SERVICES-

(1) TELEPHONE DISCLOSURE AND DISPUTE RESOLUTION ACT- Section 204(1) of the Telephone Disclosure and Dispute Resolution Act (15 U.S.C. 5714(1)) is amended to read as follows:

(1) The term pay-per-call services has the meaning provided in section 228(i) of the Communications Act of 1934, except that the Commission by rule may, notwithstanding subparagraphs (B) and (C) of section 228(i)(1) of such Act, extend such definition to other similar services providing audio information or audio entertainment if the Commission determines that such services are susceptible to the unfair and deceptive practices that are prohibited by the rules prescribed pursuant to section 201(a)..

(2) COMMUNICATIONS ACT- Section 228(i)(2) (47 U.S.C. 228(i)(2)) is amended by striking or any service the charge for which is tariffed.

SEC. 702. PRIVACY OF CUSTOMER INFORMATION.

Title II is amended by inserting after section 221 (47 U.S.C. 221) the following new section: SEC. 222. PRIVACY OF CUSTOMER INFORMATION.

(a) IN GENERAL- Every telecommunications carrier has a duty to protect the confidentiality of proprietary information of, and relating to, other telecommunication carriers, equipment manufacturers, and customers, including telecommunication carriers reselling telecommunications services provided by a telecommunications carrier.

(b) CONFIDENTIALITY OF CARRIER INFORMATION- A telecommunications carrier that receives or obtains proprietary information from another carrier for purposes of providing any telecommunications service shall use such information only for such purpose, and shall not use such information for its own marketing efforts.

(c) CONFIDENTIALITY OF CUSTOMER PROPRIETARY NETWORK INFORMATION-

(1) PRIVACY REQUIREMENTS FOR TELECOMMUNICATIONS CARRIERS- Except as required by law or with the approval of the customer, a telecommunications carrier that receives or obtains customer proprietary network information by virtue of its provision of a telecommunications service shall only use, disclose, or permit access to individually identifiable customer proprietary network information in its provision of (A) the telecommunications service from which such information is derived, or (B) services necessary to, or used in, the provision of such telecommunications service, including the publishing of directories.

(2) DISCLOSURE ON REQUEST BY CUSTOMERS- A telecommunications carrier shall disclose customer proprietary network information, upon affirmative written request by the customer, to any person designated by the customer.

(3) AGGREGATE CUSTOMER INFORMATION- A telecommunications carrier that receives or obtains customer proprietary network information by virtue of its provision of a telecommunications service may use, disclose, or permit access to aggregate customer information other than for the purposes described in paragraph (1). A local exchange carrier may use, disclose, or permit access to aggregate customer information other than for purposes described in paragraph (1) only if it provides such aggregate information to other carriers or persons on reasonable and nondiscriminatory terms and conditions upon reasonable request therefor.

(d) EXCEPTIONS- Nothing in this section prohibits a telecommunications carrier from using, disclosing, or permitting access to customer proprietary network information obtained from its customers, either directly or indirectly through its agents—

(1) to initiate, render, bill, and collect for telecommunications services;

(2) to protect the rights or property of the carrier, or to protect users of those services and other carriers from fraudulent, abusive, or unlawful use of, or subscription to, such services; or

(3) to provide any inbound telemarketing, referral, or administrative services to the customer for the duration of the call, if such call was initiated by the customer and the customer approves of the use of such information to provide such service.

(e) SUBSCRIBER LIST INFORMATION- Notwithstanding subsections (b), (c), and (d), a telecommunications carrier that provides telephone exchange service shall provide subscriber list information gathered in its capacity as a provider of such service on a timely and unbundled basis, under nondiscriminatory and reasonable rates, terms, and conditions, to any person upon request for the purpose of publishing directories in any format.

(f) DEFINITIONS- As used in this section:

(1) CUSTOMER PROPRIETARY NETWORK INFORMATION- The term customer proprietary network information means—

(A) information that relates to the quantity, technical configuration, type, destination, and amount of use of a telecommunications service subscribed to by any customer of a telecommunications carrier, and that is made available to the carrier by the customer solely by virtue of the carrier-customer relationship; and

(B) information contained in the bills pertaining to telephone exchange service or telephone toll service received by a customer of a carrier; except that such term does not include subscriber list information.

(2) AGGREGATE INFORMATION- The term aggregate customer information means collective data that relates to a group or category of services or customers, from which individual customer identities and characteristics have been removed.

(3) SUBSCRIBER LIST INFORMATION- The term subscriber list information means any information—

(A) identifying the listed names of subscribers of a carrier and such subscribers telephone numbers, addresses, or primary advertising classifications (as such classifications are assigned at the time of the establishment of such service), or any combination of such listed names, numbers, addresses, or classifications; and

(B) that the carrier or an affiliate has published, caused to be published, or accepted for publication in any directory format.

SEC. 703. POLE ATTACHMENTS.

Section 224 (47 U.S.C. 224) is amended—

(1) in subsection (a)(1), by striking the first sentence and inserting the following: The term utility means any person who is a local exchange carrier or an electric, gas, water, steam, or other public utility, and who owns or controls poles, ducts, conduits, or rights-of-way used, in whole or in part, for any wire communications.;

(2) in subsection (a)(4), by inserting after system the following: or provider of telecommunications service;

(3) by inserting after subsection (a)(4) the following:

(5) For purposes of this section, the term telecommunications carrier (as defined in section 3 of this Act) does not include any incumbent local exchange carrier as defined in section 251(h).;

(4) by inserting after conditions in subsection (c)(1) a comma and the following: or access to poles, ducts, conduits, and rights-of-way as provided in subsection (f),;

(5) in subsection (c)(2)(B), by striking cable television services and inserting the services offered via such attachments;

(6) by inserting after subsection (d)(2) the following:

(3) This subsection shall apply to the rate for any pole attachment used by a cable television system solely to provide cable service. Until the effective date of the regulations required under subsection (e), this subsection shall also apply to the rate for any pole attachment used by a cable system or any telecommunications carrier (to the extent such carrier is not a party to a pole attachment agreement) to provide any telecommunications service.; and

(7) by adding at the end thereof the following:

(e)(1) The Commission shall, no later than 2 years after the date of enactment of the Telecommunications Act of 1996, prescribe regulations in accordance with this subsection to govern the charges for pole attachments used by telecommunications carriers to provide telecommunications services, when the parties fail to resolve a dispute over such charges. Such regulations shall ensure that a utility charges just, reasonable, and nondiscriminatory rates for pole attachments.

(2) A utility shall apportion the cost of providing space on a pole, duct, conduit, or right-of-way other than the usable space among entities so that such apportionment equals two-thirds of the costs of providing space other than the usable space that would be allocated to such entity under an equal apportionment of such costs among all attaching entities.

(3) A utility shall apportion the cost of providing usable space among all entities according to the percentage of usable space required for each entity.

(4) The regulations required under paragraph (1) shall become effective 5 years after the date of enactment of the Telecommunications Act of 1996. Any increase in the rates for pole attachments that result from the adoption of the regulations required by this subsection shall be phased in equal annual increments over a period of 5 years beginning on the effective date of such regulations.

(f)(1) A utility shall provide a cable television system or any telecommunications carrier with nondiscriminatory access to any pole, duct, conduit, or right-of-way owned or controlled by it.

(2) Notwithstanding paragraph (1), a utility providing electric service may deny a cable television system or any telecommunications carrier access to its poles, ducts, conduits, or rights-of-way, on a non-discriminatory basis where there is insufficient capacity and for reasons of safety, reliability and generally applicable engineering purposes.

(g) A utility that engages in the provision of telecommunications services or cable services shall impute to its costs of providing such services (and charge any affiliate, subsidiary, or associate company engaged in the provision of such services) an equal amount to the pole attachment rate for which such company would be liable under this section.

(h) Whenever the owner of a pole, duct, conduit, or right-of-way intends to modify or alter such pole, duct, conduit, or right-of-way, the owner shall provide written notification of such action to any entity that has obtained an attachment to such conduit or right-of-way so that such entity may have a reasonable opportunity to add to or modify its existing attachment. Any entity that adds to or modifies its existing attachment after receiving such notification shall bear a proportionate share of the costs incurred by the owner in making such pole, duct, conduit, or right-of-way accessible.

(i) An entity that obtains an attachment to a pole, conduit, or right-of-way shall not be required to bear any of the costs of rearranging or replacing its attachment, if such rearrangement or replacement is required as a result of an additional attachment or the modification of an existing attachment sought by any other entity (including the owner of such pole, duct, conduit, or right-of-way).

SEC. 704. FACILITIES SITING; RADIO FREQUENCY EMISSION STANDARDS.

(a) NATIONAL WIRELESS TELECOMMUNICATIONS SITING POLICY- Section 332(c) (47 U.S.C. 332(c)) is amended by adding at the end the following new paragraph:

(7) PRESERVATION OF LOCAL ZONING AUTHORITY-

(A) GENERAL AUTHORITY- Except as provided in this paragraph, nothing in this Act shall limit or affect the authority of a State or local government or instrumentality thereof over decisions regarding the placement, construction, and modification of personal wireless service facilities.

(B) LIMITATIONS-

(i) The regulation of the placement, construction, and modification of personal wireless service facilities by any State or local government or instrumentality thereof—

(I) shall not unreasonably discriminate among providers of functionally equivalent services; and

(II) shall not prohibit or have the effect of prohibiting the provision of personal wireless services.

(ii) A State or local government or instrumentality thereof shall act on any request for authorization to place, construct, or modify personal wireless service facilities within a reasonable period of time after the request is duly filed with such government or instrumentality, taking into account the nature and scope of such request.

(iii) Any decision by a State or local government or instrumentality thereof to deny a request to place, construct, or modify personal wireless service facilities shall be in writing and supported by substantial evidence contained in a written record.

(iv) No State or local government or instrumentality thereof may regulate the placement, construction, and modification of personal wireless service facilities on the basis of the environmental effects of radio frequency emissions to the extent that such facilities comply with the Commissions regulations concerning such emissions.

(v) Any person adversely affected by any final action or failure to act by a State or local government or any instrumentality thereof that is inconsistent with this subparagraph may, within 30 days after such action or failure to act, commence an action in any court of competent jurisdiction. The court shall hear and decide such action on an expedited basis. Any person adversely affected by an act or failure to act by a State or local government or any instrumentality thereof that is inconsistent with clause (iv) may petition the Commission for relief.

(C) DEFINITIONS- For purposes of this paragraph—

(i) the term personal wireless services means commercial mobile services, unlicensed wireless services, and common carrier wireless exchange access services;

(ii) the term personal wireless service facilities means facilities for the provision of personal wireless services; and

(iii) the term unlicensed wireless service means the offering of telecommunications services using duly authorized devices which do not require individual licenses, but does not mean the provision of direct-to-home satellite services (as defined in section 303(v))..

(b) RADIO FREQUENCY EMISSIONS- Within 180 days after the enactment of this Act, the Commission shall complete action in ET Docket 93-62 to prescribe and make effective rules regarding the environmental effects of radio frequency emissions.

(c) AVAILABILITY OF PROPERTY- Within 180 days of the enactment of this Act, the President or his designee shall prescribe procedures by which Federal departments and agencies may make available on a fair, reasonable, and nondiscriminatory basis, property, rights-of-way, and easements under their control for the placement of new telecommunications services that are dependent, in whole or in part, upon the utilization of Federal spectrum rights for the transmission or reception of such services. These procedures may establish a presumption that requests for the use of property, rights-of-way, and easements by duly authorized providers should be granted absent unavoidable direct conflict with the department or agencys mission, or the current or planned use of the property, rights-of-way, and easements in question. Reasonable fees may be charged to providers of such telecommunications services for use of property, rights-of-way, and easements. The Commission shall provide technical support to States to encourage them to make property, rights-of-way, and easements under their jurisdiction available for such purposes.

SEC. 705. MOBILE SERVICES DIRECT ACCESS TO LONG DISTANCE CARRIERS.

Section 332(c) (47 U.S.C. 332(c)) is amended by adding at the end the following new paragraph:

(8) MOBILE SERVICES ACCESS- A person engaged in the provision of commercial mobile services, insofar as such person is so engaged, shall not be required to provide equal access to common carriers for the provision of telephone toll services. If the Commission

determines that subscribers to such services are denied access to the provider of telephone toll services of the subscribers choice, and that such denial is contrary to the public interest, convenience, and necessity, then the Commission shall prescribe regulations to afford subscribers unblocked access to the provider of telephone toll services of the subscribers choice through the use of a carrier identification code assigned to such provider or other mechanism. The requirements for unblocking shall not apply to mobile satellite services unless the Commission finds it to be in the public interest to apply such requirements to such services.

SEC. 706. ADVANCED TELECOMMUNICATIONS INCENTIVES.

(a) IN GENERAL- The Commission and each State commission with regulatory jurisdiction over telecommunications services shall encourage the deployment on a reasonable and timely basis of advanced telecommunications capability to all Americans (including, in particular, elementary and secondary schools and classrooms) by utilizing, in a manner consistent with the public interest, convenience, and necessity, price cap regulation, regulatory forbearance, measures that promote competition in the local telecommunications market, or other regulating methods that remove barriers to infrastructure investment.

(b) INQUIRY- The Commission shall, within 30 months after the date of enactment of this Act, and regularly thereafter, initiate a notice of inquiry concerning the availability of advanced telecommunications capability to all Americans (including, in particular, elementary and secondary schools and classrooms) and shall complete the inquiry within 180 days after its initiation. In the inquiry, the Commission shall determine whether advanced telecommunications capability is being deployed to all Americans in a reasonable and timely fashion. If the Commissions determination is negative, it shall take immediate action to accelerate deployment of such capability by removing barriers to infrastructure investment and by promoting competition in the telecommunications market.

(c) DEFINITIONS- For purposes of this subsection:

(1) ADVANCED TELECOMMUNICATIONS CAPABILITY- The term advanced telecommunications capability is defined, without regard to any transmission media or technology, as high-speed, switched, broadband telecommunications capability that enables users to originate and receive high-quality voice, data, graphics, and video telecommunications using any technology.

(2) ELEMENTARY AND SECONDARY SCHOOLS- The term elementary and secondary schools means elementary and secondary schools, as defined in paragraphs (14) and (25), respectively, of section 14101 of the Elementary and Secondary Education Act of 1965 (20 U.S.C. 8801).

SEC. 707. TELECOMMUNICATIONS DEVELOPMENT FUND.

(a) DEPOSIT AND USE OF AUCTION ESCROW ACCOUNTS- Section 309(j)(8) (47 U.S.C. 309(j)(8)) is amended by adding at the end the following new subparagraph:

(C) DEPOSIT AND USE OF AUCTION ESCROW ACCOUNTS- Any deposits the Commission may require for the qualification of any person to bid in a system of competitive bidding pursuant to this subsection shall be deposited in an interest bearing account at a financial institution designated for purposes of this subsection by the Commission (after consultation with the Secretary of the Treasury). Within 45 days following the conclusion of the competitive bidding—

(i) the deposits of successful bidders shall be paid to the Treasury;

(ii) the deposits of unsuccessful bidders shall be returned to such bidders; and

(iii) the interest accrued to the account shall be transferred to the Telecommunications Development Fund established pursuant to section 714 of this Act..

(b) ESTABLISHMENT AND OPERATION OF FUND- Title VII is amended by inserting after section 713 (as added by section 305) the following new section:

SEC. 714. TELECOMMUNICATIONS DEVELOPMENT FUND.

(a) PURPOSE OF SECTION- It is the purpose of this section—

(1) to promote access to capital for small businesses in order to enhance competition in the telecommunications industry;

(2) to stimulate new technology development, and promote employment and training; and

(3) to support universal service and promote delivery of telecommunications services to underserved rural and urban areas.

(b) ESTABLISHMENT OF FUND- There is hereby established a body corporate to be known as the Telecommunications Development Fund, which shall have succession until dissolved. The Fund shall maintain its principal office in the District of Columbia and shall be deemed, for purposes of venue and jurisdiction in civil actions, to be a resident and citizen thereof.

(c) BOARD OF DIRECTORS-

(1) COMPOSITION OF BOARD; CHAIRMAN- The Fund shall have a Board of Directors which shall consist of 7 persons appointed by the Chairman of the Commission. Four of such directors shall be representative of the private sector and three of such directors shall be representative of the Commission, the Small Business Administration, and the Department of the Treasury, respectively. The Chairman of the Commission shall appoint one of the representatives of the private sector to serve as chairman of the Fund within 30 days after the date of enactment of this section, in order to facilitate rapid creation and implementation of the Fund. The directors shall include members with experience in a number of the following areas: finance, investment banking, government banking, communications law and administrative practice, and public policy.

(2) TERMS OF APPOINTED AND ELECTED MEMBERS- The directors shall be eligible to serve for terms of 5 years, except of the initial members, as designated at the time of their appointment—

(A) 1 shall be eligible to service for a term of 1 year;

(B) 1 shall be eligible to service for a term of 2 years;

(C) 1 shall be eligible to service for a term of 3 years;

(D) 2 shall be eligible to service for a term of 4 years; and

(E) 2 shall be eligible to service for a term of 5 years (1 of whom shall be the Chairman). Directors may continue to serve until their successors have been appointed and have qualified.

(3) MEETINGS AND FUNCTIONS OF THE BOARD- The Board of Directors shall meet at the call of its Chairman, but at least quarterly. The Board shall determine the general policies which shall govern the operations of the Fund. The Chairman of the Board shall, with the approval of the Board, select, appoint, and compensate qualified persons to fill the offices as may be provided for in the bylaws, with such functions, powers, and duties as may be prescribed by the bylaws or by the Board of Directors, and such persons shall be the officers of the Fund and shall discharge all such functions, powers, and duties.

(d) ACCOUNTS OF THE FUND- The Fund shall maintain its accounts at a financial institution designated for purposes of this section by the Chairman of the Board (after consultation with the Commission and the Secretary of the Treasury). The accounts of the Fund shall consist of—

(1) interest transferred pursuant to section 309(j)(8)(C) of this Act;

(2) such sums as may be appropriated to the Commission for advances to the Fund;

(3) any contributions or donations to the Fund that are accepted by the Fund; and

(4) any repayment of, or other payment made with respect to, loans, equity, or other extensions of credit made from the Fund.

(e) USE OF THE FUND- All moneys deposited into the accounts of the Fund shall be used solely for—

(1) the making of loans, investments, or other extensions of credits to eligible small businesses in accordance with subsection (f);

(2) the provision of financial advice to eligible small businesses;

(3) expenses for the administration and management of the Fund (including salaries, expenses, and the rental or purchase of office space for the fund);

(4) preparation of research, studies, or financial analyses; and

(5) other services consistent with the purposes of this section.

(f) LENDING AND CREDIT OPERATIONS- Loans or other extensions of credit from the Fund shall be made available in accordance with the requirements of the Federal Credit Reform Act of 1990 (2 U.S.C. 661 et seq.) and any other applicable law to an eligible small business on the basis of—

(1) the analysis of the business plan of the eligible small business;

(2) the reasonable availability of collateral to secure the loan or credit extension;

(3) the extent to which the loan or credit extension promotes the purposes of this section; and

(4) other lending policies as defined by the Board.

(g) RETURN OF ADVANCES- Any advances appropriated pursuant to subsection (d)(2) shall be disbursed upon such terms and conditions (including conditions relating to the time or times of repayment) as are specified in any appropriations Act providing such advances.

(h) GENERAL CORPORATE POWERS- The Fund shall have power—

(1) to sue and be sued, complain and defend, in its corporate name and through its own counsel;

(2) to adopt, alter, and use the corporate seal, which shall be judicially noticed;

(3) to adopt, amend, and repeal by its Board of Directors, bylaws, rules, and regulations as may be necessary for the conduct of its business;

(4) to conduct its business, carry on its operations, and have officers and exercise the power granted by this section in any State without regard to any qualification or similar statute in any State;

(5) to lease, purchase, or otherwise acquire, own, hold, improve, use, or otherwise deal in and with any property, real, personal, or mixed, or any interest therein, wherever situated, for the purposes of the Fund;

(6) to accept gifts or donations of services, or of property, real, personal, or mixed, tangible or intangible, in aid of any of the purposes of the Fund;

(7) to sell, convey, mortgage, pledge, lease, exchange, and otherwise dispose of its property and assets;

(8) to appoint such officers, attorneys, employees, and agents as may be required, to determine their qualifications, to define their duties, to fix their salaries, require bonds for them, and fix the penalty thereof; and

(9) to enter into contracts, to execute instruments, to incur liabilities, to make loans and equity investment, and to do all things as are necessary or incidental to the proper management of its affairs and the proper conduct of its business.

(i) ACCOUNTING, AUDITING, AND REPORTING- The accounts of the Fund shall be audited annually. Such audits shall be conducted in accordance with generally accepted auditing standards by independent certified public accountants. A report of each such audit shall be furnished to the Secretary of the Treasury and the Commission. The representatives of the Secretary and the Commission shall have access to all books, accounts, financial records, reports, files, and all other papers, things, or property belonging to or in use by the Fund and necessary to facilitate the audit.

(j) REPORT ON AUDITS BY TREASURY- A report of each such audit for a fiscal year shall be made by the Secretary of the Treasury to the President and to the Congress not later than 6 months following the close of such fiscal year. The report shall set forth the scope of the audit and shall include a statement of assets and liabilities, capital and surplus or deficit; a statement of surplus or deficit analysis; a statement of income and expense; a statement of sources and application of funds; and such comments and information as may be deemed necessary to keep the President and the Congress informed of the operations and financial condition of the Fund, together with such recommendations with respect thereto as the Secretary may deem advisable.

(k) DEFINITIONS- As used in this section:

(1) ELIGIBLE SMALL BUSINESS- The term eligible small business means business enterprises engaged in the telecommunications industry that have $50,000,000 or less in annual revenues, on average over the past 3 years prior to submitting the application under this section.

(2) FUND- The term Fund means the Telecommunications Development Fund established pursuant to this section.

(3) TELECOMMUNICATIONS INDUSTRY- The term telecommunications industry means communications businesses using regulated or unregulated facilities or services and includes broadcasting, telecommunications, cable, computer, data transmission, software, programming, advanced messaging, and electronics businesses..

SEC. 708. NATIONAL EDUCATION TECHNOLOGY FUNDING CORPORATION.

(a) FINDINGS; PURPOSE-

(1) FINDINGS- The Congress finds as follows:

(A) CORPORATION- There has been established in the District of Columbia a private, nonprofit corporation known as the National Education Technology Funding Corporation which is not an agency or independent establishment of the Federal Government.

(B) BOARD OF DIRECTORS- The Corporation is governed by a Board of Directors, as prescribed in the Corporations articles of incorporation, consisting of 15 members, of which—

(i) five members are representative of public agencies representative of schools and public libraries;

(ii) five members are representative of State government, including persons knowledgeable about State finance, technology and education; and

(iii) five members are representative of the private sector, with expertise in network technology, finance and management.

(C) CORPORATE PURPOSES- The purposes of the Corporation, as set forth in its articles of incorporation, are—

(i) to leverage resources and stimulate private investment in education technology infrastructure;

(ii) to designate State education technology agencies to receive loans, grants or other forms of assistance from the Corporation;

(iii) to establish criteria for encouraging States to—

(I) create, maintain, utilize and upgrade interactive high capacity networks capable of providing audio, visual and data communications for elementary schools, secondary schools and public libraries;

(II) distribute resources to assure equitable aid to all elementary schools and secondary schools in the State and achieve universal access to network technology; and

(III) upgrade the delivery and development of learning through innovative technology-based instructional tools and applications;

(iv) to provide loans, grants and other forms of assistance to State education technology agencies, with due regard for providing a fair balance among types of school districts and public libraries assisted and the disparate needs of such districts and libraries;

(v) to leverage resources to provide maximum aid to elementary schools, secondary schools and public libraries; and

(vi) to encourage the development of education telecommunications and information technologies through public-private ventures, by serving as a clearinghouse for information on new education technologies, and by providing technical assistance, including assistance to States, if needed, to establish State education technology agencies.

(2) PURPOSE- The purpose of this section is to recognize the Corporation as a nonprofit corporation operating under the laws of the District of Columbia, and to provide authority for Federal departments and agencies to provide assistance to the Corporation.

(b) DEFINITIONS- For the purpose of this section—

(1) the term Corporation means the National Education Technology Funding Corporation described in subsection (a)(1)(A);

(2) the terms elementary school and secondary school have the same meanings given such terms in section 14101 of the Elementary and Secondary Education Act of 1965; and

(3) the term public library has the same meaning given such term in section 3 of the Library Services and Construction Act.

(c) ASSISTANCE FOR EDUCATION TECHNOLOGY PURPOSES-

(1) RECEIPT BY CORPORATION- Notwithstanding any other provision of law, in order to carry out the corporate purposes described in subsection (a)(1)(C), the Corporation shall be eligible to receive discretionary grants, contracts, gifts, contributions, or technical assistance from any Federal department or agency, to the extent otherwise permitted by law.

(2) AGREEMENT- In order to receive any assistance described in paragraph (1) the Corporation shall enter into an agreement with the Federal department or agency providing such assistance, under which the Corporation agrees—

(A) to use such assistance to provide funding and technical assistance only for activities which the Board of Directors of the Corporation determines are consistent with the corporate purposes described in subsection (a)(1)(C);

(B) to review the activities of State education technology agencies and other entities receiving assistance from the Corporation to assure that the corporate purposes described in subsection (a)(1)(C) are carried out;

(C) that no part of the assets of the Corporation shall accrue to the benefit of any member of the Board of Directors of the Corporation, any officer or employee of the Corporation, or any other individual, except as salary or reasonable compensation for services;

(D) that the Board of Directors of the Corporation will adopt policies and procedures to prevent conflicts of interest;

(E) to maintain a Board of Directors of the Corporation consistent with subsection (a)(1)(B);

(F) that the Corporation, and any entity receiving the assistance from the Corporation, are subject to the appropriate oversight procedures of the Congress; and

(G) to comply with—

(i) the audit requirements described in subsection (d); and

(ii) the reporting and testimony requirements described in subsection (e).

(3) CONSTRUCTION- Nothing in this section shall be construed to establish the Corporation as an agency or independent establishment of the Federal Government, or to establish the members of the Board of Directors of the Corporation, or the officers and employees of the Corporation, as officers or employees of the Federal Government.

(d) AUDITS-

(1) AUDITS BY INDEPENDENT CERTIFIED PUBLIC ACCOUNTANTS-

(A) IN GENERAL- The Corporations financial statements shall be audited annually in accordance with generally accepted auditing standards by independent certified public accountants who are certified by a regulatory authority of a State or other political subdivision of the United States. The audits shall be conducted at the place or places where the accounts of the Corporation are normally kept. All books, accounts, financial records, reports, files, and all other papers, things, or property belonging to or in use by the Corporation and necessary to facilitate the audit shall be made available to the person or persons conducting the audits, and full facilities for verifying transactions with the balances or securities held by depositories, fiscal agents, and custodians shall be afforded to such person or persons.

(B) REPORTING REQUIREMENTS- The report of each annual audit described in subparagraph (A) shall be included in the annual report required by subsection (e)(1).

(2) RECORDKEEPING REQUIREMENTS; AUDIT AND EXAMINATION OF BOOKS-

(A) RECORDKEEPING REQUIREMENTS- The Corporation shall ensure that each recipient of assistance from the Corporation keeps—

(i) separate accounts with respect to such assistance;

(ii) such records as may be reasonably necessary to fully disclose—

(I) the amount and the disposition by such recipient of the proceeds of such assistance;

(II) the total cost of the project or undertaking in connection with which such assistance is given or used; and

(III) the amount and nature of that portion of the cost of the project or undertaking supplied by other sources; and

(iii) such other records as will facilitate an effective audit.

(B) AUDIT AND EXAMINATION OF BOOKS- The Corporation shall ensure that the Corporation, or any of the Corporations duly authorized representatives, shall have access for the purpose of audit and examination to any books, documents, papers, and records of any recipient of assistance from the Corporation that are pertinent to such assistance. Representatives of the Comptroller General shall also have such access for such purpose.

(e) ANNUAL REPORT; TESTIMONY TO THE CONGRESS-

(1) ANNUAL REPORT- Not later than April 30 of each year, the Corporation shall publish an annual report for the preceding fiscal year and submit that report to the President and the Congress. The report shall include a comprehensive and detailed evaluation of the Corporations operations, activities, financial condition, and accomplishments under this section and may include such recommendations as the Corporation deems appropriate.

(2) TESTIMONY BEFORE CONGRESS- The members of the Board of Directors, and officers, of the Corporation shall be available to testify before appropriate committees of the Congress with respect to the report described in paragraph (1), the report of any audit made by the Comptroller General pursuant to this section, or any other matter which any such committee may determine appropriate.

SEC. 709. REPORT ON THE USE OF ADVANCED TELECOMMUNICATIONS SERVICES FOR MEDICAL PURPOSES.

The Secretary of Commerce, in consultation with the Secretary of Health and Human Services and other appropriate departments and agencies, shall submit a report to the Committee on Commerce of the House of Representatives and the Committee on Commerce, Science, and Transportation of the Senate concerning the activities of the Joint Working Group on Telemedicine, together with any findings reached in the studies and demonstrations on telemedicine funded by the Public Health Service or other Federal agencies. The report shall examine questions related to patient safety, the efficacy and quality of the services provided, and other legal, medical, and economic issues related to the utilization of advanced telecommunications services for medical purposes. The report shall be submitted to the respective committees by January 31, 1997.

SEC. 710. AUTHORIZATION OF APPROPRIATIONS.

(a) IN GENERAL- In addition to any other sums authorized by law, there are authorized to be appropriated to the Federal Communications Commission such sums as may be necessary to carry out this Act and the amendments made by this Act.

(b) EFFECT ON FEES- For the purposes of section 9(b)(2) (47 U.S.C. 159(b)(2)), additional amounts appropriated pursuant to subsection (a) shall be construed to be changes in the amounts appropriated for the performance of activities described in section 9(a) of the Communications Act of 1934.

(c) FUNDING AVAILABILITY- Section 309(j)(8)(B) (47 U.S.C. 309(j)(8)(B)) is amended by adding at the end the following new sentence: Such offsetting collections are authorized to remain available until expended.. Speaker of the House of Representatives. Vice President of the United States and President of the Senate.

INDEX

A

B

C

D

E

F

J

K

L

M

N

O

P

Q

R

S

T

U

V

W

Y